D0907136

*A Contextualistic Worldview*

# A Contextualistic Worldview

### Essays by Lewis E. Hahn

Southern Illinois University Press
*Carbondale and Edwardsville*

Publication partially funded by a subvention grant from the Office of the Chancellor, Southern Illinois University Carbondale.


Library of Congress Cataloging-in-Publication Data

Hahn, Lewis Edwin, 1908–
    A contextualistic worldview : essays / by Lewis E. Hahn.
        p. cm.
    Includes bibliographical references and index.
        1. Contextualism (Philosophy). 2. Philosophy, American—20th century.
I. Title.

B809.14 .H34 2001
146—dc21
ISBN 0-8093-2331-1 (alk. paper)                                        00-039504

# Contents

Acknowledgments                                                                    vii

Introduction: Broadening Our Philosophic Vision                                     ix


Part One: Contextualism

1. Contextualism and Cosmic Evolution-Revolution                                    3

2. Metaphysical Interpretation                                                      31

3. Metaphysical Inquiry                                                             40

4. Philosophy as Comprehensive Vision                                              49

5. Metaphysical Categories: Of Shoes and Ships and Sealing Wax,
   and Cabbages and Kings                                                          58

6. Psychological Data and Philosophical Theory of Perception                       69

7. Neutral, Indubitable Sense-Data as the Starting Point for
   Theories of Perception                                                          74

8. A Contextualistic View of Experience and Ecological Responsibility              82

9. Creating: Solving Problems and Experiencing Afresh                              92

10. Coping with Change: A Philosophy of Life                                       106


Part Two: Modern American Philosophers

11. John Dewey and Our Time                                                        113

12. Dewey's View of Experience and Culture                                        121

13. Wieman's Empiricism                                                            127

14. Stephen C. Pepper's World Hypotheses                                           134

15. Brand Blanshard's Worldview                                                    145


Notes                                                                              161

Bibliography of Works by Lewis E. Hahn                                             175

Index                                                                              183

# Acknowledgments

I am happy to acknowledge the warm support, encouragement, and cooperation of our publisher, Southern Illinois University Press, especially Editorial Director James D. Simmons, Managing Editor Carol Burns, and other staff of the press who worked on the final copy of the manuscript. And I also very much appreciate the continued support, understanding, and encouragement from the administration of Southern Illinois University Carbondale.

As always, moreover, I am grateful for the friendly and unfailing help in a variety of ways from the staff of Morris Library. It is invaluable for my work and that of my fellow scholars. My warm gratitude also goes to Christina Martin and the Department of Philosophy secretariat for help with numerous projects; my special thanks go to Sharon Langrand, recently retired secretary, and Frances Stanley for help with manuscripts, proofs, correspondence, and all they did and do to keep our office functioning efficiently. Thanks also go to our graduate students, Darrell J. Russell and Lucian W. Stone Jr., for their work as graduate assistants in the Library of Living Philosophers and their help with this manuscript.

Finally, for warm support, stimulation, and friendly counsel, I am most grateful to my able and resourceful pluralistic colleagues who from diverse perspectives make common cause for philosophy and for a better university.

# Introduction:
# Broadening Our Philosophic Vision

One of the primary traditional goals of philosophic vision has been to achieve a broad perspective within which all things may be given their due place. Historically, philosophers have sought to make comprehensive sense of the full range of facts from whatever field they may be drawn, whether from common sense, the sciences, the arts, religion, politics, people's working life, or their play activities. Naturally, not all persons, whether professional philosophers or concerned nonphilosophers, have sought this comprehensive vision in the same way, nor have all agreed as to its precise character. Calling it "metaphysical interpretation," as I do in chapter 2 of Part One of this volume, turns off many, even some pragmatists,[1] because the term *metaphysics* conjures up for them metaphysicians who claim that metaphysics provides absolute certainty about eternal realities and who with Plato and Aristotle regard the changing as an inferior form of existence.[2]

Not surprisingly, I shall stress the relatively recent contextualistic worldview, since over the years I have come to think of it as one of the better world hypotheses, if, indeed, not the best. By stressing the centrality of change, the intimate relationship between people and their environment, and the importance of putting things in perspective, I consider my contextualistic worldview as one of the better ways of making sense of our world and our place in it. And in using this particular world map to work on various topics, it has always suggested some fresh insights. In the first part of chapter 1, "Contextualism and Cosmic Evolution-Revolution," I have sketched a brief outline of contextualism, and this outline refers to other more extensive accounts of it. Various other parts of this chapter also deal with contextualism in relation to other philosophies. Incidentally, much of the material for this chapter, such as the debate over evolution and the implications of Darwinism for later philosophy, I used earlier for lectures in upper-division general studies courses in American philosophy. Moreover, most of the other chapters deal with or express contextualism as a form of pragmatic naturalism.

In spite of my high regard for contextualism as a worldview, however, I do not think it would be good if we were limited to a single worldview, whether contextualism or some other. Even though there may well be situations in which unanimity is deservedly highly prized, in the quest for comprehensive vision, diversity has its values. The more different views we have and the more different sources of possible light we have, the better our chances that some of these cosmic maps will shed light on our world and our place in it.

In chapter 2, I discuss metaphysical interpretation as a way of making comprehensive sense of our world and suggest that a metaphysical interpretation of any problematic feature of our world has been given when we can indicate the place of this feature in the conceptual framework of a worldview, or world hypothesis. And in agreement with Stephen C. Pepper's *World Hypotheses: A Study in Evidence* and Dorothy M. Emmet's *The Nature of Metaphysical Thinking,* I hold that such a worldview centers about a root metaphor or basic analogy from which a kind of theoretical model or map for the entire range of facts may be drawn.[3] As I have suggested above, it seems to me clear that more than one such analogy or root metaphor is worth developing, but I shall stress contextualism, a form of pragmatic naturalism, which develops from the root metaphor of historical events or happenings. Analysis for the contextualists, accordingly, is an affair of exhibiting the texture of such events in context for whatever purposes may be involved in a given problematic situation.

Chapter 3, "Metaphysical Inquiry," discusses metaphysical inquiry as a science and as an art and is one of three chapters in this book devoted to metaphysical interpretation in general. This chapter was presented originally at the Thirteenth International Congress of Philosophy in Mexico City in September 1963, just after I moved from Washington University to Southern Illinois University Carbondale. The late Wayne A. R. Leys, then of Roosevelt University, and I were cochairs of the American Philosophical Association Committee on Planning for the Congress and made an earlier trip to Mexico City to check on travel arrangements and other plans.

Chapter 4, "Philosophy as Comprehensive Vision," was the presidential address I delivered at the fifty-first annual meeting of the Southern Society for Philosophy and Psychology in St. Louis on March 28, 1959. As over against the argument that the great differences between philosophy as comprehensive vision and psychology make it unlikely that a joint society of philosophers and psychologists could be fruitful for both groups, I suggested that their differences may help make it possible for the two fields to complement each other. Important philosophical issues are raised by various psychological systems and methodologies, and some of them involve conflicting interpretations by advocates of different worldviews, and, not infrequently, a philosophical conception of what it is to be a fact serves as a presupposition of the psychologist's pursuit of facts. And on the other hand, the factual findings of psychologists are frequently crucially relevant for problems of ethics, aesthetics, philosophy of value, and theory of knowledge.

Chapter 5, "Metaphysical Categories: Of Shoes and Ships and Sealing Wax, and Cabbages and Kings," provides more details on the categories and suggests that, for contextualists, the categories for a world hypothesis afford conceptual instruments for patterning problematic situations.

Chapter 6, "Psychological Data and Philosophical Theory of Perception," applies the contextualistic categories to theory of perception and maintains that a constructive pragmatic theory of perception has little chance of a hearing unless it be granted that the determination of the relevant psychological data in solving the problems of perception is the exclusive right of no metaphysical theory or world hypothesis. What the relevant psychological facts are and just how they should be interpreted are matters that different metaphysical hypotheses may decide differently, and the proponents of no world hypothesis are entitled to assume that the facts as interpreted in terms of their categories are simply neutral facts that any and all other theories must adopt as the basis for further philosophical discussion. For that matter, many leading psychologists question the neutrality of the data of perception in view of the differing interpretative frameworks in which rival systems of psychology may place them. At any rate, pragmatists are convinced that no metaphysicians are entitled to legislate out of the realm of the philosophically significant any discussion that makes use of other data than their own. Nor should they have the right to assume that problems that arise on their view are everyone's, even if they do not happen to arise on the theory of the newcomer.

Professor Dewey happened to have an article in the same issue of the *Journal of Philosophy* in which my essay appeared, and I was delighted to receive an unexpected letter from him praising it "both for clarity of presentation and for the soundness of its point of view." He added that my article ought to call out a reply and that perhaps it would if I followed it with another one "naming names and with citations." I did not follow it shortly with another along these lines, but as a matter of fact, I had presented a paper of this sort, "Neutral, Indubitable Sense-Data as the Starting Point for Theories of Perception" (chapter 7 of this volume), before the Pacific Division of the American Philosophical Association at the University of California at Berkeley on December 29, 1938, more than three years earlier. This was my first presentation before the APA, and it too was published in the *Journal of Philosophy,* on October 26, 1939. I did not send a copy of it to Professor Dewey, but after receiving his congratulatory letter on the other article, I wrote him that I knew of no one from whom I should rather have such words of approbation. I added that the University of California Press was publishing shortly a monograph of mine, *A Contextualistic Theory of Perception,* in which I tried to do two things: (1) set forth a constructive pragmatic theory of perception suggested by the writings of Dewey and Mead, and (2) on the basis of this theory, do a detailed criticism of H. H. Price's theory of perception. I promised to send him a copy of the book when it came out and did so. He acknowledged receipt of it and said he would write after he had time to read it.

I received no letter from him about it, but surprisingly I did receive a letter from Arthur F. Bentley, to whom I had not sent a copy of my dissertation, saying that my terms were as much in need of clarification as his and Dewey's and suggesting that I join the two of them on a clarification project. But I liked some of Dewey's original terms better than some of the allegedly clarified terms the two of them came up with. I do not remember what, if anything, I wrote him in response.

I also sent a copy of my dissertation to Professor H. H. Price, who sent me a friendly, fairly lengthy longhand response to my criticism of his views, and I planned to reply to his comments as soon as I had a little more time. But what with work on the Lepley cooperative volume on value theory, a 1947 visiting lectureship at Princeton University, and a move from the University of Missouri, Columbia, to Washington University, where, as departmental chair, I helped set up a doctoral program in philosophy and took on extensive administrative work as graduate dean, the precious Price letter was set aside, always, I thought, in a safe place. However, when, after an embarrassingly long time, I finally got around to it, termites had made the material unreadable.

As I indicated above, a few years after the Bentley letter I received an invitation to participate in the Lepley volume, *Value: A Cooperative Inquiry*.[4] As Lepley notes in the introduction, the immediate stimulus to the cooperative study was a 1944 *Journal of Philosophy* article by Dewey, "Some Questions about Value," in which he formulated four groups of questions basic for value theory, offered some possible answers, and challenged other interested persons to set forth the questions and views they considered fundamental. Lepley was disappointed to find that no one had responded to the challenge by the autumn of 1945 and suggested to Dewey that a cooperative study, or symposium, on value theory might be organized that would take his article as a point of departure. Dewey, according to Lepley, agreed and mentioned some persons he would especially like to share in the symposium. These suggested a number of others, and they still more. The other thirteen selected in addition to myself, listed in no particular order, were Dewey, Lepley, Stephen C. Pepper, Charles Morris, George Geiger, E. T. Mitchell, Dewitt Parker, Henry Aiken, C. E. Ayres, H. N. Lee, Bertram Jessup, A. C. Garnett, and Philip Rice.

Each of us did a preliminary draft in answer to Dewey's questions and comments, and all these papers were mimeographed and sent to all participants for criticism. After the exchange and some further revision, our revised papers were published in Part One of the volume, and Part Two was made up of criticisms of each essay by two or more critics and rejoinders by the authors. Dewey at first planned to do a second essay for the volume but, for various reasons, did not do so.

My published paper emphasized the importance of identifying the world-view in terms of which comments on value theory were made as a way of clar-ifying and resolving basic issues in the field of values, and I identified my ap-proach as contextualistic, or pragmatic. I also stressed the need for a psychology not based on an inner-outer dualism. Instead of viewing values in terms of an "internal" or "mentalistic" framework, I prefer a broad behavioral approach, one broad enough to include all that is observable in human activities on whatever level. And, of course, a behaviorism that reduces behavior to physical or phys-iological terms is too narrow. In short, for contextualists, our value attitudes are all behavioral transactions, things open to investigation and study; and we should think of individuals as being of a piece with their social and cultural environment rather than as insulated centers of desire or prizing.

Chapter 8, "A Contextualistic View of Experience and Ecological Respon-sibility," is a paper presented originally for the Highlands Institute for Ameri-can Religious Thought Second International Conference on Philosophical Theology at the University of St. Andrews, Scotland, August 5, 1993. The ex-perts seem to agree that we and our children's children face a disturbing glo-bal environmental crisis compounded of such factors as air and water pollution, hazardous chemical waste, loss of rain forests, global warming, water shortage, ruinous erosion of the earth's surface, overpopulation, holes in the ozone lay-er, dysfunctional social practices, some ill-advised technologies in using land, and unconsidered or improperly considered actions of various sorts. A further alarming feature of these factors is the fact that of all earthlings we humans pose the gravest threat to the environment. Our increasingly aggressive encroach-ments into the earth's ecological systems and the proliferation of nuclear bombs endanger the earth's balance. We and our industrial civilization seem to have lost our sense of connection with our environment and its future.

With these things in mind, the organizers of the 1993 International Con-gress on Religious Experience and Ecological Responsibility at the Universi-ty of St. Andrews are to be commended. But as Al Gore's *Earth in the Balance: Ecology and the Human Spirit* suggests, preventing loss of the earth's balance will require cooperation on a vast scale between geographical regions, political agencies, social organizations, and individuals.

With reference to the theoretical background for ecology, however, con-textualism provides the missing sense of connection with our environment and its future. As a worldview, it conceptually places people in nature and finds a basic continuity and intimate intercourse between them and their environment, natural, social, and cultural. This intercourse is experience. What we do, we do with our environment, and we live, move, and have our being in it. We enter into more or less stable integrations with it and form uneasy equilibriums re-quiring frequent adjustments or modifications, with our very survival depending on making some of them. Where support is lacking, we have a problem and need to make use of reflective inquiry to find instruments for solving it or modify appropriately our behavior patterns. But there is more to experience than solving problems, although the latter may be more focal for environmental crises. Every texture has its own distinctive quality, and the perception or enjoyment of enhanced qualities makes life worth living. Had qualities help establish the basic continuity between us and our environment.

Contextualism, however, is not the only worldview to stress the kinship of people and nature. Both the American Indians our people found in North America and the ancient Chinese Taoists and Confucians more than twenty-five thousand years ago shared the wisdom of believing in a basic continuity and intimate intercourse between people and their environment.

Chapter 9, "Creating: Solving Problems and Experiencing Afresh," relates contextualism to philosophy of creativity by developing at some length two aspects of experience I found important in dealing with the environmental crisis: (1) critical thinking, or reflective inquiry, as a method of solving problems and (2) taking in the qualities of things, or experiencing afresh. Both increased ability to recognize and solve problems and enhanced capacity to see, hear, feel, and otherwise experience the qualities of things are creative. For each of them, we need the help of both the sciences and the arts, but the sciences are especially important for many types of problem solving, and literature and the arts are quite helpful for perceiving and appreciating enhanced qualities.

If, indeed, we live in a changing world, it is one that presents us with problems, opportunities for doing something to better our world, or make it less bad, and a rich array of enhanced qualities to share. As I indicated above, contextualism is my worldview. What is yours, and what can or should you do in yours? What does your view offer for the nonprofessional philosopher? If we pool our findings, we may better solve our problems, realize more effectively our opportunities for bettering our world, and take in more of the qualities to be shared.

Chapter 10, "Coping with Change: A Philosophy of Life," is an informal, relatively nontechnical presentation of my philosophy of life. As such, it involves both a worldview and some suggestions on what is worth seeking, doing, or being in the world outlined by our outlook. Each of the other chapters of this book offers somewhat more technical accounts of its particular topic or topics, but I am convinced that philosophy is not just for the philosophers but is rather potentially everybody's business and that, accordingly, each of us needs to think as clearly as we can about the world and our place in it. My view is sometimes called contextualism, and it holds that everything changes.

At this point, I move to Part Two, which contains the five chapters on four great American philosophers—John Dewey (1859–1952), Henry Nelson Wieman (1884–1975), Stephen C. Pepper (1891–1972), and Brand Blanshard (1892–1987).

Chapter 11, "John Dewey and Our Time," was delivered originally as a public lecture at Baylor University, where I was then distinguished visiting professor of philosophy. I touched on the Dewey Project at Southern Illinois University Carbondale but for the most part discussed four clusters of Dewey's ideas that seemed to me important for his time and still relevant for ours: (1) a new pragmatic or contextualistic worldview with emphasis on change and with it a new conception of analysis or explanation, (2) a new method of critical or reflective inquiry, (3) a new view of experience and a different conception of the role of philosophy, and (4) a conception of human growth as both the moral end and the goal of education. I tried to show what was new about these ideas and contended that they are still significant for our time.

Chapter 12, "Dewey's View of Experience and Culture," was presented originally for the October 7–10, 1976, Bicentennial Symposium of Philosophy. It discusses the concept of experience in Dewey's philosophy in the light of a 1951 draft of a new introduction for *Experience and Nature*. As late as 1951, less than a year before his death, Dewey could still say that he did not feel the need to take back any of the things he said about experience in the earlier text of *Experience and Nature;* but this statement was coupled with the declaration that "were the book that was published with the title *Experience and Nature* being written today, its caption would be *Culture and Nature* and the treatment of specific subject matters would be correspondingly modified."[5]

Chapter 13, "Wieman's Empiricism," discusses the views of a great innovative philosopher who was a member of the Department of Philosophy at Southern Illinois University Carbondale from 1956 to 1966, after twenty years, from 1927 to 1947, of distinguished service at the University of Chicago. He was a popular speaker who had numerous invitations for special lectures for relatively large audiences all over the country, but he was probably at his best in relatively small groups in which dialogue was possible. After Chicago, he taught for shorter periods at the University of Oregon, the University of Houston, Washington University in St. Louis, and Grinnell College. The acquisition of the first set of his papers in 1966 formed the initial nucleus of Morris Library's outstanding research collection in modern American philosophy. Having these papers was especially important for our getting the Foundation for Philosophy of Creativity papers, a continuing series of acquisitions. The foundation and the Society for Philosophy of Creativity were organized by William S. Minor, himself later a visiting professor in speech communication here, and as an advisor to him and as a member of the foundation board, I am happy to have helped see that these materials came to our library. Special credit is also due to Pete A. Y. Gunter, Larry R. Cobb, the late John A. Broyer, Cedric L. Heppler, Carl R. Hausman, and John Thomas, for help with the Philosophy of Creativity papers.

Wieman was the subject of volume 4 of the Library of Living Theology, edited by Robert W. Bretall, entitled *The Empirical Theology of Henry Nelson*

*Wieman.* The founding editor or coeditor of the theological series, the late Charles W. Kegley, cleared the use of the title for the series with the late Paul A. Schilpp, founding editor of the Library of Living Philosophers.

I still think my opening sentence in the chapter summarizes admirably Wieman's basic contribution. He was a prophet, philosopher, theologian, and concerned person who had a fresh vision of God as creative interchange, a strong sense of urgency, and a zeal for making his vision operative in a changing world. Although he was ambivalent about use of the term *metaphysics* to describe his philosophy and theology, there were too many major points of agreement between him and contextualism to deny that in the main he was contextualistic. In the postscript to *The Source of Human Good,* in spite of his misgivings about being identified with contextualism, he admits that the metaphysics of contextualism is a recurrent theme in the book.[6]

The important thing for him was achieving a better understanding of "the creativity which transforms all systems to meet the demands of human existence as it undergoes transformation,"[7] and he preferred for his key fact, or root metaphor, creative interchange rather than the historical event. But most of the basic categories of contextualism have prominent roles in his metaphysics.

As I indicated in this chapter, Wieman thought the contextualists go too far on change. In his view, in addition to changing things, there is a law or order to which change conforms, and the latter is a changeless form.[8] As noted above, he was theistic, whereas most contextualists tend to be humanists. But both Wieman and contextualism are naturalistic, and both are committed to the method of reflective inquiry as the basic method of investigation for our problems, whether practical, scientific, religious, or metaphysical. Both share roughly the view of experience set forth in chapter 8 on experience and ecological responsibility.

Chapter 14, "Stephen C. Pepper's World Hypotheses," surveys some characteristic theses of one of the most original and suggestive philosophers of our time. In a field in which some of the great philosophers have adamantly insisted that their account of what is and how we come to know it is certainly true, Pepper devotes the first part of his *World Hypotheses* to arguing against claims to certainty, whether in the form of infallible authority, self-evident principles, or indubitable data, and spends most of the rest of the book discussing what he takes to be the best we have in this field, namely, some relatively adequate hypotheses. What we should seek in developing a world hypothesis, according to Pepper, is not certainty but converging lines of evidence, and if we have more convergent lines than one, so much the better, for we have more possible sources of light. Since a world hypothesis by definition aims at unlimited scope, we frame it in terms of convergences and corroborations.

At this point, Pepper's root metaphor theory comes in. Since we are puzzled about the nature of the universe, we look back over our past experience to see if we can find a good sample of the nature of things. This is our basic analogy. Can we generalize its structure to apply significantly to the interpretation of other areas, perhaps to any other area? Thales looked long ago and came up with water. Later, others discovered that better root metaphors were such things as machines, organisms, or historical events. Can we find a still better analogy?

This theory sheds fresh light on the nature of worldviews and their categories, shows their relation to common sense, and provides a basis for describing, classifying, and criticizing world hypotheses. But in view of the low esteem many logicians have for analogical reasoning, perhaps it took a philosopher with a rich background in the arts who sought in worldviews a means of grounding art criticism to find in metaphor a key to understanding world hypotheses both historically and epistemologically. At any rate, Pepper has helped many of us see a larger role for metaphor.

At least two other features of his views have been particularly important for creative interchange. In the first place, his pluralism has opened the way for accounts of creativity on the part of each relatively adequate worldview. In the second place, for him, how well world hypotheses handle values is a primary consideration; and he wrote several books on empirical aesthetics, ethics, and general theory of value. What enterprises, if any, afford greater opportunity for creativity and creative interchange than do empirical attempts to make sense of values?

Chapter 15, "Brand Blanshard's Worldview," discusses some of the central theses of Absolute or Hegelian Idealism. Pepper called the view organicism and regarded it as one of three or four relatively adequate alternatives to contextualism. Blanshard, who tells us in his autobiography for the Schilpp volume of the Library of Living Philosophers that he and Hegel shared the same birthday, August 27, was an ardent, fresh, and lucid advocate of Hegelianism long after it had fallen from general popularity among British and American philosophers; and for that matter, young John Dewey, before he turned to instrumentalism and contextualism, also vigorously espoused the view. George Sylvester Morris, who was one of Dewey's teachers at Johns Hopkins University and a senior colleague of his at the University of Michigan, was a strong and persuasive advocate of Absolute Idealism.[9]

Blanshard was known internationally for his literary clarity and felicity of style, and he was much sought after as a speaker on philosophy and general topics. His 1940 two-volume work, *The Nature of Thought,* was rated by a committee of the American Philosophical Association as one of the ten outstanding works published in the United States since 1900. Among his many memberships and special speaking engagements, he was a member of the American Academy of Arts and Sciences, corresponding fellow of the British Academy, Dudleian Lecturer at Harvard in 1945, Hertz Lecturer of the British Academy in 1952, Gifford Lecturer at St. Andrews University in Scotland in 1952–53, Adamson Lecturer at the University of Manchester, England, in 1953, Howison Lecturer, University of California, Berkeley, 1954, Carus Lecturer, 1959, and Whitehead Lecturer at Harvard in 1961.

The Schilpp volume in the Library of Living Philosophers, *The Philosophy of Brand Blanshard,* is one of the finest volumes in a series concerned to set up a dialogue between the critics and the great philosopher. From autobiography to bibliography, it fulfills admirably the basic purpose of the series in that it aims not at refutation or confrontation but rather at fruitful joining of issues and improved understanding of the positions and issues involved. The autobiography traces the course of his career and affords in addition a survey of major issues and movements in contemporary philosophy along with helpful references to the history of philosophy. His volume, moreover, initiates a new LLP pattern for placing criticisms/descriptions and replies. Instead of the standard mode of having a section on criticism and description followed by a section of replies, in his pattern there is one section on criticisms/descriptions and replies with a specific response after each critical/descriptive essay; and for the most part, this practice leaves both critics and readers better satisfied.

Viewing his philosophy as a whole from the perspective of contextualism, however, I have four sets of questions. First are some queries concerning Blanshard's explanatory ideal, the Absolute, and his account of explanation. For him, we start with incomplete fragments and move inexorably toward the Absolute, in terms of which everything is explained; and then it turns out that the Absolute was already present all the while. Second, I have grave misgivings concerning the place of change and novelty in his view. For me, they are the heart of things in process, neither unreal nor secondary. In the third place, his account of individuals sounds like a way of explaining them away. Finally, Blanshard departs somewhat from traditional organicism in rejecting the notion that the world is both logically, or intelligibly, and morally perfect, but how does any imperfection comport with the Absolute? And can any adequate survey of the evidence fail to find some imperfection in our world?

# Part One

## Contextualism

# 1

# Contextualism and Cosmic Evolution-Revolution

ineteenth-century developments in biology and geology helped trigger a series of remarkable developments in other sciences and helped make for a radically new way of seeing our world and our place in it, giving rise to a host of philosophical interpretations. Central in the biological developments was the Darwinian notion of evolution, and a cluster of pragmatic views constituted one of the most interesting of the philosophical outlooks. In this essay, I should like to outline some features of the revolutionary changes in worldview and relate them to contextualism as typifying some of the major pragmatic emphases. In this connection, it seems to me, contextualism is both an expression of evolutionary theory and a way of interpreting it. Accordingly, I shall begin with a brief account of contextualism, follow this with a discussion of the philosophical significance of the debate over evolution, next treat contextualism as an expression of the changed outlook stemming from this debate, and conclude with some comments concerning a contextualistic interpretation of evolution.

## Contextualism

In treating any form of pragmatism, questions are fairly sure to be raised concerning both the name "pragmatism" and whether what it refers to has sufficient unity for the designation to be illuminating unless otherwise qualified. A full answer to these questions, moreover, might well take far more space than we have at our disposal; but some brief comments may be helpful. As to the name, most of the proponents, living and dead, of what we may call pragma-

From *Evolution-Revolution: Patterns of Development in Nature, Society, Man and Knowledge,* ed. Rubin Gotesky and Ervin Laszlo (New York: Gordon and Breach Science Publishers, 1971), 3–39; also in *Philosophy Forum* 11 (Mar. 1972): 3–39. Reprinted by permission of Gordon and Breach Science Publishers.

tism apparently prefer to characterize their views by some other name. For example, William James, who perhaps did most to bring it to the attention of the philosophical world and who helped frame the issues which divided it from other positions, spoke (in the Preface to *Pragmatism*) of not liking "pragmatism" as a name for the movement or collection of tendencies but thought that it was probably too late (1907) to change it. Although the term does not occur in Charles Sanders Peirce's famous essay of 1878 in the *Popular Science Monthly* on "How to Make Our Ideas Clear," that essay is usually said to be the first clear-cut formulation in print of the view; and years later he explained how he took over from Kant the adjective *pragmatic* to stress the relation of thought and knowledge to definite human purposes.[1] But he later decided to use the label "pragmaticism" as one ugly enough to protect his views from unwanted associations going with pragmatism.[2] John Dewey, the one who gave the view its most nearly definitive formulation, for many years preferred to call his view instrumentalism or perhaps experimentalism.

With reference to the matter of unity, few would be willing to argue that pragmatism as "a new name for some old ways of thinking" designates a single well-unified movement from the early 1870s to the present rather than a cluster of tendencies and movements. Indeed, it seems clear that a movement which at one time or another included such diverse thinkers as Peirce, James, Dewey, Mead, F. C. S. Schiller, Chauncey Wright, John Fiske, O. W. Holmes, Jr., J. H. Tufts, E. S. Ames, A. W. Moore, C. I. Lewis, George Boas, H. C. Brown, D. A. Piatt, Josiah Royce, Charles W. Morris, Sidney Hook, E. A. Burtt, Irwin Edman, S. Morris Eames, Van Meter Ames, Max Otto, George Geiger, John L. Childs, and George Counts, to mention only a few, is not likely to be reducible to a single doctrine or even a simple set of views. Except possibly for periods like the one from 1894 to 1904 for the Chicago School few would be willing to claim that pragmatism was a unified movement, and even then Peirce and James were holding forth along rather different lines. Perhaps we should not expect too much unity for an outlook in which such a critic as A. O. Lovejoy in 1908 rather impatiently professed to find thirteen logically independent varieties, not all of which the pragmatists themselves could recognize.

At any rate, in point of fact pragmatism is a name which has referred to many varieties of doctrine, as one might infer from the reservations many leaders of the movement had about calling themselves pragmatists lest it commit them before the philosophic public to various doctrines they could not accept. And I shall not attempt to discuss all these variations. But I should like to direct attention to one important unifying factor in this body of doctrine since James, at least: namely, the attempt to take time seriously—time as passage, as ongoing process, as felt duration. Most of the great pragmatists since James have been concerned with things in time, things in process, changing realities, patterned events. With James, moreover, they have insisted that the truly empirical philosopher is concerned not with eternal or static realities but with things in the

4

making or in the process of becoming. In Dewey's words, for the pragmatist "every existence is an event"—a history.[3] Although some things change at a slower rate and thus give a relative stability, no concrete thing exists apart from temporal process. The pragmatist argues that the things that seem to "exclude movement and change" are only "*phases* of things," perhaps legitimate abstractions but not concrete things.[4] Things in process, histories, changing events, with their mixture of contingency and stability, are thus basic for any adequate metaphysics or worldview. These patterned events have within them movements from and toward other events, and they always occur in certain contexts and have reference to other events within these contexts.

No two pragmatists, it is true, treat these basic facts in quite the same way, and some prefer other realms of discourse than the metaphysical, but between the accounts of any two of them there is likely to be a large measure of continuity, frequently accompanied by major differences. Consider, for example, the approaches of Dewey, James, Schiller, and Stephen C. Pepper, remembering that James credits Peirce with much of his view. As I put it in another study of pragmatism some years ago:[5]

> Dewey, coming at events, histories, occurrences, primarily from the point of view of the experimental scientist interested in effecting change, noticed that certain events could be used to direct the occurrence of others. They could be used as instruments. If any particular event could be brought within the context of certain other events, control of consequences was effected. Here was a natural means of rendering good things more stable and bad ones less persistent. Experimentation was necessary to determine just what kind of events were valuable for controlling any special type of existent; and until a possible means of control was tried out, it was impossible to say whether or not it would work. The ultimate criterion, however, was whether or not the intended consequences turned up. And fortunately enough, this process of bringing a particular set of events into a control context seemed to be a way of solving any empirical problem including those of philosophy. Hence Dewey set about hammering home the importance of setting up such relations between complexes of events and thereby making such a process an instrument for bringing about desired consequences. Because of his emphasis upon this aspect of pragmatism, his view came to be called Instrumentalism.
>
> James before Dewey, of course, had stressed the temporal character of reality and the importance of consequences. He discerned the vital significance of the fact that events may lead to or refer to something beyond themselves, and about this fact he built up his pragmatic theory of meaning and truth. An idea means what it leads to, and the test of its truth is whether or not it leads as was expected.

Specific consequences provide the test. If there is no difference in the specific consequences, James maintained, there is no practical difference in meaning.

Schiller was profoundly impressed by the shift in emphasis produced by such a view. Instead of speaking in terms of meta-physical entities often far removed from the empirical level, instead of stressing what seemed to him impossible idealistic goals somehow concerned with Absolutes rather than with human affairs, this view brought philosophical discussions back to the realm of human endeavor. He called the view Humanism.

Interested primarily in what pragmatism had to offer for aesthetic theory, Pepper was struck by the significance of context for aesthetic quality. Histories, patterned events, are not isolated affairs. They occur in certain contexts of other events; and differences in context may make important differences in quality. To control the quality of an event, one does not isolate it, but rather surrounds it with a suitable context; and given the proper context, practically any event may have the enhanced quality of beauty. Nor, Pepper was convinced, is context significant merely for aesthetic matters. It occupies an equally important place in other fields. Hence for that form of pragmatism which stresses this fact he coined the name Contextualism.[6]

In terms of my own commitments and reservations the form of pragmatism I am most interested in is contextualism, an outlook which finds much of value in the other approaches listed above. I think of contextualism as a form of pragmatic naturalism which takes as its basic fact or root metaphor patterned events, things in process, or historical events.[7] The main traits of such events constitute the fundamental categories of the view I hold, and may be used to characterize or explain any set of problematic facts. Though there are various alternative statements of these categorial features,[8] one convenient grouping divides them into (1) a set of filling or textural traits which indicate the nature or "stuff" of an event, and (2) a group of contextual or environmental traits which denote the place of the event in relation to other events. The textural categories include *texture, strand, quality, fusion, and reference* (direction-distance values), whereas the most important contextual ones are perhaps *environment, initiations, means* (or *instruments*), *consummations,* and *frustrations* (blocking).

The patterned event or affair with which the contextualist starts is not a discrete atomic unit but rather a complex interrelationship of tendencies all interwoven into an integral whole with its own individual character or quality. As the term *texture* (borrowed from the weaver's art) suggests, each historical event is a web or network of happenings (strands), a focal center into which features of other histories somehow enter. Textures may be analyzed into constituent strands, and texture, strand, and context are relative to each other. What is strand or detail in a larger context may become texture in another. As a detail of a texture a strand reaches out into the context and brings some of the quality of the latter into the texture. Since the character of a texture is a fusion of the qualities of its strands and the latter are partly from its context, analysis of a texture takes us into the texture of other events.

References are both part of the character or nature of an event and links with its context. Strands reach out or refer to other textures. They move from initiations through means-objects or instruments to frustrations or consummations, and to control the direction of affairs we must direct our attention to the means.

We shall want to elaborate on certain of these categorial features later; but perhaps already enough has been said to suggest that the language and categories of the contextualist reflect in various ways developments in evolutionary theory; and I hope that a survey, to which we now turn, of some of the issues in the debate over evolution will make this plainer.

## Debate over Evolution

In some ways the debate over evolution after the publication of Darwin's *The Origin of Species* in 1859 was livelier and more heated among theologians, philosophers, scientists from fields other than biology, and popular writers than among biologists; and we may wish to distinguish with A. O. Lovejoy and Philip Wiener between evolution as a scientific theory in a special field and evolutionism as a generalization invading every field from biology and cosmology to sociology and philosophy of history.[9] At any rate, writers in many diverse fields, some of them remote from biology, found or thought they found that Darwinian theory had implications for their field; and the end in this process has not yet been reached. The theory seemed to raise basic questions as to the nature of reality, law and design in nature, human beings and their place in the cosmos, human experience, knowledge and the methods of knowing, morals, and religion. Darwin was apparently headed for a career as a clergyman when his appointment as naturalist for the famous Beagle expedition provided experiences which changed his outlook and his vocation; but he himself avoided the wider implications of his view. In spite of his reluctance to speak out on some of these matters, debate over the scientific issues, however, seemed to make the broader implications stand out all the more clearly for others, and it has become obvious that a revolution has taken place in our ways of thinking. Indeed, it has become increasingly clear that whatever the reservations of his fellow biologists concerning his interpretation of natural selection, sexual selection, and the agencies of evolution, the fact or principle of evolution is well established by a host of different lines of evidence from many fields: for example, paleontology, embryology, comparative anatomy, analysis of the blood and other fluids of various species, vestigial organs, geographical distribution of plants and animals, and plant and animal breeding.

But why, it may be asked, should the general public get so excited over a scientific principle, even if it be one which ranges from stardust to people? Perhaps a sampling of some of the issues will help make clear the reasons for the heat and liveliness of the debate. The issues ranged from whether man is a brother to the apes or a Son of God and whether the species are products of special divine creation or of natural selection through whether the Bible or science affords the more trustworthy account of creation, whether human reason is a relatively perfect mirror of reality or an instrument of adjustment, and whether analysis is a matter of reducing a complex to permanent elements or of tracing a pattern of changes, to broad questions of naturalism versus super-naturalism and of change or permanence as the touchstone of the real, with a host of associated issues.

The issue of whether man is a brother to the apes or a Son of God is one as to whether man is a part of the animal kingdom and the natural order or a member of a distinct and higher spiritual order. The traditional Christian out look had assumed that man was a creature apart, a being set over against his world. One set of principles applied to his world and the animal kingdom, another to man. To be sure, man was set down for a time in this vale of tears to enact his drama of salvation; but it was clear that this natural order was an alien realm and that man was destined for something higher. Thus the Darwinian notion that man was a part of the animal kingdom and the natural order seemed to many an affront to the dignity of man. The more the Darwinians traced continuities within the animal kingdom and the more they spelled out man's place in nature, the more insulted many became. It was as if one had a choice of one's ancestors and kinship groups, God and the angels, on the one hand, or on the other, the apes; and faced with this choice, the Darwinians, it seemed to many devout individuals, deliberately and perversely chose to align them-selves with a base, brutal realm rather than with a glorious spiritual order. A favorite ploy was for a speaker to retort that he or she did not know about the relatives of Darwin and the Darwinians but that he or she was quite sure that there were no monkeys among her or his own kinfolks. Lest one think that this issue faded out more than a century ago, perhaps a reminder of the famous Tennessee Scopes trial of 1925, with Clarence Darrow and William Jennings Bryan as opposing lawyers, is in order. Their debate, as contemporary newspa-per accounts show, echoed the line of argument sketched above and took up various of the other issues I have mentioned.

A closely related issue was whether man and other living creatures were products of a special divine creation or of natural selection. It was sometimes formulated as a question of divine selection or design as opposed to natural selection and chance. Could any species of living things, much less man, have come about as a result of small chance variations appearing spontaneously in the individuals of a species struggling to survive in a world in which there al-ways seemed to be too little food and too many offspring? Granted that in some instances small variations taken in conjunction with just the right external conditions might mean the difference between a species making an appropriate adjustment and surviving or failing to adjust and perishing, is the origin of species to be explained in terms of this sort of natural selection? Can the instances of a species having just the right conditions of climate and food supply for its maintenance be explained in terms of an unplanned, fortuitous natural process? Could a giant crab, say, with just the right pincers for stripping coconut husk from the three-eye holes of the fallen nut and the right secondary pincers for extracting the meat have come about by any unplanned process? Or is this not rather an illustration of the admirable provision of Infinite Wisdom by which each created thing is adapted to the place for which it was intended? Is not speaking of natural selection another way of saying that no intelligence made the selection, or, indeed, that no selection occurred at all? And are there not too many regularities in nature for one not to seek some design or plan? How could people who were brought up in a tradition which accepted the Bible and held to divine providence find the doctrine of natural selection credible? Faced with a choice between divine foresight and a blind, brutal, natural process, the choice in favor of the former was easily made by many. To decide otherwise seemed to them to rob the world of meaning and strip man of his focal place in the universe. The evolutionary explanation seemed to threaten Christianity and a religious view of man and his world.

This second issue was closely intertwined with a third as to whether the Bible or science affords the more trustworthy account of creation. Since many believed the Bible to be divine revelation, it seemed clearly more certain than the admittedly fallible, hypothetical account of the scientists. Why settle for a fallible version when infallible truth was at hand? Some thought, moreover, that the Biblical account interpreted in terms of Bishop Ussher's chronology was a great deal more plausible than the scientific estimate of the age of the earth. According to the former, the world was only about six thousand years old, but the changes the scientists spoke of would have required millions of years, and the great time periods seemed incredibly long. There was the further fact that the Bible spoke of a special creation which gave man a central place in the scheme of things whereas on the other interpretation man was a tiny detail, one instance among an indefinitely large number selected blindly by natural process, in a vast evolving universe.

These first three issues, however, were in a sense all subordinate to the great issue of naturalism versus supernaturalism. Is it possible to account for natural events wholly in terms of other natural events without going outside the system, or must we not bring in God and/or supernatural agents to account for what we find in our world? Some argued for a supernatural agent in terms of revelation and the authority of the Bible, but most philosophers have become convinced that the problems of determining whether a revelation is genuine and of justifying the choice of an authority drive us to a consideration in terms of the evidence available to human thinkers; and if we must use ordinary reflective thinking to decide these matters, why bring in revelation and religious authority?

Others argued for a supernatural intelligence as a first cause, holding that God is necessary to set the natural process in motion. After the system of nature is started off, perhaps it can take it from there; but how could it have started if there were no outside intelligent agent to get it going? The naturalists have replied by asking who caused or started the outside supernatural intelligence or God, and upon being told that God is self-causing and needs no further causative agent, they have inquired why we should not stop the regress one step sooner and treat nature as the self-sufficient system instead of moving to the deity and then stopping there.

Others have held that getting things started is not the only reason why God is needed to explain the evolutionary process, that there are also various gaps in the line of development from the inorganic to the organic realm, and that supernatural powers are needed to bridge them. The naturalists have conceded some gaps but have pointed to the impressive progress science has made in filling them in and have indicated that it seems reasonable to expect further progress along these lines. In the long run, they have argued, reliance on the working hypotheses of the scientists affords a more hopeful prospect than acceptance of religious dogmas of revelation.

Some other defenders of supernaturalism maintained that the admirable adaptation of organism to environment and the regularities in nature, the lawful character of nature, were clear indications of design and that the very evidence the evolutionists had piled up made design all the more evident. Men like Asa Gray, Fiske, and McCosh held that one could retain belief in God and combine it with evolution properly interpreted. Perhaps the creation was spread over a longer time than was previously thought and the whole evolutionary process of the Darwinians was simply God's way of carrying out His design for creation. Although the Biblical account was not to be taken literally, some noted, it suggested the general nature of the development described by the scientists; and the evidence from design could be used as the deists claimed to establish the existence and nature of God. One would not have to have a special revelation. All the key facts of design could be read in the great book of Nature. But the facts of evil in the world seemed to many to raise insuperable difficulties for any attempt to prove the existence and nature of God from His works. And if the deistic way was blocked, some theists thought the supernaturalists had to depend on some antecedent revelation or some other way of first establishing the deity so that it might then be possible to show how evil somehow fitted into the divine design.

The naturalists tended to argue that, on the one hand, the supernaturalistic special creation explained too much or too little and that, on the other hand, a prior intelligent causal agent to plan and preordain organic adaptations was unnecessary. So long as we stress the fact that nothing is beyond the power of the deity, any kind of universe or any kind of happening in it may be explained as stemming from the divine will, but surely this is to "explain" too much in that any and everything is undifferentiatedly attributed to the divine will. And if we insist on a differentiated account, some things being more an expression of the divine will than others, the naturalist questions whether the supernaturalist has explained enough. How illuminating it is to be told that God created the world, of course, depends partly on what kind of deity is the creator; and the naturalist wants something more than an alleged revelation to establish a benevolent deity. Once we accept the idea of an external supernatural power in terms of some revelation, we seem to be operating primarily within the domain of our ignorance rather than building on what we have learned through critical inquiry. Without extensive supplementation by what we have discovered through the sciences, the supernaturalistic account tells us very little about what kind of world has been or is being created, and the supernatural base and the scientific developments seem to require radically different assumptions as to how to get knowledge. If we accept the Darwinian account or some outgrowth of it, moreover, the supernatural base is not needed. Organic adaptations may be explained in terms of constant variations and the elimination of harmful variations in the struggle for existence engendered by excessive reproduction and limited food supply.

Another issue concerned knowledge and the role or character of reason or intelligence. Although the Calvinists had thought of human reason as basically depraved and sadly insufficient as a substitute for revelation, many pre-Darwinians, taking their cue from the Greeks, thought of reason as a mirror of the real. They adopted a spectator view of knowledge and thought of reason as surveying and simply noting what was real. To be sure, according to this outlook, prejudices and biases may distort one's vision of reality, but pure reason reflects fairly perfectly what is there in nature or the external world. With Darwin's account, however, came the suspicion that intelligence is a device for adjusting to a favorable or hostile environment rather than for providing a purely rational carbon copy of the real. Whatever pure reason might provide, what we have is something much less pure; and such being the case, context, or situation, and conditions of observation become significant in determining or interpreting what is perceived. In terms of the opposition between pure reason and intelligence as an agent of adaptation or adjustment, once more some felt that the evolutionists were denigrating man and conceiving of him as a brute rather than as a rational spirit.

In many ways, however, the issue with the greatest revolutionary impact was that of change or permanence as the touchstone of the real. For two thousand years in field after field permanence and perfection tended to be equated; and during this period, as John Dewey wrote in a famous essay on Darwin,[10] the ruling conceptions in the philosophy of nature and knowledge had rested on the assumption of the superiority of the fixed and final. Absolute permanency marked at one and the same time the height of reality and perfection; and the species or forms typified fixity and perfection. Becoming, originating and passing away, change, these were signs of defect and unreality, at best the marks of a lower reality. Imagine, then, the impact of a soberly reasoned, massively detailed treatise with the title of Darwin's book, *The Origin of Species*! Here was an account of the coming to be and passing away of what had been taken to be fixed and inflexible. In the light of his account no longer can they be regarded as fixed forms of inflexible species; rather they become alterable characters,[11] and a last major fixity thereby comes to be expelled from nature. If even the species change, changing reality becomes something to be reckoned with; and some began to suspect that the fixed and permanent, far from being signs of perfection, are expressions of the dead and outmoded.

This is not to say, of course, that everyone agreed at once that change rather than permanence is the mark of the real, for many are still unconvinced. Old ways of thinking, especially ones grounded in numerous traditions, are hard to dislodge, and patterns of thinking have tended to change slowly. Nor is it to say that most people saw the full implications of the Darwinian revolution with reference to change and permanence. I suspect that we are still far from seeing all of them. What is perhaps most noteworthy about the Darwinian revolution is not that one scientist spoke of the origin of what had been assumed to be fixed and permanent, remarkable though that be. Still earlier Galileo and others had spoken of the earth as the setting for incessant alterations and generations and had shifted their interest and attention from the permanent to the changing. It is rather that most of his fellow scientists by now, whatever their reservations about his account of natural selection, assume his big point that species come into being and pass away and offer their version of the origin of species and evolutionary change.

The issue as to whether analysis is primarily a matter of reducing a complex to permanent or fixed elements or an affair of tracing a pattern of changes is obviously closely related to the one we have just been considering. The advocates of the latter interpretation of analysis charged the proponents of the former with reductionism and were answered by the charge that they were confusing logic and psychology. Is analysis an affair of timeless distinctions or one of distinguishing temporal patterns? Or does it depend on what one is attempting to analyze and why? At any rate, more and more explanations were being given in terms of origin and development, in terms of phases of a career or history, whether with reference to the stars and galactic systems, or to the constituents of matter, or to plants and animals, or to linguistics, or to economic institutions, or to religion and cultural patterns. And increasingly the genetic emphasis has entered into the analyses of investigators in such fields as experimental physiology, experimental psychology, ecology, physical and cultural anthropology, social psychology, sociology, comparative religion, institutional and historical economics, linguistics, and a host of new social sciences appearing in the late nineteenth and early twentieth centuries.

There were, to be sure, other important issues involved in the debate over evolution, some of which—for example, the implications for ethics—are treated in other parts of this symposium; and certain of these other issues also helped make for a lively, heated discussion. But I hope that the sampling of questions we have considered will help make clear both the revolutionary impact the theory of evolution has had on our ways of seeing and reacting to our world and some of the reasons for the general concern with the implications of evolution. Perhaps one of the most vivid ways of pointing up the differences between the world before Darwin and the new world is to note the character of some of the debates. For example, the idea that man is a part of the animal kingdom, which seemed like an outrageous proposal in the 1860s and 1870s, is now pretty much accepted as a commonplace.

Perhaps the review to which we now turn of contextualism as an expression of the changed outlook stemming from the controversies over evolution will shed further light on some of the remaining issues and afford a measure of clarification of the new evolutionary outlook.

## Contextualism and the New Outlook

How does contextualism express the Darwinian outlook? A complete answer would require volumes, but, fortunately, the main outlines can be suggested in fairly brief compass. Central for the contextualistic philosophy in this regard are (1) change and the ways of dealing with the changing and (2) a naturalistic approach framed in terms of the biological matrix of experience; and it is difficult to discuss either of these sets of points in such fashion as to illuminate the changed outlook stemming from the controversies over evolution without assuming the other. So there will be a measure of arbitrariness as to which points we discuss under which heading as well as in the order of discussion. In the first place, then, contextualism expresses the Darwinian outlook in its wholehearted acceptance of change. For contextualists the key fact about our world is the fact of change, and they find it wherever they look throughout the universe, whether in the vast galaxies of stars, the constitution of the atoms, or human affairs. Every existence is an event or history, with its own point of initiation, qualitative changes, and point of termination. Each thing in the universe comes into being, undergoes qualitative changes, and dies, making way for other individuals. A fixed world of static things is foreign to the outlook of the contextualists and post-Darwinians. Nature, on this view, is a complex of affairs, transactions, histories, marked by incessant beginnings and endings. In our changing world we may expect unpredictable novelties, qualitatively new things, incomplete things still in the making, uncertain, unstable situations as well as relatively stable ones, genuine contingencies; and to meet the challenges this kind of world presents we must try to work out ways of intelligently redirecting ongoing affairs. We need to stabilize patterns we find good and to seek ways of averting, reconstructing, or living acceptably with patterns we find bad. As Dewey argued in *The Quest for Certainty,* our concern as empirical philosophers is not the quest for the immutable or the pursuit of changelessness but rather finding patterns of change, constant or relatively invariant relations between changes.

The more we concentrate upon specific changes in the natural order, the clearer it becomes that the affairs constituting our world are many and varied; and this notion too seemed to be an expression of the Darwinian approach. Heterogeneity and diversity rather than homogeneity and sameness characterize existent things; and as William James never tired of saying, our world is not a monistic block universe but rather one with a plurality of specifically diverse, heterogeneous existences. Those views that make our world out to be more like an empire or kingdom than some sort of federation are fairly sure to be suppressing differences and underestimating the variety in it. Although, he admitted, there are many ways, mainly abstract or mechanical, in which we may refer to the universe as one, there is no way of reducing all things to a common denominator in any very significant, concrete sense; and James, like the contextualists in general, was suspicious of theories which make the world out to be all crystal clear with each part fitting into a tightly ordered logical system. The kind of world we find in experience seems rather to be one with some mud and chinks in it, with some portions shadowy and others shrouded in darkness; and although we seek to shed what light we may on these dark areas, we must not make the mistake of assuming that the significance of an item is always directly proportional to its clarity. There may, indeed, be things not dreamt of in our philosophy.

James was convinced that the pragmatic difference between pluralism and a monism of some sort hinged on the reality or unreality of novelty, and concrete novelty was for him so obvious a fact that the issue was readily resolved. It seemed clear to him that reality as perceptually experienced shows us a world of change—one shot through with novelties and risks, struggles, real losses, and genuine gains; one having a place for freedom.

Or, as James sometimes put it in a characteristically contextualistic vein, the difference between pluralism and monism or absolutism turns on the legitimacy of *some*.[12] Instead of speaking always in terms of *all* and *none,* we need to recognize that each part of the world is in some ways connected with its other parts and in others separated from them, and just how much union there is can be investigated empirically. For that matter, in discussing the range of realities in our world the contextualist feels more comfortable in speaking of *each* than of *all* in the sense of the total collection. For the former we may have a sample; for the latter our best enumeration may leave something out.

In dealing empirically with a world made up of a plurality of specifically diverse, changing affairs, there is no place for indubitables or claims to certainty. Rather a method or approach on the order of Peirce's fallibilism and probabilism seems more appropriate; and this, once more, seems to be an expression of the Darwinian outlook. Although in ordinary speech there may be justifiable ways of speaking of "practical certainty," ones which, paradoxically, leave open the possibility of our later discovering that we were in error, cognitive certainty in principle regarding matters of fact seems unattainable. Accordingly, contextualists challenge claims to certainty, whether based on infallible authority, either of God, His representatives, a sacred book, or the established doctrine of an Aristotle or a Marx, or on self-evident principles, or on indubitable data of some sort. According to the contextualists, such claims operate as devices for shutting off or blocking further investigation, and with Peirce they want to keep the road to inquiry open. At most the feeling of certainty is an evidential item which needs to be weighed with other evidence, and the feeling has been reported for so many highly uncertain claims that it is properly suspect. Whether in terms of current evidence or the historical record, where can we find another equally large and varied set of allegations with a poorer record of substantiation than the assertions of indubitability or certainty?

Contextualists agree with Peirce that attempts to base our reasoning regarding matters of fact on indubitables are likely to lead to skepticism or irrationality. We neither find indubitable axioms nor need we find them. We may base our account on a number of lines of evidence each of which is only probable; but if they converge, we get a belief that is highly probable and a much better guide to action than a so-called indubitable. If, as Peirce held, our reasoning is a kind of sampling operation in which we judge concerning the nature of a whole on the basis of the proportion found in our sampling of it, our judgments are, of course, fallible; but we can by increased sampling improve on our accuracy. With appropriately selected thimbles of wheat, we can judge the quality of a shipload of wheat just as with a random selection of hookfuls of cotton we can estimate the quality of a trainload of bales of cotton, and similarly for other areas.

Mechanistic determinists have sometimes looked to scientific laws for illustrations of certainty and universality and have reasoned from them to each and every instance covered by a particular law; but according to Peirce, this procedure is largely due to the fact that the individuals who reason in this way are unfamiliar with measurement and the actual procedures involved in formulating laws. In interpreting scientific laws in the light of radical change or basic novelty, on his view, we do well to remember that these formulations are statements of uniformities, statistical averages. Such necessity as they may have is a nomic necessity, not an empirically derived one. Although they may be reasonably accurate for large classes of instances, they may be inapplicable to specific items. In this respect they may be more like the actuarial charts of the life insurance companies than the mechanistic ideal. These charts may predict fairly accurately how many people of, say, our age will die in a given year but not whether a specific person of that age will die in that year.

If we seek to avoid one set of consequences or stabilize another in a changing world, we need something better than authoritarianism, a priori formulas, simple guesswork, or merely waiting for events to run their course. Here, according to the contextualist, a frankly experimental approach is needed, and the more significant the issues at stake, the more clearly is this the case. This is something we shall comment on later in connection with an analysis of critical thinking or reflective inquiry, but here I want at least to note the importance pragmatists have always attached to experimentation as a way of dealing with change. It is a way of getting more accurate predictions and better control in a problematic situation. An experiment is a program of action to determine consequences and is thus a way of introducing intelligence into a situation. It is an intelligently guided procedure for discovering what adjustments an organism must make to its environment to ward off ills or secure goods. For that matter, of course, experimentation is relevant not merely on the individual biological level but also, as John Dewey spent a lifetime reminding us, wherever planned reconstruction of a situation may help effect desired transformations—for example, in social planning or in education. Although experimentation will not and need not provide certainty, it may help us achieve a greater measure of security in the face of a hostile environment, biological or social. For if through experimentation we can discover or introduce appropriate instruments, we may better stabilize our responses or adjust with a greater measure of success to a hostile environment.

Persistent, careful concern with specific things changing and the ways of introducing desired changes, as the contextualist sees it, introduces a basic relativism, which is also quite in keeping with Darwinism. This relativism is to be opposed to absolutism and is a way of stressing the importance of context, situation, relationships. To take things out of context is to risk distortion and loss of meaning and value.[13] Place a texture in a different context, and you change its quality. Whether the change is significant for a given purpose, however, may depend on the purpose or the context. At any rate, constancy of quality from one context to another is not something to be assumed but rather something which may have to be worked for. It may require planning and setting up appropriate control textures. Absolutes, accordingly, are ruled out on this view, and unqualified generalizations are likely to be misleading. Contextualists suggest that characterizing any affair or specifying its relations is rarely simple and usually proceeds more clearly if we can indicate for what purpose, in terms of what standards, in what respects, or under what conditions it may be so characterized. Fortunately, the context commonly makes these matters clear enough for everyday purposes.

At any rate, a response that is appropriate to one environmental situation, as Darwin's investigations repeatedly showed, may be disastrous in another. A teaching technique which works very well relative to students with one set of backgrounds and interests may prove quite inappropriate for students with different backgrounds and interests. A type of pine which flourishes under most soil conditions in Southern Illinois may fare very poorly under standard conditions in Northern Illinois. An economic policy or a plan of action is good relative to a specific situation which makes it desirable. A knife may be good for sharpening a pencil and bad for cutting a rope; but to speak of it without qualification as good or bad is quite misleading.

The contextualistic account of analysis also expresses the Darwinian mode in a number of ways: for example, in its rejection of the idea that analysis is primarily a matter of reducing a complex to permanent or fixed elements, in its acceptance of the notion that analysis is an affair of tracing patterns of change, and in its recognition of the importance for many purposes of a genetic account of events. Contextualists deny the possibility of element analysis in the sense of breaking a whole down into atomic units or irreducible constituents of some sort. Analysis for them, as Pepper notes,[14] is an affair of exhibiting the texture of an event, and this involves discrimination of its strands, but the strands derive part of their quality from the event's context and have a way of leading off into it. So analysis becomes a matter of following references from one texture to another, and how far we follow them or which ones we trace depends on the problem which occasions our analytic inquiry. But we never reach ultimate elements.

We may trace the strands of a given texture into convenient control textures (schematic textures, or schemes) such as the color cone or a musical scale, and these in turn may be traced into schemes of light wave or air vibrations. These latter schemes are tied in with the system of schemes constituting physics and are interknit in various ways with the schematic structures of the other sciences. Any color may be located rather precisely as to hue, saturation, and value on the color cone, and once so located we have a basis for producing it in the future. A Chopin piano piece may be analyzed in terms of notes on a staff, thus giving us the musical score of the composition, whether we think of this score as something transcribed from hearing the piece or as Chopin's own analysis of the texture he sought to provide; and with this scheme a pianist can follow its references to the keys of a pianoforte keyboard and produce a set of tones constituting her or his version of the Chopin piece. Thus these schemes give us systems of references and suggested operations for producing textures of some specified character. They guide us to the objects or textures indicated.

Platonic realists and mechanistic naturalists traditionally have assumed that any whole can be analyzed completely and finally into its constituent elements. What the elements are may be debated, but that it is possible to reduce a whole to such constituents they never doubted. This possibility, however, is categorially denied by contextualists. On their categories there is no final and complete analysis of anything; and to speak in these terms shows a lack of understanding of analysis. Analytic inquiry involves both discrimination of constituent strands of a texture and relevant contextual references, and the traditional accounts have tended to limit it to a special form of the former. When we analyze a given event into A, B, and C, this is not to say that the event is divided without remainder once and for all into constituents A, B, and C, but rather that it is possible to trace a pattern of relations connecting the event with A, B, and C. And, of course, it does not rule out the possibility of tracing another pattern of relations between the event and D, E, F, or between it and an indefinitely large number of other possibilities. Ultimate cosmic units or elements are, for contextualists, dubious entities, and to speak of somehow reducing things into them as final constituents is to misinterpret analytic inquiry.

There is, of course, for the contextualist, no such thing as *the* analysis of anything. The texture of an event may be exhibited in any number of different ways, depending upon the purpose of the analysis or the nature of the problem generating it. The quality of an event is a fusion of the qualities of its strands, and part of the quality of any given texture accrues to it because of the quality of its environing textures, whose qualities, in turn, depend partially on the qualities of still other textures in their contexts, and so on—a process which drives the analyst beyond the event being analyzed. So depending upon which referential strand we follow and which environing texture we trace it into, we may have any number of analyses, each of which may be more or less adequate for its purpose.

If, then, analysis is an affair of exhibiting the texture of an event, a genetic account in terms of conditions and consequences is very much in order, for this is an important way of exhibiting the texture in question. Nature, for the contextualists, is a scene of incessant beginnings and endings; and initiations, consummations, blockings, with connecting references and intervening means-objects or instruments operating within a certain context, are categorial for them. These categorial distinctions, moreover, are ones in a temporal process, and an analysis which neglects this fact, contextualistically speaking, omits or slurs over something of vital importance. Although such an analysis may provide timeless logical distinctions, it is unlikely to exhibit the texture of an event with temporal spread. For that a genetic account may prove more illuminating.

If, for example, we are analyzing the death of JB, it will not do to say that whatever the cause, he is nonetheless dead, and no considerations of attendant circumstances or of anything before or after the instant of death are needed. Which considerations of this sort are relevant will depend, of course, on the purpose of the analysis. If homicide is suspected, the attendant circumstances may be crucially important for the police investigator. The act of dying, moreover, is not a matter of a knife-edge instant; it takes some time, sometimes relatively little and sometimes a fairly long time. And what happens within that time varies with the cause of death. Hence, although, to be sure, after the fact JB is equally dead whatever the cause, the police investigator's analysis of his death will be different in significant ways depending on whether the cause is asphyxiation, cyanide poisoning, food poisoning, strangulation, a stab in the heart, a blow on the head, cancer, or something else. Death from one of these causes will lead into different environing textures and will involve different control textures, observations, laboratory reports, and so on. And an adequate analysis of JB's death for the purpose cited needs to exhibit the distinctive features of the total texture stemming from whichever cause or complex of causes with whatever pertinent ramifications in more or less distant environing textures may be required.

In terms of contextualistic analysis we might well develop still other points connected with the respects in which the contextualistic philosophy expresses the Darwinian outlook in its acceptance of change and in its development of ways of dealing with the changing, for the entire philosophy centers about these topics. But the contextualist's naturalistic approach framed in terms of the biological matrix of experience is also an expression of the Darwinian perspective, and some of the key doctrines may be more conveniently discussed under this second heading than under our first or temporalistic one.

At any rate, contextualists reject supernaturalism with its doctrines of special creation, miracles, and revelation and attempt to account for natural events wholly in terms of natural principles without going outside the system of nature. They are concerned with questions growing out of affairs within nature rather than with attempts to discover some divine design for the totality of things. They reject the notion of a deity who intervenes in arbitrary fashion through special supernatural measures. One of the lessons of Darwin for philosophy, according to Dewey, is the forswearing of "inquiry after absolute origins and absolute finalities in order to explore specific values and the specific conditions that generate them,"[15] to investigate the ways in which one set of changes serves concrete purposes and another defeats them.

In spite of their forthright rejection of supernaturalism various pragmatists have used the term *God,* but in each case the traditional idea has been reinterpreted in naturalistic terms, usually in terms of values, and they have sometimes noted that the ideas with which they are concerned can be formulated without using the term. James and Dewey both spoke of God and religion in terms of values, and even so some of his associates criticized James as too supernaturalistic. Dewey, in *A Common Faith,* spoke of God as an active relation between the ideal and the actual rather than as an eternal, completed Being. Another contextualistically oriented philosopher, Henry Wieman, speaks of God as the source of human good, the set of forces making for creativity. John Fiske thought of the deity as guiding the natural evolutionary process, but his deity works through nature.

The naturalistic approach of the contextualists assumes a basic continuity between lower, less complex forms of existence and higher, more complex ones such that the latter grow out of the former. This is not to say that higher forms and activities are reducible to lower level ones; but it is to recognize the fact that life, conscious activities, linguistic communication, and forms of culture develop in a natural order from lower forms in which these features were not present. Precisely how any one of these higher level affairs develops is a matter for reflective inquiry or scientific investigation, but contextualists adopt a genetic point of view which maintains that in principle it is possible to trace lines of development from the lower to the higher stages. Using this genetic hypothesis, moreover, it has been possible time after time to work out or follow the patterns of change involved. But the matter of levels of existence is a topic to which we shall return after noting some features of the biological matrix of experience.

Pragmatists have long recognized that one's interpretation of persons and nature is intimately tied up with the psychology one adopts. If one starts with the traditional introspective psychology of Locke, Berkeley, and Hume which describes experience in terms of relatively distinct sensations or impressions and ideas somehow brought together by association, it may appear that a yawning chasm separates persons and their world. If, however, one adopts a newer psychology which draws upon developments in physiological and experimental psychology and describes experience in terms of ongoing courses of purposive behavior, it becomes apparent that persons are parts of nature and that the biological matrix of experience is central. This newer psychology is so focal for pragmatism or contextualism that George Herbert Mead regarded it as a primary source of this outlook. According to him, the sources of pragmatism are two: (1) a behavioristic psychology which enables one to put intelligence within conduct and to state it in terms of the activity of the organism, and (2) the research process, which comes back to the testing of a hypothesis by its working.[16] And whether these be called sources or perhaps rather essential constituents of pragmatism, they are indeed basic for the view. Both, moreover, have occasioned a storm of criticism, the former sometimes on the ground that the pragmatists have confused psychology and theory of knowledge. But clearly any theory of nature or knowledge which accepts the psychological theory of its rivals places itself at a decided disadvantage.[17] Mead, moreover, himself both a social scientist and a philosopher, saw the relations between the pragmatic philosophy and its psychological base more clearly than many who have not had his combination of interests; and he early took the lead in developing a behaviorism of the sort mentioned above.

It should be noted, however, that this behavioristic psychology must be distinguished from Watsonian behaviorism, which is fundamentally individual, mechanistic, and antithetical to introspection. It is rather a purposive behaviorism which starts with behavior on a molar rather than a molecular level and finds a place equally for the usual observational material and for that which is open mainly to the observation of the acting individual. Behavior, on Mead's account, is basically social, and language as an instrument of socialization is a form of interaction within a social group rather than something to be explained simply in terms of movements within the larynx of the individual. Mind or consciousness, according to Mead, instead of being something to be ruled out of account, is something to be explained in relation to conduct; and the distinction between inner and outer, instead of being one between disparate metaphysical realms, is one made within experience.

E. C. Tolman's *Purposive Behavior in Animals and Men* offers an excellent systematic formulation of a purposive behaviorism of this general type, and the wealth of experimental material summarized in it both fits in with and uses the contextualistic categories. It needs supplementation in terms of social and cultural considerations, but the biological matrix of experience comes out clearly in this account. Tolman assumes that molar behavior-acts are correlated in significant ways with facts in physiology and physics, as might be expected from our earlier account of contextualistic analysis; but he holds that each such act has its own identifying properties. To identify it, in the first place, we describe "(a) the goal-object or objects being got to or from; (b) the specific pattern of commerces with means-objects as involving short (easy) commerces with means-objects for thus getting to or from."[18] In the second place, identifying the act also involves specifying two additional sets of properties: (1) initiating causes, namely, (a) environmental stimuli and (b) initiating physiological states; and (2) behavior determinants, namely, (a) purposive and cognitive immanent determinants (which should include behavior adjustments, Tolman's substitute for the conscious awareness and ideas of the mentalist), and (b) purposive and cognitive capacities.

As I have indicated elsewhere,[19] the outstanding feature of such molar behavior, whether in the lower animals or in men, is its purposive character, the fact that it is motivated by some drive. Certain states of affairs or ends are sought and achieved. Other results are to be avoided. Such behavior is carried out for the sake of satisfying various demands, to get to or from a given instance or type of environmental presence or of physiological quiescence or disturbance, to overcome problems in connection with food, water, or any of the multifarious wants and needs of a living organism. It is an attempt of the organism to maintain the organic or environmental conditions necessary, if need be, to change them to bring about the fulfillment of these demands. Upon its degree of success in fulfilling certain of them depends the very preservation of the organism or the species. Fundamental physiological drives form the core of purposive behavior, but the demands of an adult human being are far richer and more varied than this central core might suggest.

As might be expected from the above, the naturalistic approach of the contextualists places persons in nature and assumes a basic continuity between them and their environment, natural, social, and cultural.[20] As living organisms they have commerce with their environment in multitudinous ways. They enter into multiple interactions or transactions with it, some of them so integral to the events related that the distinction between organism and environment becomes a functional one which may be drawn in different ways, depending on the interaction. Their environment supports some interactions and fails to support others. It enters both directly and indirectly into one's life-functions. Thus organism and environment enter into more or less stable integrations, form uneasy equilibriums requiring frequent adjustments or modifications, with the survival of the organism depending on making some of them. Darwin and James have helped us see the focal importance of the living creature adjusting or adapting to its environment and to view intelligence as a distinctive form of behavior, one concerned with choosing appropriate means for the attainment of future ends. Whatever else mind may be, it is at least a means of controlling the environment in relation to the ends of the life process.

In terms of their acceptance of the notion of a basic continuity between organism and environment, contextualists reject such dualisms as those between the self and the world, mind and matter, and subject and object. If interaction or transactionalism be accepted, these dualisms are untenable. The relation between a self and its world, according to the contextualists, is not one of confrontation between hard and fast, sharply defined, relatively unmodifiable objects that change in little but position but rather, as we have seen, a far more intimate form of intercourse. The conception of a private inner mind-set over against an external material world does not accord with the contextualists' idea of a texture and its context, with strands of reference running from one to the other in such open and aboveboard fashion that in principle there are no inaccessible textures or realms of textures. Nor is the notion of a self-contained subject which somehow knows an equally self-contained but alien object any more acceptable, contextualistically speaking. We start not with subject and object but rather with a total affair or situation within which, for purposes of practical or intellectual control, we may distinguish, say, a subject as experiencer from an object as experienced or a self from its not-self. Contextualists have similar reservations, of course, about attempting to turn a functional distinction between the organic and the inorganic into a hard and fast distinction between two separate, mutually exclusive realms of life or living things and matter or material things. And they find it not surprising that, depending on how one draws the line, viruses, say, might be in either domain.

Accordingly, when one speaks of levels of existence, from the point of view of the contextualists, this is not to assert that matter, life, and mind, say, are separate and distinct kinds of Being. Rather they might better be thought of as different modes of interconnection and operation, different ways of characterizing diverse particular fields of interacting events. In Dewey's language, they are consequences of interactions of varying complexity, scope, and degrees of intimacy.[21] And depending on the problem at hand, we might distinguish dozens of "levels" or modes of interconnection and operation, each with its own distinctive marks. In *Experience and Nature*, however, Dewey characterized the three levels mentioned above roughly as follows: (1) the physico-chemical level of mass-energy interactions on which the physical sciences seek to discover the properties and relations of things in terms of which they may serve as means or instruments; (2) the psycho-physical or organic pattern of need-demand-satisfaction activities; and (3) the level of mind or human experience in which social transactions involving language and meaning come in. These types of interactions exhibit different degrees of complexity, diverse functions, varied sets of consequences, and variegated qualitative patterns.

What we call material things, living organisms, or mind (persons, or personalities) involve in each case abstractions from concrete transactions or situations. For example, depending on the problem, we may think of material things as behavior-objects, or we may think of them as physical stimuli, as abstractions the physical scientists make from the immediacies of specific concrete behavioral situations to get generalized supports for any and all possible operations and thus provide instruments for as wide a range of interactions as possible. Physical stimuli may be described in terms of, say, air vibrations of a given frequency or in terms of mass. If we have a formula calling for a given mass, it does not matter whether that is provided by a thimble, a coin, a plant, a section of human tissue, sheets from a musical score, or pages from a manuscript on philosophy. All are equally masses. Physical schemes are constructed to provide a wide range of applications; if they do not afford such a range, we revise them to get more adequate coverage; and the possibility of locating a given strand in one of them accordingly is useful for a broad range of problems. The key thing about such a physical object or a statement involving it is whether it enables us to predict accurately and thus solve the problem for the sake of which we traced the strand into the schematic textures of physics.

Thus statements made at the physico-chemical level may be very useful for a wide range of problems, but for some problems something much more illuminating can be provided by a botanist concerning a plant or by a composer about a musical score; and the contextualists would not think of saying that something at the organic level or at the level of mind was nothing but a combination of physical or material elements or that things at these two levels should be described exclusively in terms of the laws and generalizations of the physical sciences. Nor would they wish to maintain that an organism is nothing but a material thing plus this or that additional item any more than they would wish to hold that a man is only a child plus a few additional items: such statements do not begin to do justice to the different types of interactions involved, with their diverse functions and consequences.

From the point of view of the contextualists, with their acceptance of change and fallibilism, there are new things under the sun. New qualities do emerge; and recognition of this fact, far from being simply a way of foregoing explanation, may provide added understanding. It seems to be an irreducible fact that life and mind have evolved from states of affairs in which they were absent; and *after* the fact we can show how potentialities in the former, specifiable directions of change present there, when taken in conjunction with appropriate occasions and supporting conditions, pointed toward the state which has evolved. But we make our predictions in the face of change with the knowledge that they are fallible and with the expectation that through observation and experiment we may make them better.

Another distinctive doctrine of the contextualists which clearly reflects the Darwinian biological matrix of experience at the same time that it exemplifies genetic analysis is their analysis of reflective thinking, scientific method, or critical inquiry. Although critical thinking is by no means limited to practical problems of adjustment of an organism to its environment or ones affecting either its survival or that of its species, such problems come in for special emphasis, and the characteristic pragmatic descriptions of such thinking manifestly grow out of an attempt to take seriously the contributions of biology. These accounts, moreover, express succinctly a number of ideas central for both the naturalistic and biological emphases of contextualism and provide, indeed, a kind of outline of the entire philosophy.

What, then, is critical inquiry or reflective thinking? The process has been described in somewhat different terms in various versions, but in general contextualists have thought of it as a problem-solving or doubt-resolving affair; and they are convinced that the pattern exemplified in it is applicable, with appropriate modifications, to the full range of problems facing us in this changing world. From Peirce on, however, they have maintained that these problems are specific and concrete, or can be made so; and so long as we can formulate our problems in these terms we can deal with them, work at overcoming them. If, however, we try to make a problem of everything at once or the universe at large, we have no way of solving it; and escape or despair is the response. Uneasiness about the world at large may produce a profound malaise, but it is not likely to be effectively reconstructive. Descartes's universal doubt, according to Peirce and his fellow pragmatists, is a fake: we do not doubt in general or wholesale fashion. It is only when we have some question about a specific item that doubt occurs, and this is possible because, for the moment, we accept without question a context of beliefs. This is not to say, of course, that these other beliefs are indubitable, for another time they may be questioned but once more within a context of accepted beliefs or habits of action.

Granted, then, that reflective thinking is a problem-solving or doubt-resolving process, what are the main steps or phases involved in it? The contextualistic reply finds its fullest expression in the writings of John Dewey, who has set forth his answer to this question in many different books and articles, perhaps in its simplest terms in *How We Think* (1910, 1933) and in a fuller, more sophisticated version in *Logic: The Theory of Inquiry* (1938). For present purposes we may say that there are five main steps in a complete act of reflective thinking.

(1) The first step is the appearance of the problem. This may be marked by a more or less vague sense of something having gone wrong, a breakdown in habitual responses or modes of action. Our usual patterns of response do not

seem to be working or have run into difficulty. The situation may be one of practical friction or strain, conflicting tendencies, perplexity, ambiguity, or doubt. One of us comes thirsty to the familiar water hole or spring in the wilderness and finds no water or perhaps hears an insistent rattling as one bends to drink. (2) The second step or phase is the clarification of the problem. Through analysis and observation we gather the data needed to formulate the difficulty or define the problem. The more or less vague feeling of something amiss is replaced by a clearly formulated problem. We establish that the spring is dry or that a rattlesnake is rattling and proceed to state our problem. (3) Having it clearly stated, we are ready for the third stage, that of suggested solutions or hypotheses as to how to solve the problem. Various ideas as to how it may be solved occur to us, and these ideas suggest further observation and help point to other pertinent facts. The more adequately we have stated the problem, of course, the more expeditious our search for possible solutions. (4) The fourth step is that of deductive elaboration. We reason out the implications of the various hypotheses, noting what we may expect if we take the first, the second, the third, and so on. In some instances further information may be needed before we can deduce the implications of a given hypothesis. Then on the basis of our survey of the probable consequences of the various proposed solutions we decide which to put to the test of action. (5) The fifth and final step is that of verification or disconfirmation. Through observation or experiment we test the most promising hypothesis or hypotheses. If one of them works out, our problem is solved, the difficulty is cleared up, the doubt or perplexity is resolved; and once more stable lines of action are resumed.

This pattern is somewhat oversimplified, and the stages do not always come one right after another in the order in which I have listed them. For example, the probable consequences of the proposed solutions may look so unpromising that we may go back to the second and third steps, rethink our problem, and see if we cannot think of other possible solutions. Nor are the stages always as distinct as may appear from this analysis; some telescoping or merging of stages may occur. But ordinarily for the solution of a difficult problem the stages need to be outlined clearly.

In spite of its simplicity, however, the above account seems to me basically accurate. This is what is involved in problem-solving activity whether it is a personal problem, a major social issue, or a significant scientific problem; and it is difficult to overestimate the survival value of this method for the human species. Indeed, if its past record of achievement should lead to its more extensive use with reference to such problems as those of war, poverty, population, and pollution, my optimism concerning our future survival would be greatly strengthened. In any event, the method of critical inquiry is a tremendous advance over the trial and error method of resolving difficulties, having the advantage of both solving a problem and providing some descriptive or explanatory statements about how it was solved.

Going hand in hand with this account of critical inquiry is a view of experience which incorporates findings and emphases of biological science and focuses upon the fact that experiencing means living in and by means of an environment, natural, social, and cultural. Experience is the entire range of our relations, interactions, and commerces with nature. It includes our enjoyments and appreciations, our consummations and sufferings, as well as our reconstructive or adjustive activities. We experience nature in manifold manners and modes, and things interacting in certain ways constitute experience.

The contextualistic interpretation of experience is very well summarized through a series of contrasts with what he called the orthodox view in Dewey's famous essay on "The Need for a Recovery of Philosophy."[22] As contrasted with the orthodox notion that experience is primarily a knowledge affair, Dewey insisted that it is a matter of intercourse between us as living beings and our physical and social environment, a process of doings and undergoings in which we employ direct environmental supports in order indirectly to help effect changes favorable to our further functioning. Far from being an invidiously subjective inner affair, separate and distinct from objective reality, it is of a piece with an objective world in which and by means of which we live, move, and have our being. Whereas the proponents of the orthodox conception have been preoccupied with what is or has been given in a bare present of some sort and have tended to look toward the past if they have passed beyond the present, the thrust of this new outlook stresses the contextual, situational, transactional, or field character of experience as opposed to a particularism which neglects connections, relations, and continuities and concentrates on more or less disconnected sense data, impressions, and ideas. Finally, instead of holding that experience and thought in the sense of inference are antithetical, the contextualists see experience as full of inference. For them it is loaded with references which trace directions and relations and pregnant with imaginative forecasts of future trends and movements. How could it be otherwise if we seek to eliminate environmental incidents hostile to our future life activity and to insure conditions favorable to the process? What else should we expect if we wish not merely to live but to live well, to enrich and enhance the qualities of experience and to share their enjoyments?

In keeping with this view of experience, ideas for the contextualists are not more or less miraculous psychical carbon copies of real but never given external objects. They are rather, in their distinctive role, hypotheses, plans of action, suggested solutions for problematic situations. They function as tools or instruments, anticipatory sets for guiding desired changes. With this conception goes an operational theory of truth. Truth is a matter of how ideas work out in practice, whether they lead as expected or predicted, whether they provide qualitative confirmation.

Knowledge too needs to be placed within the context of the problematic situation and reflective inquiry. But here there are some terminological differences among the contextualists. Bergson's *Introduction to Metaphysics* distinguishes between intuition or the realization of quality and analytic, relational knowledge, holding that only the former affords genuine knowledge. In *A Contextu-alistic Theory of Perception* I have maintained that perception has the two limit-ing poles of aiming at the realization of quality or at identifying qualities and things for the furtherance of a practical drive and that it is not a question of one being more genuine than the other. Pepper declares that the intuition of quality is as informative of the nature of things as analysis and should, of course, be considered equally a form of cognition.[23] Dewey grants, in an essay on "Qualitative Thought," that Bergson is correct in contending that intuition as the realization of quality precedes conception and goes deeper but wishes to reserve the term *knowledge* for the latter, for relational knowledge;[24] and in general pragmatists have followed this usage. So long as it is clear that both of these things have important places in the contextualistic system, for present purposes I am willing to go along with this practice.

Dewey has stressed the pervasive quality which characterizes a total prob-lematic situation and guides the course of inquiry, and it seems reasonable to hold, as Iredell Jenkins has persuasively argued, that vivid realization of this unique quality is significant not merely for aesthetics but for human surviv-al.[25] The more novel the situation and the more rapidly changing the course of events, the more useful it is likely to be for adaptive or adjustive purposes to intuit this quality.

When all this is noted, however, it is nonetheless the case that the knowl-edge needed for implementing a practical drive is more than immediate aware-ness or the presence of sense data. Hence, as Dewey insisted, the senses are not primarily pathways to knowledge but stimuli to action; sensations are not so many pellets of knowledge but signals to redirect action, or signs of problems to be solved. Having quality before us may be a condition for knowing or the begin-ning of relational knowledge, but this type of knowledge is an affair of the use we make of sensory discriminations. It is inferential, and the problem is how the processes of inquiry are to be guided to trustworthy or warranted conclusions. It involves operations of controlled observation, testing, and experimentation. It is a product of inquiry—the steps in a complete act of reflective thinking.

In like fashion the contextualistic account of moral values may be treated in the context of the problematic situation and critical inquiry, but we have space for only a few brief comments. Here too, moreover, the account reflects Darwinian evolutionism in its emphasis on improving or bettering our present situation rather than upon good or bad in some absolute sense. A moral end or standard is a hypothesis as to how to overcome a moral problem. The good, if one is to speak of the good rather than the better, is what will enable us to solve the problem or difficulty, and since each problematic situation is unique, values are also unique. Problems are connected in various ways, however, and a career may be charted in terms of their sequence. Accordingly, we try to solve our current problems in ways which will not block the path to the solution of foreseeable future ones. This, I think, may be part of what Dewey had in mind in holding that if a general end is to be specified, it should be one on the order of growth, education, or continued problem-solving. In this connection we may note that our personal problems are related in various ways to the problems of others and that we have enough common problems that we may need to think in terms of our society or culture and the human situation. If shared experience is truly the greatest of human goods, the basis for this may be found in our common problems.

A naturalistic account of morals may be framed not merely in terms of adjustment, adaptation, and problem-solving, however, but also in terms of our likings, enjoyments, and desires. But contextualistically speaking, although consummations and fulfillments are categorial, there are ways and ways of achieving them; and what is good is not raw likings or satisfactions. Rather it is ones which still look good after critical scrutiny. We need to test them by checking on their conditions and consequences; and this involves running through the steps in a complete act of reflective thinking. It is not simply a question of whether as a matter of fact we do or do not enjoy or like something but whether this enjoyment or liking meets the test of reflection. Is it worthy of being desired, demanded, or enjoyed? An affirmative answer constitutes a claim that future consequences will be such as to meet the test of reflection.

I find the context of the problematic situation and critical inquiry a highly fruitful one,[26] and still other topics might be discussed in terms of it. For example, the contextualist also has a place for human freedom, and part of what helps bring it about is the delay between stimulus and response which makes it possible for reflective consideration of alternatives to become a factor in the decision process.

By way of summary, then, in this section I have tried to suggest some of the respects in which the contextualistic philosophy, through (1) its acceptance of change and its ways of dealing with the changing and (2) its naturalistic approach framed in terms of the biological matrix of experience, expresses the Darwinian outlook. In this connection, as we have seen, a great deal of contextualistic interpretation of evolution also has been given, thus anticipating the concluding interpretive comments of the final section of this essay.

## Concluding Contextualistic Notes on Evolution

In tracing the implications of evolutionary theory for various aspects of philosophy I have already sketched the main outlines of a contextualistic interpretation of evolution, but in this section, for emphasis and further clarification, I should like to present four or five points in this interpretation in somewhat different terms and supplement briefly my earlier account of some of them. Perhaps the dominant theme running through all of them is the fact that from the point of view of the contextualists change is a central feature of the cosmos, and evolution and revolution are important patterns of change.

In a world of change novelties and contingencies are to be expected, and in terms of the contextualistic categories a number of kinds of novelty may be noted. First is novelty as uniqueness. William James insisted that every event is unique. Even if it could recur, it would be different at least in terms of its antecedents. Pepper suggests four types of novelty: intrusive, emergent-qualitative, emergent-textural, and absolute or naive novelties;[27] and there is no question about the first three. Intrusive novelty occurs when a referential strand is blocked or intercepted by a conflicting line of action. This unexpected opposition draws attention and generates enhanced perception of the situation. Emergent qualitative novelty is also to be expected. A new quality comes into being with every event as a look from this page to something over your shoulder suggests. With the constant involvement through its strands of a texture in its context and with the complex changing from moment to moment, the total texture at moment two is different from that at moment one, and accordingly, each has a different quality. One character is gone and a new one has come to be. Emergent textural novelty results from the integration or fusion of its substrands. The integration is something new. In all these cases of novelty, however, it is possible after the fact to trace strands leading up to the novel quality or texture, and in general contextualists tend to assume that continuities or connections may be traced between any two states of affairs. Nor would they hold that this casts any doubt on the genuineness or importance of the novelties.

Pepper's fourth category of novelty, however, raises a question as to whether there are not novelties of a more radical or absolute type. Are there textures or strands such that no previous event ever referred to them, one whose initiation is not an integration or fusion of other strands? And in like fashion are there absolute endings in the sense of strands with no connection with an actual present or future event, ones which disappear without a trace? There is nothing in the contextualistic categories, according to Pepper, to exclude such textures; but even if this be true and maximum allowance be made for it, as he adds, we still need more to make an affirmative case than absence of evidence to the contrary. It seems to me, moreover, that the category of context and the contextualists' operational procedure point in another direction. Loss of context in the fashion suggested by an absolute novelty or ending does not seem to me to have a contextualistic ring. Insulated or isolated entities and absolutes are questionable on contextualistic grounds, and the fact (mentioned by Pepper) that many references believed to be untraceable have later been traced would seem to provide some grounds for skepticism concerning this type of novelty.

Contextualists find both continuities and discontinuities in nature, and such being the case the interpretation given either set of facts should not be such as to rule out the other. As I have tried to show earlier in this essay, contextualistic analysis is admirably fitted to do justice to both features, which contextualists find both at the level of individual textures and at that of patterns of vast complexes of events. Habits, dispositions, and regularities, say, point toward continuities, and diversities, novelties, and irregularities suggest discontinuities.

A mutation marks a discontinuity, but even here there are traceable connections. A major discontinuity in some larger pattern of events we may call a revolution, but the course of evolutionary development includes revolutions as well as more gradual changes. It has a place for cataclysmic as well as for graded change. Indeed, as the history of science suggests, discontinuity and revolution are rather more common than we may have suspected.[28] Emergents signalize the combination of discontinuity and continuity of which we have been speaking. They may be novel and at least partially unpredictable relative to our best present knowledge, but after the fact it is possible to trace their coming to be, and in the light of our experience with them we work at developing better conceptual instruments in order to improve on our future predictions.

Contextualists tend to be dubious of any grand overall evolutionary scheme. If we take seriously the notion that the stars as well as the firm earth are in process, we are not likely to think that everything is all finished and done or that some pattern of cosmic development which will account for all new species is already set and that all we have to do is make note of eternal perfection or seize upon some simple formula. The cosmos in general and our world in particular are vastly more complex and diversified than some of our formulas may suggest; and we have a staggering if not almost overwhelming amount to learn about them, but through the method of reflective inquiry we are making a beginning on learning more about the world and our place in it.

Contextualists find no inevitable tendency toward progress in evolution, nor, unlike Hegel, Marx, and Fiske, do they discern any set of necessary stages through which the life of spirit, social or economic systems, or the biological order must move in the developmental process. Successful adjustment to one state of affairs may render a species incapable of responding successfully to a markedly different set of conditions, as the number of extinct species may suggest. There clearly is change, and sometimes progress, but not a necessary or inevitable progress.

In keeping with our naturalistic approach, we contextualists reject any supernatural theistic design, nor do we find acceptable an Aristotelian final cause for the universe. Purposive behavior we do observe in both animals and people, and we have no need or wish to reduce it to anything else. But we have discovered no cosmic goals or plans. The only designs or plans we know of are those of finite planners, and we are convinced that through the proper use of intelligence our human plans can be greatly improved with a consequent strengthening of our capacity to come to terms with the problems confronting us. I share the hope of John Dewey that philosophy can contribute to the betterment of our human situation through helping inform our action at all levels with vision, imagination, and reflection to bring clearly to mind future possibilities with reference to attaining the better and averting the worse.

# 2

# Metaphysical Interpretation

One of the primary goals of philosophic vision has been to achieve a broad perspective within which all things may be given their due place. The philosopher has been particularly sensitive to the dangers of the sort of narrow specialization which either refuses to look beyond its own little province or treats as nonsensical any attempt to go beyond it. Traditionally, the philosopher has sought to make comprehensive sense of the full range of facts from whatever field they may be drawn, whether from common sense, the sciences, the arts, religion, politics, people's working life, or their play activities.

Naturally, not all philosophers have sought this comprehensive wisdom in the same way, nor have all agreed as to its precise character. Whereas some look for it through metaphysical speculation, an increasing number of thinkers make the avoidance of metaphysics a condition of talking sense. Some of the latter group find the key to the wider view in a systematic study of language in its semantic, syntactic, and pragmatic dimensions and feel that through the judicious use of logical analysis the major problems of philosophy may be cleared up. Instead of asking about the nature of reality, these individuals may prefer to inquire about what distinctions we mean to express through our use of the words *real* and *unreal*. Not infrequently, however, it turns out that for this group *metaphysics* has become a smear word for designating views they oppose, and their own position, or set of stipulations, assumes without explicit recognition of the fact, the basic outlines of some one of the familiar metaphysical theories.

I should like, therefore, in this paper to explore briefly certain aspects of metaphysical interpretation as a way of making comprehensive sense of our world. Without attempting an exhaustive account, I hope to suggest something of the nature of metaphysical interpretation, its scope, its method, its aim, its relation to science, and of how we check on the adequacy of a system of in-

From *Philosophical Review* 61.2 (Apr. 1952): 176–87. Copyright © 1952 Cornell University. Reprinted by permission of *Philosophical Review.*

terpretation. By metaphysical interpretation, in general, I have in mind explanation or analysis in terms of the categories, or fundamental concepts, of a worldview. A metaphysical interpretation of any problematic feature of our world has been given when we can indicate the place of this feature in the conceptual framework of a worldview. With Stephen C. Pepper[1] and Dorothy M. Emmet[2] I think that such a worldview centers about a root metaphor or basic analogy from which a kind of theoretical model for the entire range of facts may be drawn. It seems to me clear, moreover, that more than one such analogy is worth developing. With Whitehead[3] I hold that the notion of importance or the presupposition of importance and the notion of matter-of-fact are crucial ones for any attempt to survey the whole of things and that it is the former which brings order in the realm of matter-of-fact or which imposes a perspective. Some one fact or cluster of facts seems to a given creative thinker to be especially important for an understanding of things in general. An insight into the structure of this fact seems to afford a master coordination of facts. Accordingly, he or she attempts to spread that structure to worldwide scope. If it can be given this scope—if, that is, it can be applied with precision and without serious inconsistency to the illumination of any fact or any range of facts— we have a worldview with high claim to our thoughtful consideration.

Perhaps here I should make clear that in spite of my reference to root metaphors and my feeling that something akin to poetic—or, should I say, scientific?—imagination is involved in the initial insights of a metaphysical outlook, I do not think of a metaphysical system as merely a useful myth. A measure of idealization of key fact may enter in, but the idealization is for the sake of more comprehensive knowledge.

It may be urged, however, that the procedure which has just been outlined is a confusion of what is important for a person, or what is impressive for an individual, with what is existential, or with what characterizes anything whatsoever. Because one philosopher is impressed with the transiency of things or feels that it is important to plan with change in mind does not justify holding with a Heraclitus or a Bergson that everything is in change any more than another philosopher's sense of the abiding character of reality justifies the position of a Parmenides or a Bradley. Indeed, the critic[4] may continue, ultimate importance for the organization of experience around humanly basic interests needs to be sharply distinguished from ultimate reality or what characterizes everything real. I should agree with the critic that the fact that I prefer a key fact or regard it as important does not make it a criterion of ultimate reality. The basic question is not whether I prefer change, or permanence, or the mechanical, or some other fact but rather what viewing the world in terms of these facts can do by way of plausible ordering of the rest of the realm of facts. If we place ourselves sympathetically within the intellectual framework determined by the basic structural features of one of these key facts, how far will it take us in the organization of the entire realm of facts—in giving what appears, in the light of all the available evidence, to be a reasonable ordering of the facts? Does taking the structure of a particular fact as basic lead us to regard most of the other facts as mere appearances or nonentities, or does it rather illuminate a wide range of other facts? If the former, it is relatively inadequate as a basis for a worldview, and its claim to special significance is in so far unjustified. If the latter, it gives greater promise as the basis for a worldview and has a type of importance which is significant for a study of what is. This importance is a matter of its explanatory value in the broad sense. It consists not simply in congeniality to temperamental bias or to individual preference but rather in the aid it offers for detailed understanding of the realm of facts. If it helps make clear connections which other views have perhaps left opaque or unnoticed or if it suggests solutions for philosophical problems difficult or impossible of solution on other views, it gains added corroboration. And, on the other hand, of course, if it does not seem especially helpful in ordering the facts in a given area or has less suggestiveness for further investigation than alternative views, its position is weakened. I might add that, even though importance for the organization of experience around humanly basic interests is not to be confused with being pervasively characteristic of reality, the fact that interpretation in terms of a given set of categories achieves this end is surely not irrelevant to its claim to be able to order the totality of facts.

The kind of check which we can make of our most promising worldviews, however, does not offer conclusive proof for them. This, of course, is a difficulty which applies not merely to traditional metaphysical systems but also to the model languages proposed by such antimetaphysicians as Carnap and Neurath, and Neurath has an interesting discussion of some of these difficulties in the first pages of an article, "Universal Jargon and Terminology."[5] The practice of testing, he maintains, depends upon the limitations we give to the respective "area" in question, and the more comprehensive the "area," the more difficult it is to compare different "possibilities."[6] "Moreover," he adds,

> building up a Universal Jargon [his name for the model language he proposes for general use] needs a comprehensive training, which is connected with an alteration of our whole attitude. One is hardly able to apply alternatively an empiricist's language with all its implications and a non-empiricist's language with its implications. What comes from an "experiment" with a modified scientific language will be analysed by a man who is modified by his "experiment," which is more than an experiment: it performs a kind of self-education.[7]

These are genuine difficulties; and I am not willing to claim a ready solution for them; but perhaps the long history of metaphysical systems provides somewhat more basis for dealing with them than the relatively short history of the search for a universal jargon of Neurath's type affords. Metaphysicians have long been aware of the fact that discussions of different metaphysical views are likely to be colored by the metaphysical preconceptions of the one discussing them, and any survey of the relative merits of different views may reflect this too. For that matter, it may be clear to you that the present discussion reflects my pragmatic or contextualistic leanings. At any rate, metaphysicians have learned to identify interpretative biases, and they have had an opportunity to see how well certain modes of interpretation stand up under centuries of criticism. Some teachers of philosophy, moreover, seem to have developed considerable skill in this difficult art.

Though the long period of criticism I referred to a moment ago has served to eliminate a good many worldviews from serious consideration, it has not succeeded in narrowing the field down conclusively to one view. Indeed, it seems to me to suggest that claims to indubitable certainty for any position are quite dubious. Where does this leave us? It seems to me to leave us with the sort of tentative approach characteristic of the wider scientific theories. Unless we are willing to claim an immediate guarantee of the certainty of some view—a claim which seems to me to go beyond the evidence—we marshal circumstantial evidence after the manner of an investigator attempting to solve a crime—except that we attempt it on a worldwide scale. Each evidential item adds support or the reverse according as it fits or does not fit a given pattern of interpretation—according as it has or has not a precise and plausible place in the ordering delineated by our view. The fact that metaphysical interpretations remain hypothetical in character, as such philosophers as H. N. Lee and Pepper have maintained, does not mean that all of these hypotheses are of equal weight. Some offer a far more adequate interpretation than others. Metaphysicians may differ with reference to which hypothesis is more adequate, and much has been made of their differences; but there would be scant question among contemporary metaphysicians that the worldview of Thales and the Milesians is far less adequate than that of, say, Aristotle, or Democritus, or Hegel, or Dewey—whatever misgivings they may have concerning the views of this second group of philosophers. Any one of this latter set of views derives corroboration from diverse evidential items which do not seem to support Thales. Each one of them seems to explain the facts better than does the water hypothesis. And, while on this matter of agreement, I might add my suspicion that contemporary metaphysicians would agree that the basic outlook of a Carnap or a Neurath offers something a good deal more adequate in the way of a worldview than the writings of Comte.

It may be suggested, however, that the reason for the failure to arrive at some one well established worldview is not the difficulty of getting at the facts on this scale. It is rather that the metaphysician is not concerned with factual questions. The outstanding peculiarity of metaphysical difference, it may be claimed, is that the differing metaphysicians agree on all the facts—a claim sometimes made perhaps on the assumption that metaphysical differences are inconsequential and arbitrary. John Wisdom is one who holds that metaphysicians are not concerned with factual questions. In an article, "Metaphysics and Verification, I,"[8] he maintains that in asking a metaphysical question you are asking something on which no expert can help you. You already have all the relevant facts. "What you are asking for is a decision and the reasons for it *in the sense in which reasons can be offered for a decision* (by barristers for and against). But these as a matter of fact you have already set out."[9] The question is one of whether one set of facts, say X-facts, is to be identified with another set of Y-facts. So interpreted, Wisdom asserts that "metaphysical paradoxes appear no longer as crude falsehoods about how language is actually used, but as penetrating suggestions as to how it might be used so as to reveal what, by the actual use of the language, is hidden. And metaphysical platitudes appear as timely reminders of what is revealed by the actual use of language and would be hidden by the new."[10] I am pleased to find this support for my belief that metaphysics may offer penetrating suggestions about matters which might otherwise be hidden. I agree, moreover, that there is pretty clearly an element of persuasion or decision in a worldview, and I am convinced that the terminology used in setting forth a view is frequently of crucial importance; but the linguistic considerations seem to me to grow out of basic interpretations of the facts. The linguistic usages are likely to parallel and reflect more fundamental differences regarding the nature of a fact. Languages are developed to deal with some subject matter. Determining that something is a fact is usually far easier than securing agreement on its relevance or its significance or on what a fact is. The agreement on all the facts as between different worldviews—if one takes the full range of facts—I think has been greatly exaggerated. It does not seem to me that the Hegelian idealist and the Aristotelian agree on all the facts but add as a kind of afterthought that the one regards them as of the nature of ideas and the other demurs in certain respects—the relation between interpretation and what is interpreted is more intimate than that; or, if they do agree on the facts, it is on a rough common-sense basis with both of them convinced that these facts are in need of much further analysis or refinement. The interpretive attitude and the categories in terms of which facts are interpreted are of crucial significance, and it seems to me far from arbitrary which attitude and categories one takes.

John Dewey, in *Philosophy and Civilization,* has a passage on the quality of persons or historic events which seems to me suggestive of the difference different metaphysical interpretations can make. He writes:

> We follow, with apparently complete understanding, a tale in which a certain quality or character is ascribed to a certain man. But something said causes us to interject, "Oh, you are speaking of Thomas Jones, I supposed you meant John Jones." Every detail related, every distinction set forth remains just what it was before. Yet the significance, the color and weight, of every detail is altered. For the

quality that runs through them all, that gives meaning to each and binds them together, is transformed.[11]

In a sense the same common-sense facts are presented to different metaphysical interpretations, but the transformation may be far more sweeping—so much so that the set of details reported by one interpretation may be recognizable by advocates of another view only in terms of the intermediary common-sense facts.

In speaking of a worldview as offering even hypothetical knowledge, however, it may appear to some that I am offering metaphysics as a kind of substitute for science. And, it will be asked, is not science far more adequate in the field of knowledge than is any metaphysical insight and particularly than one which professes to show that science somehow falsifies the basic nature of reality? My answer is that I do not conceive of metaphysics as a substitute for science or specialized knowledge; and any metaphysics which interprets the results of science as illusory has, it seems to me, quite a handicap. I agree that our most reliable knowledge is scientific in character, but it is always more or less specialized whereas metaphysical interpretations seek expertness in things in general. A scientific hypothesis delimits an area and justifiably, for its purposes, rules out as irrelevant facts from other areas. It seeks to illuminate a limited area in terms of methods and techniques appropriate to that subject matter; and the more inclusive the subject matter, the greater the similarity to the work of the metaphysicians. Metaphysics, on the other hand, tries to include all facts. It has for its subject matter the totality of things and understandably has greater difficulty in working out precise knowledge of this broader scheme of things. An adequate metaphysics, I think, would take account of scientific knowledge, but it would seek to indicate the place of religion, art, play, and any other major interest or activity as well as that of science in a wider scheme of things. In so doing, it would, like science, aim at consistency and empirical adequacy. Its method is that of critical thinking everywhere. If scientific method be thought of in terms of some such analysis as Dewey's steps in a complete act of reflective thinking, we may say that the method of metaphysics is scientific in this broad sense. Perhaps the most important difference between any one of the sciences and a metaphysics comes in the scope of their respective subject matters; and I dare say that such differences in method as there may be between metaphysics and the more specialized sciences stem from this difference in scope.

It may be argued, however, that I misstate the case in contrasting metaphysics and particular sciences. The contrast rather should be between the sciences as a group and metaphysics, and, considered in this light, science includes all subject matters. What we need is unification of the sciences, not metaphysical interpretation. There is a science, actual or possible, for every subject matter; and all knowledge is thus scientific. Anything else claiming cognitive import speaks nonsense. Metaphysics accordingly has the choice of duplicating unnecessarily what the sciences already provide or of being nonsense from this point of view. This, of course, is a familiar positivistic line; and we might interrupt at this point to inquire which of the sciences has for its subject matter statements or stipulations of the above type. My candidate, and the one which has traditionally handled such questions, is metaphysics. It seems to me that any other answer, if offered as more than an arbitrary stipulation, is pretty sure to be less inclusive in scope. If it is equally inclusive, however, I should regard it as a worldview to be judged in terms of its handling of the total range of interests and activities and not merely in terms of scientific ones. If all activities—artistic, religious, or what you will—are to be interpreted as scientific, I think it is worth noting that the term *scientific* takes on a new meaning which is much less clear-cut than its usual meaning. It may be further observed that there is a sense in which both the arts and religion may claim that nothing is foreign to their domains, and there are interesting metaphysical questions regarding their relations to the world of science.

The attack on metaphysical interpretation, however, may take a somewhat different form. It may be argued that such interpretation is distortive rather than illuminative. Everything is just what it is and not something else; and no fact can have any tendency to support or conflict with any other fact. In the kingdom of facts all are equally facts, and no fact is to be minimized or excluded as the price of preferential treatment for another. Metaphysical interpretation accordingly systematically distorts the facts. If only we would come to the facts without metaphysical presuppositions and confine ourselves to logical analysis, we would have a far clearer and much more adequate account of the world. This line of argument, it seems to me, makes the highly questionable assumption that the facts are given innocent of interpretation or that it is a relatively simple matter to single out and eliminate any theoretical admixture they may contain; and this, of course, is an assumption not limited to the positivists. Most metaphysical theorists probably hold that their categories reveal the facts in their stark reality as contrasted with the obviously interpretive material introduced by the categories of opposing views. Eliminating theory for metaphysicians usually means reading out of the facts the interpretations of other views. In the light of these considerations common-sense facts seem pretty clearly to be mixtures of "fact" and theory, and the major philosophical writings with which I am familiar, including those which set forth such arguments as the one I have just outlined, do not seem to me to offer merely neutral fact. In this connection I have been very much interested to note the way in which one generation of positivists points out the metaphysical assumptions of an earlier generation of positivists—or should I say, pseudo positivists?—and occasionally singles out for criticism the metaphysical aspects of contemporary members of this school.[12] In a way this is more eloquent testimony to the lack of neutrality of their facts and analyses than Warner Wick's able discussion of their speculative doctrines in his *Metaphysics and the New Logic,* in which he groups them with Plato, Hegel, and the pragmatists in what he calls the holoscopic tradition.

I incline to agree with Stace that "analysis usually implies speculative doctrines, however hard the analyst usually fights to show that it doesn't" and that the fact that "analysis always, or at least often, implies speculative doctrines, should be an important part of any complete defense of speculative philosophy."[13] In the same article Stace declares: "You may call Aristotle's view an analysis of the individual object. But it implies the speculative proposition that all objects in the universe are compounded of matter and form. Berkeley's analysis implied certain speculative doctrines about the world; so did Hume's analysis of causation. You cannot put a wall around analytic philosophy and stay consistently inside it."[14]

With reference to the contention that in the kingdom of facts all are equally facts, and no fact is to be minimized or excluded as the price of preferential treatment for another, two observations are in order. In the first place, the advocates of every worldview claim to do justice to all the facts; but they differ as to what is the due of the various facts. I see no reason, however, why their claims should not be examined on their merits unless one adopts what J. Loewenberg[15] has called the a priori principle that the data of common sense must remain inviolate. At any rate, a comparison of worldviews suggests that each of them tends to give preferential treatment to some facts, and some metaphysicians frankly admit this, which brings me to the second observation. Facts are indeed equally factual in the sense that all evidence is equally evidence or that all testimony is equally testimony; but would anyone seriously urge that all evidence or testimony is of equal weight? It does not seem to me that all testimony in the realm of metaphysics is of equal weight either. Though we cannot afford to exclude any fact from our reckoning, some facts are more important than others for an understanding of the total range of facts. An understanding of these key facts may afford a master coordination of facts; and once more I see no a priori reason for denying this and a great deal of empirical evidence in its favor in that theorizing in any field seems to involve selection and principles of selection with a consequent weighting of the facts.

If it be admitted that the major views give a preferential status to some facts, would it not be better to say to the metaphysicians as some critics do: "A plague on all your houses! The advantages any one of you may have are simply corrections of overemphases of others of your kind. I will avoid your slantings and maintain a neutral, impartial attitude in the interpretation of all the facts"? But can our antimetaphysicians maintain a purely neutral attitude in the interpretation of all the facts? That they can avoid the emphases or overemphases of any one metaphysics may be granted, but does this mean that they can interpret the full range of facts and avoid all metaphysical emphases or biases? I doubt it. Procedurally, therefore, it seems to me that this allegedly impartial, neutral attitude is likely to be more confusing than helpful. For large scale organization of facts some judgments of significance or importance seem to me essential. The facts do not come neatly ordered or arranged in their proper systems or tagged with cosmic place cards. Hence the so-called impartial, neutral attitude in the pursuit of comprehensive wisdom is likely to result in the implicit acceptance of the metaphysical assumptions explicitly denied—a result we see recorded many times over in the history of philosophy. Such implicit assumptions submitted under the guise of neutrality are far harder to recognize and allow for than an acknowledged metaphysical bias. It seems to me that a more acceptable neutrality may be achieved by comparing the various interpretations of the facts and trying to see not merely what is distinctive of each, though this is important, but also what is common or relatively invariant as between them. I may add that because no one point of view seems to us entirely satisfactory or adequate does not mean that we must or should seek absence of all points of view. Or to vary the figure, the fact that no metaphysical system seems fully adequate as a conceptual tool or instrument of interpretation—if it be a fact—is hardly the basis for abandoning metaphysical technologies in favor of some positivistic back-to-simple-fact movement.

But whether or not metaphysical interpretation is inescapable, which of the major divisions of philosophy is free from it? Not philosophy of religion, ethics, aesthetics, general theory of value, theory of knowledge, logic, or philosophy of science. The writings of philosophers in all these areas give evidence of metaphysical assumptions. Even those who see in their own position a logic or an epistemology or an aesthetics without ontology find that the positions of others in the field are loaded with metaphysical assumptions; and the latter group may speak of the pragmatic or naturalistic outlook of the former. For that matter, metaphysical assumptions have played an important role in many fields other than philosophy. It may be, of course, that those philosophers who assert that this simply illustrates the pervasive misuse of language are right; but even so, understanding of the literature of the field of philosophy is facilitated by interpretation in terms of the categories of various worldviews; and much of the history of philosophy would be a closed book without such interpretations. I incline to think therefore that, instead of limiting our philosophic endeavors to attempting to show the meaninglessness of works not developed in terms of our particular categories or our particular "language," we might profitably devote some time to trying to see if interpretation in terms of the categories of another worldview does not render apparent the meaning of these works and perhaps add to our comprehensive understanding of the world.

# 3

# Metaphysical Inquiry

etaphysics, as one recent study notes, "has a unique power to attract
or repel, to encourage an uncritical enthusiasm on the one hand, an
impatient condemnation on the other."[1] Some regard it as the heart
of philosophy as it is and should be. Somerset Maugham, a novelist with a pas-
sion for philosophy, declares that metaphysics deals with the whole of knowledge, appealing both to our imagination and our intelligence, and does this for
both the amateur and the professional.[2]

Others speak of it as a disorder which with proper treatment, linguistic and
psychoanalytic, we may overcome. Still others regard it less optimistically. For
example, Kant, with all his misgivings about it, regarded it as inevitable; Hampshire speaks of it as a hopeless temptation. F. H. Bradley, one of the great metaphysicians of our day, in an oft-quoted passage referred to it as "finding bad
reasons for what one believes on instinct."

At any rate, few fields have stimulated more vigorous discussion, both from
within and without. The metaphysicians differ sharply from each other and react
forcefully to the critics from outside. In view of what is frequently referred to
as the notorious lack of agreement among metaphysicians, general statements
concerning the field are unusually perilous; and strictures or praise of one form
of metaphysics may turn out to be inapplicable in another. This makes brief
surveys of the field especially difficult; and in what follows I shall not attempt
to survey the history of metaphysics or even the range of contemporary positions. Instead I want to explore briefly certain points in connection with metaphysical inquiry as a science and as an art.

Before proceeding with this discussion, however, perhaps a brief statement
concerning my conception of metaphysics may be helpful. As I have indicated
elsewhere, I think of metaphysics in the broad sense as being concerned with
what is and how we come to know about it. It is an attempt to make comprehensive sense of the full range of facts from whatever field they may be drawn

Presented at the Thirteenth International Congress of Philosophy, Mexico City, Sept. 7–14, 1963.

and thus may be thought of as aiming at a worldview. Any such view claims to offer a set of basic concepts in terms of which any and everything can be interpreted. It constitutes a hypothesis to the effect that each and every fact can be given its proper place in an overall scheme of things. It seeks to detect and describe the basic generic traits of existence. It deals with what constitutes a fact, or what it means to be, as well as with the organization of all facts.

No account of what is, moreover, is complete without some indication of how we know it. With Hegel I agree that a theory of knowledge and a methodology are not independent of each other, but rather are implicative of each other, and that both imply some account of being. At any rate, among the facts which must be explained or interpreted are those of knowledge, and some account of the latter is at least implicit in any worldview or hypothesis. For that matter, an explicit account of either being or knowing is likely to carry, explicitly or implicitly, some version of the other. If a thing must exist to be known, it is also true that our views as to what exists depend on what we have experienced of it or what we know about existence. Thus what is and how we come to know about it are intimately interrelated so much that I prefer to think of metaphysics in the broad sense as including both being and knowing.

At least one further notion should be noted in our brief preliminary characterization of metaphysics: namely, that of importance, or the presupposition of importance. With Whitehead[3] I hold that this notion is of crucial significance in helping order the realm of facts. Some facts or some traits of reality seem to be more important than others for an understanding of the total range of facts. This is not, I hasten to add, simply a matter of congeniality to temperamental bias or individual preference but rather a matter of aid afforded in the understanding of other facts. The fact that I am impressed by or prefer change, or permanence, or the mechanical, or organic wholes, or "reflection" upon "acts" of spontaneous knowledge, or linguistic usage of some sort, or patterned events, or something else, is not basic for this purpose. What is basic for it is what light or aid, if any, one of these facts can afford for interpreting and ordering other facts—whether its structure affords a key to the understanding of the total range of facts.

## Metaphysical Inquiry as a Science

If we ask whether metaphysics is a science or not, our answer will depend partly on our conception of science and partly on our account of metaphysics; and I have sketched above my conception of the latter. We may interpret science in such fashion as to include only the natural sciences and mathematics, or we may interpret it broadly as any branch of knowledge or study concerned with establishing and systematizing facts, principles, and methods. Perhaps, however, instead of attempting a definition of science, we may find it more helpful for present purposes to note certain respects in which metaphysics appears to resemble the generally accepted sciences and other respects in which it seems to be quite different.

Without wishing to deny certain significant differences between metaphysics and other types of investigation, we may hold that in at least three respects there are important similarities between metaphysics as I conceive it and the commonly accepted sciences: namely, (1) in the use of the method of critical or reflective inquiry; (2) in aiming at consistency and empirical adequacy; and (3) in providing certain distinctive information. Let us examine each of these points briefly.

(1) Scientific method is frequently described in terms of some such analysis as Dewey's steps in a complete act of reflective thinking, and if we speak of scientific method in these terms, metaphysics is a discipline making use of scientific method. Some prefer to say that the method of metaphysics is that of critical thinking everywhere and that the sciences have offered their version of this basic method. In any event metaphysics proceeds in terms of the five steps in Dewey's analysis. The problem or difficulty in metaphysics may arise because some accepted belief is questioned or because the status of a given area of experience within the conceptual framework of a worldview is unclear. The clarification of the problem requires analysis and, sometimes, obtaining additional information. Once the problem is clearly defined, one may proceed to suggested solutions for it. The consequences of these proposals may be developed deductively, and it is then possible to see whether one or more of them affords a plausible means of clearing up the initial difficulty. Checking on whether one conceptual ordering better illuminates the facts or promotes better understanding of them than another or on whether the facts fall into place better on one view than another is something involving a somewhat broader range of acceptable answers than might be true of most scientific problems; but it is possible to say that various modes of ordering facts—for example, those of Plato, Aristotle, Lucretius, Wittgenstein, Dewey, or Hegel—appear to be clearly superior to, say, Thales's account in terms of water or Anaximander's in terms of the boundless.

In *A Contextualistic Theory of Perception*[4] I attempt to set forth at length an account of perception along the lines suggested above.

(2) Metaphysics, like the commonly accepted sciences, aims at consistency and empirical adequacy. The first of these aims perhaps needs no comment here, but the second requires a word of explanation. Metaphysics shares with the other sciences a concern with facts, and from the nature of this mode of inquiry it has a concern for more facts than any other sciences—a concern for all facts. In a sense all of the sciences stem from the initial philosophic wonder about the world and one's place in it, and the various sciences may be thought of as contributing to the metaphysician's goal of achieving a reasoned view of the full range of facts. In attempting to give each and every fact its appropriate place in the categorial framework of a worldview, it offers a world hypothesis. Such hypotheses are better or worse, more adequate or less so, in ordering the total range of facts; but in dealing with facts on so comprehensive a scale, there is

understandably room for differences of opinion among metaphysicians as to the adequacy of different hypotheses; and much has been made of these differences. Perhaps, however, in view of the scope or scale of these hypotheses, the marvel is that there should be as much agreement as there is.

Many metaphysicians speak of world hypotheses as true or false to help emphasize their empirical or evidential character, but when one marshals evidential items on a worldwide scale, the designations "true" or "false" are perhaps less helpful than "adequate" and "inadequate."

(3) In the third place, metaphysics, like the commonly accepted sciences, provides certain distinctive information. In the case of metaphysics this information includes a) the meaning of factuality, b) the knowledge involved in a comprehensive view of the full range of facts or experiences, and c) the knowledge that comes from attempting to see the place of specific facts in an overall scheme or framework. The first type of information is concerned with such questions as: What is a fact? What does it mean to be? What constitutes evidence or evidential items for a worldview? What is a key fact, basic analogy, or root metaphor?

Clarification of these concepts and questions constitutes an important part of the metaphysician's task. Though each fact must be taken into account and given its proper place, certain facts are more important than others in giving an insight into the nature of factuality and in providing a basis for a worldview. The structure of these key facts or experiences, basic analogies, or root metaphors provides the categories of a worldview, and what it means to be or what the nature of a fact is may be given largely in terms of these categories. An element of decision enters into the selection of a key fact, whether this be thought of essentially as a decision to use language in a certain way or as one to explore the total range of facts in terms of the structure of one fact; something of insight is required for discriminating the traits of the key fact; and checking on the wisdom of the initial selection and the adequacy of the key fact for developing a worldview brings in the whole range of facts or evidence.

The second type of information afforded by metaphysics is the knowledge involved in a comprehensive view of the full range of facts or experiences. This includes material on the categories which outline the overall structure of the worldview. In terms of these categories one attempts to set forth relations between facts and assess priorities. For a comprehensive view no simple compilation or assemblage of facts—common sense, scientific, or other—will do. Interpretation of the various facts is essential; and a priori there is no reason why common sense facts or ordinary language about them must be accepted without interpretation or modification.

The third type of knowledge the metaphysician provides is that that comes from attempting to see the place of specific facts in an overall conceptual scheme or framework. Tracing out the place of such facts in the categories of a worldview is what is meant by explaining or interpreting them. One set of categories may well help make clear connections in experience slurred over by another set, or it may afford solutions for philosophic problems which alternative sets handle less capably. In any relatively adequate view categorial analysis or interpretation is fairly sure to bring to light distinctions or similarities which would otherwise be overlooked.

So much, then, for three important similarities between metaphysics and the commonly accepted sciences. Let us now turn to three or four significant differences which are pointed up by an examination of the following topics: (1) the scope of metaphysics, (2) its mode of dealing with facts, (3) the character of the questions it asks, and (4) the lack of agreement among metaphysicians.

(1) Perhaps the most important difference between any one of the sciences and a metaphysics comes in the scope of their respective subject matters. A scientific hypothesis is always more or less specialized. It delimits a specific area and rules out as irrelevant facts from other fields. The methods for checking on facts within this area are those which seem appropriate for this restricted domain. A metaphysical hypothesis, on the other hand, claims to be all-inclusive in scope, and in one sense no fact may be excluded. The metaphysical hypothesis must have a place for any and all facts, and it cannot maintain that any facts are irrelevant or need not be accounted for. If the metaphysician has discriminated generic traits of existence, any body of facts should be illustrative of them.

(2) At least part of the difference in mode of dealing with facts stems from the difference in scope. The more specific the hypothesis, the more closely it is geared to specific items of fact; and the more general the hypothesis, the less it is tied to any specific fact and the more it is likely to be concerned with various ways of fitting facts into a pattern. More general scientific hypotheses thus tend to be more like metaphysical hypotheses in this respect. A second consideration in connection with the mode of dealing with facts is that whereas the scientist is often primarily concerned with gathering facts, the metaphysician is primarily interested in interpreting facts.

(3) In the third place, the questions raised by the metaphysician are significantly different from those dealt with by the commonly accepted sciences. This, however, is in large part something to be expected from the fact that metaphysics affords distinctive information of the sort discussed above. If it did not provide such information, it would be even more different from the sciences than now appears. But the metaphysician does discuss such questions as the following: What is a fact, or what do we mean by a fact? What constitutes evidence for a worldview? What is a key fact? What kind of pattern can we find in the full range of facts? How can we make comprehensive sense of all the facts, or how can we achieve comprehensive vision? How does this, that, or the other fact fit into the categories of a worldview? And these are not questions raised by the commonly acknowledged sciences.

"What is the nature of a metaphysical question?" and "What is anything really?" are requests for analysis, but analysis of a distinctive type. These questions ask for analysis or interpretation in terms of the categories of a worldview; and though it may be argued that in asking these questions we are asking not so much for facts as for a decision regarding our manner of speaking, or our way of dealing with facts, the answers we make may be (1) incorrect in that the categories of the worldview in question require a different answer, or (2) questionable in that the answer in these terms is not very illuminating, or (3) inadequate in that it is less helpful or illuminating than an answer given in terms of another metaphysics or worldview.

Largely as a result of the writings of Wittgenstein, Wisdom and others have come to say that the metaphysician is concerned not so much with a set of problems to be solved or a set of questions to be answered as with an assortment of perplexities to be cleared up or resolved. Certain puzzlements are removed.[5] Which puzzlements or perplexities are the metaphysician's to deal with, however, becomes clear only in terms of the background of the traditional discussions of metaphysics. But in any event understanding rather than solution of problems seems to be the metaphysician's goal.

(4) In the fourth place, whereas in the sciences there is a high degree of unanimity on major points, in metaphysics, Lazerowitz and others have noted, there is a notorious lack of agreement. As Lazerowitz puts it:

> But although metaphysics looks like science, it differs from science in an important respect, a respect which is overlooked by philosophers but which is a source of profound disturbance to intelligent outsiders. No one, except a person who must for some reason blind himself to the facts, can fail to contrast the special sciences, with their imposing edifices of solid results, and metaphysics, with its chronic condition of endless and unresolved debates.
>
> Theories which are accepted as undeniably true by many philosophers are rejected as certainly false by others. And what is perhaps even more perplexing, demonstrations which, according to the considered opinion of some philosophers, are absolutely conclusive are, according to the considered opinion of other and equally able philosophers, inconclusive or mistaken.[6]

Nor, Lazerowitz adds, is the disagreement resolved by confrontation with facts, for the metaphysician seems to be curiously impervious to facts.[7]

If, however, the metaphysician is primarily concerned with interpreting facts and if the facts may be interpreted differently in terms of the categories of different worldviews, some diversity is to be expected. Among metaphysicians working within the categories of a single worldview the disagreements are likely to be less pronounced and more readily resolvable. But if understanding or vision is our goal, some diversity may be wholesome.

## Metaphysical Inquiry as an Art

Though on the whole it seems to me that metaphysics may have more in common with the sciences than with the arts, we have seen that it differs significantly in certain respects from the commonly accepted sciences, and we may find it interesting to note a few points of agreement and difference between it and, say, poetry. For example, metaphysics and poetry have some similarities in their (1) use of metaphor, (2) concern for making or creating as opposed to discovering, (3) criteria of success, and (4) expression of values. Let us consider these points briefly.

(1) Both poetry and metaphysics make use of metaphor. The poet Robert Burns, for example, writes:

> O my luve is like a red, red rose,
>> That's newly sprung in June;
> O my luve is like the melodie
>> That's sweetly played in tune.

And a metaphysical hypothesis may claim that everything is like a central experience or key fact—say, a machine, a living organism, or a vision of "form" and "matter"—and that the total range of facts or experiences may be ordered in terms of the central root metaphor or basic analogy. Thus, Dorothy M. Emmet maintains that a metaphysician constructs

> an imaginative theoretic model, drawn by analogy from whatever it is which has seemed to make most sense within his own experience. His system is a *Weltanschauung,* that is an intuition of and response to the world from the standpoint of some particular kind of intellectual or spiritual experience. So the first step in seeking to understand his system is to try to appreciate the kind of intellectual or spiritual experience through which he sees the world; and if we can enter into this with intellectual sympathy, if we gain nothing else, we should at least have the enlargement of imaginative vision which would come from seeing what the world looks like from this perspective.[8]

Stephen C. Pepper gives the following account of the origin of metaphysical hypotheses in root metaphors:

> A man desiring to understand the world looks about for a clue to its comprehension. He pitches upon some area of common-sense fact, and tries if he cannot understand other areas in terms of this one.
>
> This original area becomes then his basic analogy or root metaphor. He describes as best he can the characteristics of this

area, or . . . discriminates its structure. A list of its structural characteristics become his basic concepts of explanation and description. We call them a set of categories. . . . Since the basic analogy or root metaphor normally . . . arises out of common sense, a great deal of development and refinement of a set of categories is required if they are to prove adequate for a hypothesis of unlimited scope. Some root metaphors prove more fertile than others. . . .[9]

Morris R. Cohen argues that literal truth grows out of metaphors and that they are not merely artificial devices for making discourse more vivid and poetical, but are also necessary for the apprehension of new ideas. Metaphors, he declares, express "the vague and confused but primal perception of identity which subsequent processes of discrimination transform into the clear assertion of an identity or common element (or relation) which the two different things possess."[10]

(2) In the second place, both metaphysics and poetry contain an element of creativity as opposed to purely factual discovery. The poet creates for us a work of art which may or may not reflect some feature of objective reality. Instead of simply presenting the actual he may make for us a new world. The metaphysician, though concerned with seeing what the world of the full range of facts is like, does not simply report on what he finds or discovers. Facts do not come categorized and neatly labeled with their proper cosmic identification tags. The metaphysician must frame a set of categories that will enable him to do justice to the complex diversity of facts, and metaphysical interpretation proceeds in terms of these categories. Determining what the facts are is itself a complex interpretative process, poles removed from the model of plucking pure facts as one might gather daisies. The option is not that of either choosing pure facts or accepting facts distorted by metaphysical interpretation. Interpretation seems to me inevitable, but framing a system of interpretation that will do justice to all the facts is a major creative enterprise; and if the facts shine forth in their clarity, it is likely to be a tribute to the system of interpretation and not simply a reflection of the natural luminosity of the facts.

(3) In the third place, poetry and metaphysics have certain resemblances with reference to their criteria of success. Negatively, for neither of them is truth or falsity in a clear and straightforward sense the criterion, though perhaps for somewhat different reasons. The sense in which either a poem or a metaphysical system is true requires considerable discussion and interpretation. A poem is not thought of ordinarily as providing discursive or descriptive truth, and we are more likely to speak of the adequacy, illumination, or vision provided by a metaphysical system than of its truth. Positively, certain of the criteria of excellence in a work of art apply also to metaphysical systems or hypotheses. We may value either of them for its suggestiveness and its expressiveness or for the insights it provides. A good part of our sense of appropriateness in either a

scientific or a metaphysical hypothesis stems from aesthetic considerations; and Professor Dorothy Emmet suggests that our hypotheses may be strengthened by and appeal to our sense of aesthetic fittingness which may also be used to discipline our basic analogies.[11]

(4) Both poetry and metaphysics are expressions of values, both individual and social. In the case of poetry this is perhaps too obvious to require comment here. In the case of metaphysics I shall make only two or three brief comments. First, since metaphysical hypotheses are human creations, it is not strange that the marks of a great personality or a cultural milieu are on occasion reflected in a metaphysics. In the second place, the selection of a root metaphor itself involves a presupposition or judgment of the importance of that key fact, and the degree to which a given analogy illuminates facts depends somewhat on the background of the individual and the culture of the person's time. For example, the received tradition of one's church or the accepted tradition of science may afford the point of departure for a metaphysics, and the manner in which a metaphysical analogy is developed may reflect such considerations. In the third place, the major shifts in emphasis upon different philosophical systems in different periods of history, the fact that types of philosophy recur, and the further fact that philosophical systems are more likely to be abandoned as irrelevant than disproved suggests that these systems are at least in part expressions of value.

These points of similarity between poetry and metaphysics are, I think, significant; but they need to be considered in connection with at least three points of difference between the two with reference to (1) the aim of consistency and empirical adequacy and relevance, (2) the use of the method of critical or reflective inquiry, and (3) their attitude toward knowledge and information. On each of these points the metaphysician seems to have more in common with the scientist than with the poet; and the metaphysician's stand on these I have sketched above in connection with the similarities between metaphysics and science.

1. The aim of metaphysics and poetry seems to be quite different so far as consistency and empirical adequacy and relevance are concerned. Poets are not bound by considerations of empirical adequacy or relevance, and they have far less emphasis on consistency.

2. Perhaps partly because of the difference noted in the preceding paragraph, the poet's method seems to be quite different from that outlined for science and metaphysics in our discussion of similarities between the two.

3. Poets need not be concerned with conveying any information or with ordering it to show its place in a systematic view or perspective. Expressing feelings clearly and vividly may be all they are concerned with in a given poem. Metaphysicians, however, do have a basic cognitive concern. They seek to make comprehensive sense of the full range of facts.

# 4

# Philosophy as Comprehensive Vision

The fact that I have the happy privilege of addressing this distinguished audience of psychologists and philosophers stems at least partially, I take it, from the fact that the founders of this Society and those who have helped it to grow and flourish had some appreciation of the traditional aims and activities of philosophy and of their relevance for psychology. Many philosophers and psychologists now feel, however, that a survey of the history of philosophy and psychology shows that this appreciation rested on a serious misconception and that the direction of history points toward a sharper and sharper separation of the two fields. I have no wish to deny that both psychology and philosophy have distinctive functions, methods, and subject matters; but in the course of this paper I should like to stress the importance of close relations between the two fields and to express my conviction that the idea of having a joint society of philosophers and psychologists rests upon a sound insight. Some of those who are dubious of close relations between the two fields, however, have been particularly critical of one of the traditional philosophic goals I should most like to re-emphasize: namely, that of achieving a broad perspective within which all things may be given their due place; for I feel that, in spite of the difficulties involved, it is important that the philosopher seeks to make comprehensive sense of the full range of facts from whatever field they may be drawn, whether from common sense, the sciences, the arts, religion, politics, people's working life, or their play activities. The dangers of the sort of narrow specialization which either refuses to look beyond its own province or treats as nonsensical attempts to go beyond it far outweigh the risks of attempting a worldview. Hence I feel that it is important that at least some philosophers conduct their criticism, analysis, and interpretation within as broad a perspective as possible.

From *Philosophy and Phenomenological Research* 22.1 (Sept. 1961): 16–25. Presidential address delivered at the fifty-first annual meeting of the Southern Society for Philosophy and Psychology in St. Louis, Mar. 28, 1959. Reprinted by permission of *Philosophy and Phenomenological Research*, Brown University.

But let us examine what these critics feel to be the lessons of history regarding the relations between philosophy and psychology and see what light this examination may throw on the conception of philosophy as comprehensive vision. The word *philosophy,* as we are often reminded, comes from the Greeks and means the love or pursuit of wisdom, and with the Greeks almost all forms of knowledge or learning were included under the term. With the passage of time, however, theology, physics (or natural philosophy), and the various sciences branched off from the central body of philosophy and set up their own methods for dealing with their particular subject matter. Psychology was one of the more recent sciences to branch off, but its progress since becoming separated from philosophy, like that of the other sciences, has been rapid. Its knowledge has gained in exactness, clarity, and definiteness. There is a tendency toward a larger measure of agreement among workers in the field. Its problems are formulated with increasing precision, and testable hypotheses are proposed for their solution.

Philosophy, on the other hand, relies heavily on meditation, conjecture, imagination, and speculation, all of which make for a high degree of tentativeness or uncertainty and permit vague, ambiguous, and somewhat fanciful developments. Instead of verifiable experimentation, we may have what is sometimes referred to as pure reason at work, with logic being used to discount or negate the evidence of the senses. Conflict between opposing schools and failure even to agree on what are the significant questions are more likely to be found among philosophers than agreement or cooperation. Whereas in the sciences present inquiry is likely to mark so much of an advance over earlier work as to leave the older out of the discussion, among philosophical systems it is difficult to demonstrate that any is definitely wrong, and the speculation of the ancients may demand as much attention as the latest thinking on the subject. The present subject matter of philosophy includes a group of embryo sciences—like logic, aesthetics, and possibly theory of value or ethics—which may be splitting off before many decades from the central body of material, which is largely metaphysical or epistemological. If we note that logic, for example, has been making remarkable advances within the past one hundred years and that its distinguishing characteristics are contrary to much of what we have been saying about philosophy, it may be urged that this simply affords evidence that basically, it is a science which is nearing the point of becoming a separate discipline. Thus in philosophy we seem to be moving in the direction of having what can be given definiteness and precision separate off to develop sciences, leaving a more and more restricted body of material of an increasingly unscientific character.

In the light of this historical development it may well be suggested that the less psychology has to do with philosophy, the better for it; and the hope of the philosopher may well be to align himself with one of the embryo sciences and help cultivate it, or to develop a different type of philosophizing, or at least get some sharply different subject matter to investigate. Some philosophers, on the other hand, apparently have felt that the close relations between philosophy and psychology have created a dangerous situation for the former. Many of them since before the time of the founding of this Society have insisted that philosophers stick to what they took to be the philosophical issues and avoid bringing in psychology. They have stressed the importance of not confusing philosophical theory of knowledge and logic with psychology and have charged advocates of philosophical positions other than their own with palming off psychological data or facts for philosophical theory. Lotze, for example, accused his opponents of confusing the history of the growth of knowledge with the theory of the character of knowledge. Another great philosopher, the centennial of whose birth we are celebrating this year (1959), John Dewey, charged that some of the critics of his instrumental or pragmatic outlook were making the reverse error. They mistook their theory, he maintained, for psychological fact and were guilty of "a wholesale mistaking of logical determinations for facts of psychology."[1] Dewey was not, of course, using this argument to show that philosophers needed to know less about psychology; and the remedy for this sort of confusion would appear to lie in the opposite direction.

Though I confess to great difficulty on occasion in distinguishing between the philosophical and the psychological in some important studies of ethics, aesthetics, theory of value, and psychological theory, my plea for closer relations between psychologists and philosophers is not intended as an argument for either merging philosophy and psychology or urging either to try to take over the tasks of the other. It does seem to me, however, that the lessons of history may be read with a vastly different import from either that suggested by those who cite history as an argument for having psychologists abandon concern for philosophical issues raised by their field or that proposed by those who regard the psychological data their own position rests on as simple fact and reserve the term *psychology* for material they regard as irrelevant to philosophical issues.

At any rate, the position of philosophy as mother of the sciences does not suggest to me that this is a field which any self-respecting scientists would feel it their duty to keep as far away from as possible. Quite the contrary! That from the initial philosophic wonder about the world and our place in it should have come most of the sciences would seem to point rather clearly to philosophy as a subject worthy of careful consideration. That disciplines like physics, political science, economics, sociology, and psychology, to mention a few of the major ones, should have sprung from philosophy in the past 250 years affords impressive evidence of its rich potentialities. Historically considered, it contained within its sprawling domain the seeds of new and significant growth; and there are clear indications that even now the field contains at least in embryo yet other such developments. That its offspring should have developed so rapidly, with such distinction, and in such divergent directions after leaving the central body of philosophy would seem to be a cause for congratulation rather than a warning against philosophy.

The argument that the differences in method between philosophy and psychology or, for that matter, any of the other sciences are so great that the scientist can find little of value or pertinence for his field in philosophy does not seem strong to me. There are great differences between the method of mathematics and that of the experimental sciences, but this does not prevent mathematics from being of great value for the sciences. In like fashion the methods of the logician and the metaphysician are significantly different, but logic may be quite helpful for metaphysics. Hence a priori I see no reason why the differences between philosophy as comprehensive vision and psychology should make either of them of little value for the other. An examination of certain of these differences, moreover, suggests that they help make it possible for the fields to supplement each other. Whereas a primary task of psychologists or other scientists is determining, establishing, or gathering facts, philosophers are more likely to be concerned with the attempt to explain what it means to be a fact or with the interpretation of a body of facts and theory. They aim at understanding, at seeing things in a framework which makes sense of them. Without the facts philosophers have nothing to interpret, and for many problems in theory of value, ethics, aesthetics, and theory of knowledge the findings of psychologists are of crucial relevance.[2] More often than not a philosophical conception of what it is to be a fact serves as a presupposition of the psychologist's pursuit of facts. The philosopher's characteristic concern with the presuppositions of psychology, with its methodology and logic, and with attempting to place its findings and conclusions in a wider context, moreover, appears to be one shared by many psychologists.

Part of the difference in method and results between philosophers and scientists turns about the scope of their respective subject matters. A scientific hypothesis is always more or less specialized. It delimits an area and rules out as irrelevant facts from other fields. It seeks to illuminate a limited area in terms of methods and techniques appropriate to that subject matter. In philosophy as worldview or comprehensive vision the same sort of delimitation is not possible. No area of facts can be ruled out because philosophers are attempting to show that any and every fact may be given a place within their system. If they have discriminated generic traits of existence, any body of fact should be illustrative of them. Their categories, if adequate, must afford illumination for any problematic area; but by the same token no single item of fact is peculiarly or crucially relevant. Hence the worldview is not closely geared to specific factual items after the fashion of a specialized scientific hypothesis. For that matter, however, more general scientific hypotheses are less closely tied to specific items of fact and more concerned with various ways of fitting facts into a pattern. Thus the broader and more general the scientific hypothesis, the more it is likely to resemble philosophy as worldview.

In terms of this difference in scope it is not surprising that our most precise and reliable knowledge comes from the sciences; and philosophers who do not have a place in their system for the methods and conclusions of the sciences thereby convict their view of inadequacy. Including something which conflicts with specific scientific findings would be viewed by most philosophers as even more risky.

It is sometimes maintained, however, that it is not the difference in scope between scientific hypotheses and philosophical views which is troublesome. It is rather a difficulty of determining what problem, if any, philosophers are trying to solve. There appears to be no specific item of information or fact which, if established, would show that their view is correct or incorrect. The positivists have pushed this line of criticism periodically, sometimes arguing that their non-positivistic philosophic brethren and sisters were dealing with pseudo-problems rather than genuine problems. Unless, however, one proposes by definition to deny problematic status to all questions which turn about something other than specific points of fact, there is no reason to deny that philosophers have their problems. They are likely to turn about matters of clarification or interpretation rather than specific matters of fact; but they almost always involve a marshaling of evidence, and their pattern is that of critical or reflective thinking in general. In terms of Dewey's famous five steps in a complete act of reflective thinking, the problem or difficulty may arise because some accepted belief is questioned or because the status of a given area of experience within a conceptual framework is unclear. The clarification of the problem requires analysis and sometimes obtaining additional information. Once it is clearly defined, one may proceed to suggested solutions for the problem. The consequences of these proposals may be developed deductively, and it is then possible to see whether one or more of them affords a plausible means of clearing up the initial difficulty. Checking on whether one conceptual ordering better illuminates the facts or promotes understanding of them than another or on whether the facts fall into place better on one view than another is something involving a somewhat broader range of acceptable answers than might be true of most scientific problems; but it is possible to say that various modes of ordering facts appear to be clearly superior to, say, Thales's account in terms of water.

One familiar illustration of a philosophical problem is what has been referred to since Descartes as the problem of perception. Traditionally it has been formulated in terms of a metaphysical theory or worldview which sets up, on the one hand, an external world of real things in a spatiotemporal field of location and, on the other, an "inner" domain of mind or consciousness which contains the rest of the world. Within this second realm, according to this view, fall the data of perception or what is given in perception. The problem is that of passing beyond the "inner" data to the "external" physical world, making sure that the inner subjective data correspond to the real external things. How, it may be asked, can we be sure that the object perceived presents the thing as it exists unperceived? How can we be sure that an inner reality corresponds to a never given external object? Many philosophers refuse to accept the mechanistic naturalism in terms of which this question is formulated, but perhaps the main solution within this framework is to say that though the entities immediately given in sense perception are not identical with the physical thing, they may somehow correspond with it. When they do, we have veridical perception. When they do not, we have perceptual error. Material things may appear to exist or to have properties which they do not really have because what is given is a set of data belonging to a quite different kind or order of reality from the material things themselves.

The difficulties of determining, on the basis of dualistic presuppositions, whether or not the given corresponds with the external world, however, have led mechanistic theorists to attempt other ways of solving the problem. These non-dualistic solutions ordinarily consist of wiping out one or the other of the dualist's domains and attempting to expand the other to cover what previously the two included. Others have sought a solution for the traditional problem in terms of an analysis of language. They maintain that the problem is not one of how to get from an inner realm of subjective data to a real external world but rather one of how to relate the language of sense data to the language of material things or of otherwise properly minding one's language.

Seeking a solution for the problem is largely a matter of clarifying meanings and achieving a clearer vision of the nature of perception rather than of getting additional information. If further facts are sought or additional evidence adduced, it is for the sake of seeing more clearly what the place of perception is within the conceptual framework of this worldview. If we step outside this framework, the problem may appear to be a pseudo-problem; and from this outside point of reference one of the chief arguments against the mechanistic naturalist's position may well be that it gives rise to this problem of the external world, a problem which does not arise if we start with certain other assumptions. If we accept his basic categories, however, this is a genuine enough philosophical problem; and so persuasively and so frequently in modern times has it been set forth for us that many philosophers who do not share the assumptions which gave rise to it still feel impelled to start from this formulation if they are discussing perception.

But it is by no means the only philosophical problem of significance in connection with perception. Hence referring to it as *the* problem of perception is misleading. If one is to speak of the problem on a more inclusive basis, it is that of showing the place of perception within the conceptual framework of a worldview; and, accordingly, there may be at least as many sets of problems as there are worldviews. The Platonist, the Hegelian, and the contextualist, to mention only three, all have somewhat different problems from the Cartesian; but all of them have to have some account of sense perception. Whatever the view, there are situations in which things are perceptually accepted as having values which they turn out not to have in the test situation. This fact—that of perceptual error—as well as the further fact of veridical perception each view must account for in terms of its basic categories. This raises, of course, the question both of what evidence there is and what evidence we require in justification of our perceptual claims and beliefs. Each view must also have a place for all the main types of perception, not merely for ordinary perception or any one special kind, but for any and every kind, aesthetic, disinterested scientific, or other. Any view, moreover, must be able to give an account of the perceptually accepted object—of what it is that we perceive. Hence the problem of perception turns out to be a cluster of problems, and these problems will be handled somewhat differently by the proponents of various worldviews.

The problems of perception arise in connection with difficulties in interpreting a particular body or area of facts—commonsense facts, everyday experiences in regard to habitual patterns of behavior as well as ones concerned to realize or enjoy quality, and psychological data of various sorts; and philosophical theories or views of perception offer interpretations of these facts or data—ones which are the special concern of psychology. Any reasoned view of these matters, I take it, must draw upon some psychological data; but what the relevant psychological facts are and just how they are interpreted are matters which different systems of psychology as well as different worldviews may decide differently. Tolman or Koffka may pattern them differently from Clark Hull or Spence or Freud. Accordingly, the advocates of no system or worldview are entitled to assume that the data as they see them are simply neutral facts which all others must take as their starting point. We cannot expect T. H. Green or James and Dewey to accept the conceptions of experience and perception held by Plato or by Locke and Hume any more than we can expect the latter three to start with the views of the former; and no one of these philosophers is entitled to urge that whereas he or she speaks of what is philosophically significant in setting forth his or her conception of experience, the others treat simply of psychology.

With reference to the obscurity or lack of clarity with which philosophy is charged, though I do not wish to counsel our philosophic brethren and sisters to any greater obscurity, it may be worth remembering that clarity and significance are not identical and that it is far more important to become clearer about something significant than simply to be clear; and a resolute adherence to being clearer and clearer about less and less is probably not the best way to discovery in any field. Friedrich Waismann, who started his philosophizing with the Vienna Circle, puts the case even more strongly, declaring,

> There is nothing like clear thinking to protect one from making
> discoveries. It is all very well to talk of clarity, but when it becomes
> an obsession it is liable to nip the living thought in the bud. This, I

am afraid, is one of the deplorable results of Logical Positivism, not foreseen by its founders, but only too striking in some of its followers. Look at these people, gripped by a clarity neurosis, haunted by fear, tongue-tied, asking themselves continually, "Oh dear, now does this make perfectly good sense?" Imagine the pioneers of science, Kepler, Newton, the discoverer of non-Euclidean geometry, of field physics, the unconscious, matter waves or heaven knows what, imagine them asking themselves this question at every step—this would have been the surest means of sapping any creative power. No great discoverer has acted in accordance with the motto, "Everything that can be said can be said clearly." And some of the greatest discoveries have even emerged from a sort of primordial fog. . . . I've always suspected that clarity is the last refuge of those who have nothing to say.[3]

It would be equally erroneous, of course, to maintain that wherever we find obscurity we therefore have significance or something of momentous import, but new and significant insights do appear to develop with sufficient frequency from fumbling, ambiguously expressed or vaguely felt beginnings to suggest that the philosopher's occasional lack of clarity is not in itself sufficient reason for advising the psychologist to steer clear of philosophy.

Nor is the lack of agreement among philosophers the unmitigated evil some would make it out to be. I doubt if there are any philosophers who have not had at least occasional pangs of regret that their colleagues did not group themselves solidly and unequivocally behind the truth as they see it instead of viewing it with varying degrees of skepticism and displaying their customary heterogeneity or diversity of outlook; but in terms of the quest for comprehensive vision, this diversity has its advantages. If we seek vision, unanimity is less important than light; and who are there among us who have not learned much from views sharply different from their own? The more different views we have and the more different sources of possible light we have, the better our chances that some of these philosophies will shed light on our world and our place in it.

The criticism that the central body of philosophy concerned with the generic nature of what is and how we come to know about it shows its lack of progress in its continuing interest in the views of the ancients—for example, Plato, Aristotle, Democritus, and Lucretius—also has its more hopeful side; for this suggests that these ancient systems may contribute to our efforts to make comprehensive sense of the full range of facts. Their insights and those of other pre-twentieth-century philosophers still afford clues to a clearer vision. We are richer, not poorer, in finding that their analyses and interpretations still have something of value for our time. There is a sense in which each of us must think through for oneself and see for oneself what a given philosophical system or approach to philosophy has to offer, but this thinking through and vision are greatly furthered by the suggestions and guidance of previous thinkers.

At any rate, my reflections on the history of philosophy and on its methods and aims lead me to feel that the goal of comprehensive vision remains one of paramount importance for philosophers. It is true that they may devote their major efforts to the development of some one of the embryo sciences still within the field of philosophy. For example, they may center their study upon science, studying the methods, operations, and objectives of the sciences as they study the segments of nature they take for their own. They may concern themselves with a type of logical or linguistic analysis which focuses upon the specific and attempts to avoid ontological speculation. But it is not essential that they turn in any one of these directions; and if they do take one of them, it will still be necessary for someone operating in terms of the traditional goal of seeking to make comprehensive sense of the full range of facts to try to see how these activities fit into a more inclusive scheme of things.

Making comprehensive sense, moreover, is not simply a matter of assembling the conclusions of the various sciences. For comprehensive vision selection and emphasis are unavoidable; and it is difficult to overestimate the significance of key facts or basic analogies in effecting a master coordination of facts. It seems clear that some facts or clusters of facts are more important than others for an understanding of various ranges of facts. By this I do not mean merely that a given philosopher may prefer, say, change to permanence or a live organism to a machine or the like. Rather what I have in mind is that if we place ourselves sympathetically within the conceptual framework determined by the basic structural features of some one of these key facts, we may be able to effect a plausible ordering of the entire realm of facts. The extent to which this can be done in illuminating fashion affords a check on the adequacy of the worldview generated by this key fact. The matter of tests of adequacy of worldviews, however, is a topic for another occasion; and here I should like merely to note that though no view has been so successful as to preclude the search for more adequate ones, still careful study of even inadequate views may contribute to a clearer understanding of things. Hence it seems to me that the philosopher has no more important or central task than that of attempting to make comprehensive sense of the full range of facts.

# 5

# Metaphysical Categories:
# Of Shoes and Ships and Sealing Wax,
# and Cabbages and Kings

"The time has come," the Walrus said,
  "To talk of many things:
Of shoes—and ships—and sealing wax—
  Of cabbages—and—kings—
And why the sea is boiling hot—
  And whether pigs have wings."
      —Lewis Carroll, *Through the Looking-Glass and What Alice Found There*

When the time comes to speak of many things, of shoes and ships and sealing wax, and cabbages and kings, it is necessary to categorize these things; and a perennial concern of the philosopher has been the character of the categories. Is there any order among the categories such that one may think of some as more basic than others? If so, what are the fundamental categories? How may they be characterized? Are they pervasive characteristics of reality, forms of conceivable objects, basic modes of thinking about reality, typical forms of discourse, guiding principles of action, absolute presuppositions of experience, or what? What is their function? How many of them are there? How are they related to each other and the things categorized? In this paper I should like to discuss at least some of these questions; for, as Professor Albert Hofstadter has very well said, "unless we have some modicum of clarity" on questions about the categories, "we are liable to be misled, either in attempts at metaphysical construction or in criticism of their possibility."[1]

Presidential address delivered before the annual meeting of the Southwestern Philosophical Society at the University of New Mexico, Albuquerque, Dec. 19–21, 1955. Originally published in *Journal of Philosophy* 55.2 (Jan. 1958): 45–57. Courtesy of *Journal of Philosophy*.

## Fundamental Categories

Though in popular speech "category" is a name used for any class, genus, species, family, or other division—from shoes and sealing wax to cabbages and kings—in philosophical usage it has ordinarily referred to some fundamental trait or grouping—to a key concept. Aristotle's categories, for example, offer ten ways in which Being may be asserted—ten classes of Being. Kant's categories are forms or classes of conceivable objects—forms of judgments about objects, or fundamental concepts or forms of the Understanding. In post-Kantian usage, by and large, any basic or fundamental philosophical conception has been known as a category.

If at this point, however, one turns to the question of what are the fundamental categories, the answer may take the form of another question: fundamental for what purpose? And if the answer to this is in terms of categories fundamental for worldviews, we see that philosophers or metaphysicians not merely speak of many things and note that they may be categorized; they seek to find some order in the multiplicity of things—some set of principles which will enable them to discuss, interpret, or order anything and give it its proper place—whether ships or cabbages or boiling seas or kings. They attempt to fit all these things into some larger scheme of things, and the basic instruments for doing this are the categories of their view. For their view they are the most fundamental categories.

## How May the Categories Be Characterized?

Discussing the categories raises a number of problems. One of these is the difficulty of explaining in what terms we are to discuss them or how we are to characterize them. In terms of them we characterize everything else; but can we discuss them or characterize them at all? Some explanation of them each view must have, or it convicts itself of inadequacy. But can any attempt to discuss or explain the categories avoid falling into either irrelevance (and hence failure) or circularity (and hence no illumination)? If the categories are to be categorized or explained, it would appear to be either in terms of something else or in terms of themselves; and if it is the former, is not this an affair of explaining the categories in terms of something more basic and hence a denial of their categorial status? If the latter, is it not circular and not illuminating?

If something is the subject matter of inquiry, is not this a fairly sure sign that it is not a basic concept or category? In this case is it not being considered in terms of something else, some more fundamental presupposition or category; and if so, is not the discussion concerned at best with something mistaken for a category rather than with a genuinely basic principle? Thus our discussion, so the argument runs, would appear to be irrelevant to the nature of the categories and our attempted discussion a failure. And if the discussion proceeds in terms of the categories themselves, the proponent of this position would argue, it is circular—simply a matter of saying that $A$ is $A$ when we are eager to learn what $A$ is or how it is characterized.

I do not think that the situation is as bad as these questions may suggest. Indeed, it appears to me absurd to argue that the mere fact that something is the subject of inquiry—in this case, the categories—shows that it cannot be what we are discussing. The fact that we take ourselves to be discoursing concerning the categories does not seem to me to show that we must really be discussing something else—a pseudo- or sub-category. That the categories are claimed to be ordering principles for all things surely does not prove, apart from an additional theory of types (which, incidentally, I regard as a development from a particular set of categories other than my own), that they must order less—that they order all things *except* categories. Anything may be a subject of inquiry—including the categories. Though the fact that discourse proceeds in terms of the categories tends to focus attention upon the material organized rather than upon the organizing principles, the presence of alternative sets of candidates for *the* basic principles of explanation aids us to discern them.

If by characterizing the categories one has in mind describing or explaining them in terms of something more fundamental, the advocates of each worldview would find this impossible; for the categories of a view are the fundamental concepts or key principles in terms of which everything is to find its place. To assert that they can be explained in terms of something more fundamental is indeed to deny their categorial status and to offer another set of categories.

It seems to me, however, that we may discuss the categories without attempting to explain them in terms of something more fundamental. After reflective inquiry makes us aware of them, we may at least point to or designate the categories—as in fact we have been doing in referring to them as ordering principles or concepts; and the basic instrumentality for achieving this end would be the categories of the view within which we are operating. On a common-sense level, moreover, we may compare categories of one view with those of another; and such comparison may well suggest the need of more thorough consideration—which each worldview is ready to provide for the categories of other views as well as for its own categories. To be unable to provide this would be an indication of inadequacy on the part of the view; for, after all, the categories do constitute a most important area of fact—the basic ordering principles; and each worldview attempts to find a place for everything.

But does not this offer an undesirable and unilluminating circularity to explain the categories in terms of themselves? It is a form of circularity, I grant, but not an undesirable one. It seems to me, moreover, that it may be highly illuminating. In the first place, finding the place of the categories themselves within their own conceptual framework is likely to focus attention upon some one or two of them. For any given purpose the entire set is likely to be subsumed under some one of them instead of offering merely an $A$ is $A$ statement; and to know which of the categories this is may be quite illuminating. For example, for the contextualist categories find a place in the main under the category of the instrument as conceptual tools or instruments for patterning the generic or pervasive traits of existence. This does not mean that means-objects or instruments are the most important or fundamental category for the contextualist. It simply means that if the question is where to locate the categories themselves within the conceptual framework of this view, this is where to look. For another question some other category may come to the fore. In the second place, insofar as characterizing the categories involves more than subsuming the set under some one of them—involves possibly the entire set—this, too, need not be unilluminating. In effect this would be a way of showing forth or rendering obvious what the fundamental concepts of a view are—and not an explanation of them in other terms. To designate them as ordering principles does not require explaining order in terms of something more basic than order.

The first step in showing forth or attempting to make obvious a categorial system might well be to indicate the key insight, basic analogy, or root metaphor from which it stems; for, with Stephen C. Pepper[2] and Dorothy M. Emmet,[3] I think that a worldview centers about a root metaphor or basic analogy from which a kind of theoretical model for the entire range of facts may be drawn. The basic traits of this key fact—whether it be water, a machine, an organic whole, matter and form, historical events, reflection upon spontaneous acts of knowledge, or something else—constitute the categories of a view. Hence, insight into the structure of this key fact or cluster of facts affords a clue to the understanding of anything whatsoever and thus a master coordination of facts. A worldview constitutes a claim that the basic traits of this central fact are what characterize any and all facts, or, in other words, that understanding them will illuminate any problematic area of fact.

The next steps, of course, in showing forth a categorial system involve applying it to these problematic areas to see what guidance or illumination it affords, both with reference to the material organized and the organizing principles themselves. The problematic area with which we are concerned in this discussion is that of these organizing principles, the categories; and the place they are given will vary with the worldview. Hence it is important to specify the conceptual framework within which one is working. It may be argued, indeed, that which worldview we take is less important than that we indicate clearly which it is; and though this seems to me to be an overstatement, I recognize that highly illuminating interpretations may be had from more than one view and feel that a view which dismisses all others as sheer error is itself less likely to afford adequate vision.

At any rate, at this point I may serve notice that in this paper I am operating within the contextualistic conceptual framework—one which I have attempted to characterize at some length elsewhere.[4] Contextualism I think of as a form of pragmatic naturalism which takes as its basic fact patterned events, things in process, or historical events. The main traits of such events constitute

the fundamental categories of the view and may be used, I think, to characterize or explain any set of problematic facts. Though there are various alternative statements of these categorial features in the writings of Dewey, Pepper,
Hook, and others,[5] one convenient grouping, which I set forth in *A Contextualistic Theory of Perception,* divides them into (1) a set of filling or textural traits
which indicate the nature or "stuff" of an event, and (2) a group of contextual
or environmental traits which serve to denote the place of the event in relation
to other events. The textural categories include *texture, strand, quality, fusion,* and
*reference* (direction-distance values), whereas the most important contextual ones
are perhaps *environment, initiations, means* (or *instruments*), *consummations,* and *frustrations* (blocking).

In terms of this set of categories the most promising place to look for a place
for the categories themselves is to the category of reference (direction-distance
values) or to that of instruments, and the character of the categories for a contextualist may be indicated fairly readily under either of these headings, with
the difference between them being largely one of emphasis. This point serves
to illustrate the contextualist's contention that it is impossible to do justice to
the nature, "stuff," or quality of an event without bringing in the context or
relations, and the other way around. If we think of the categories as types of
reference, they are the most general forms of reference, cosmic direction-val-
ues; and in this sense all of the contextual categories—environment, initiations,
instruments, consummations, and frustrations—are forms of reference. If we
think of the categories as instruments or means, the direction-distance values
offer ways of spelling them out and evaluating them. Thus, starting with either
category, I think we should come out with much the same general formulation. Two considerations, however, incline me to discuss the categories as instruments. In the first place, the direction-distance values are primarily concerned with characterizing individual events or textures, whereas the category
of means or instruments places the emphasis upon the relations between events;
and the chief problems of the categories turn about relations. In the second
place, moreover, not merely do the problems turn about relations, but they
center on functions, and this is an affair of instruments. The categories, then,
for the contextualist may perhaps best be thought of as conceptual instruments
for classifying, interpreting, or ordering the entire range of facts.

It may be noted that the contextualist's conception of the categories encourages comparisons between views. In thinking of categories as conceptual
instruments, we are urged to ask which set of categories best serves to perform
their common function. From the vantage point of contextualism, to be sure,
the contextualistic categories may well appear to be much more adequate tools
for patterning the pervasive traits of existence than do the categories of alternative views; but my point is that the very notion of instruments forces contextualists to consider alternatives and to inquire about means of improving their
own conceptual instruments. I shall not claim cosmic provincialism is impos-

sible for contextualists, the difficulties at best of achieving comprehensive vision being what they are; but it seems to me clear that their categories actively encourage open-mindedness and full consideration of alternatives.

## Function of the Categories

In the preceding section we have seen that what a category is, or how it may be characterized, is perhaps best indicated for the contextualist in terms of its function; and I have suggested that the function of the categories is to help us make comprehensive sense of the full range of facts from whatever field they may be drawn. A set of categories, then, is a conceptual instrument (or set of them) for patterning or ordering facts, and metaphysical interpretation proceeds by explaining or analyzing facts in terms of such categories. A metaphysical interpretation of any problematic feature of our world has been given, as I have suggested elsewhere,[6] when we can specify or trace out the place of this feature in the categories of a worldview. If these fundamental concepts can be applied with precision and a fair measure of consistency to the illumination of any fact or any range of facts, they show themselves to be conceptual tools of high adequacy and the worldview to be one worthy of our thoughtful consideration.

But how, it may be asked, do the categories help us make comprehensive sense of the entire range of facts? In the first place, as we have suggested above, they offer a classificatory scheme in which anything may be located. In terms of this scheme we may order facts, for the categories are pervasive traits of existence as we have experienced it. Secondly, as significant characteristics of a key fact, or cluster of facts, they help direct attention upon significant features of other facts. Not merely, then, do they offer pervasive traits of existence in terms of which a useful classification may be had, they also afford guiding principles of action. The classificatory scheme affords principles of orientation, cosmic signposts in terms of which we can take our bearings. The relationships in the categorial system suggest looking for similar relationships in the problematic area. What proved useful as a means of treating this key fact may be helpful in the case of another. Implicit in the scheme, moreover, is a logic or methodology which seems appropriate for this master fact and which affords its criteria of understanding. In terms of these criteria each worldview develops its account of proper procedure, truth, and adequacy.

## Empirical Relevance

These last remarks raise certain questions concerning the empirical relevance or applicability of the categories; and the manner of developing some categorial systems is such as to raise serious doubt about their applicability. They afford beautiful ontological schemes, but, we may ask, do they fit our world, and if so, how? And this question is pertinent for more adequate categorial systems as well. How does one determine their adequacy or inadequacy? In what sense can any empirical fact make a difference in them? Is the construction of categorial systems something which proceeds with such sweeping disregard for the realm of facts that one may have a universal and necessary system of categories which is irrelevant or inapplicable to these facts? One contemporary writer avers that the choice between universality and necessity, on the one hand, and empirical objectivity, on the other, is a central dilemma for metaphysicians. "From Aristotle to Whitehead," he writes, "the crucial problem of all categoriology has been this: How can the categories be at the same time both universally valid and empirically objective? How can they meet the requirement (specified by Whitehead) of being a 'coherent, logical, and necessary system of general ideas,' and still prove to be 'applicable and adequate' for the interpretation of the external world given in experience?"[7]

This formulation has at least a hint of the mechanistic naturalist's inner-outer dichotomy, and in this form contextualists would hesitate to claim it as their own; but if forced to make a choice on these terms, their emphasis would be on the side of empirical relevance. Ordering or interpreting common-sense facts is primary with them. Their categorial system aims at or intends universality rather than starts with it. Observed failure to encompass any fact would require modification of their set of categories.

But, it may be asked, is not a set of categories in the nature of the case an analytic or a priori affair rather than one involving the possibility that a body of empirical knowledge may change it? I should like to answer: "Not completely so." It is true that there is anticipation of experience in that our categories may be accepted prior to this, that, or the other experience, and acceptance of a set of categories involves a decision to sort things or classify them in certain ways. We are not sure what experiential items will turn up tomorrow, but we contextualists would expect to classify whatever turns up in terms of our categories. Why, then, do we suggest that there is an empirical aspect to the categories?

In the first place, it is empirical in that this is an expectation of applicability rather than a foregone conclusion. We go on the assumption that new facts or areas of experience will also prove to be like our key fact or basic analogy; that the central features of this fact will turn out to be applicable in illuminating fashion to any fact; and that they will thus show themselves to be pervasive traits of existence. But we are ready to add that we may find a better way of categorizing things; and our insistence upon an empirical aspect is grounded in our conviction that something sufficiently new may turn up to require a re-working of our categories. There is, moreover, the standing possibility that the categories of a philosophy may leave large areas of fact unclassified, unordered, or unilluminated, so that a critical Hamlet may justifiably charge that "there are more things in heaven and earth . . . than are dreamt of in your philosophy."

Finding such gaps in the classificatory system of one of the major worldviews is unlikely, but the fact that it may occur in any classificatory system claiming universal scope is sufficient to remind us of the empirical relevance of such systems in general. If there appears to be no place for a fact in a categorial system or if it appears to be singularly unilluminating to place it under what appears to be the proper category in this system, revision of the system or substitution of another for it is a live possibility. It is always in order, moreover, to inquire whether a given set of categories affords what appears, in the light of all the available evidence, to be a reasonable ordering of the facts; whether accepting these categories leads us to regard most areas of common-sense experience as sheer appearances or nonentities, or whether it rather illuminates a wide range of facts; whether one set of categories helps make clear connections in experience slurred over by another set and affords solutions for philosophical problems for which alternative sets have less to offer.

At this point, however, it may be objected that it is all very well to speak of categories as illuminating wide ranges of fact; but is not this a highly subjective affair such that one may profess to find illumination where another fails to find it? Is it not, therefore, doubtful whether metaphysical categories illuminate anything? Perhaps the best answer to the question of whether or not they afford illumination is to urge the questioner to place herself or himself sympathetically within the framework of a worldview and analyze some problematic area of experience in terms of its basic concepts and then see if this does not lead to a better understanding of this area. Of those who have carried through this type of experiment a sufficient number, including some nonmetaphysicians, report increased understanding to make me feel confident that analysis in terms of these categories does afford clarification. There is, in addition, a high degree of agreement as to, say, a half dozen or so worldviews being more adequate than a corresponding number which may be selected from the history of philosophy. On the other hand, however, there is enough difference of opinion among able individuals of good will as to the relative adequacy of different sets of categories to lead me to conclude that one categorial system may be more helpful and afford greater illumination for one person than for another and that, accordingly, the pursuit of comprehensive wisdom will be furthered by leaving open the possibility of more than one worldview. This is better even than making contextualists of all philosophers!

## Categorial Sets or Systems

When we talk of sets of categories or categorial systems, however, this may have us thinking about how many fundamental categories there are in such a set and how they are related to each other. What sort of thing is a system or set of categories? This is far too extensive a topic for adequate consideration here, but I should like to comment briefly on both the number of the categories and the nature of categorial systems.

Clearly there must be a sufficiently large number of fundamental categories to provide a basis for interpreting the great variety of facts, but the number of basic concepts should not be so large as to raise serious question of which is the more complicated—the facts or our concepts for interpreting them. It is not the function of the categories to duplicate the realm of existence but rather to order or interpret it—to help us get a worldview; and if this is the case, there are obvious advantages in having a set which comes fairly readily within the limits of attention. This is not to maintain, please note, that the limitations of human understanding or comprehension can set a limit to the complexity of the realm of facts. It is rather to suggest something concerning the conditions of effective use of instruments for understanding our world. It is not even to set a limit to the total number of concepts or to the number of ways of analyzing events. There may be, as Whitehead suggests,[8] an indefinitely large number of ways of analyzing experience; and the number of derivative concepts may be indefinitely extended so long as we are clear regarding their relation to the basic categories. Thus, though Whitehead says that in a sense "there are an endless number of categories of existence,"[9] he lists eight and notes that among the eight, two, actual entities and eternal objects, "stand out with a certain extreme finality."[10]

The more numerous the fundamental categories, however, the more framework for grouping them we have to have—so that one may get the impression of undue or misplaced abstractness of which Whitehead on occasion complained as the other side of misplaced concreteness. The abstractions become involved in ordering other abstractions and these yet others, with the concrete events we hope to order or interpret growing ever more remote from our discourse. Interestingly enough, however, most of the major worldviews have had a comparatively small number of fundamental categories.

But, in any event, how do we group the categories of a worldview? What constitutes them a system? Whatever it may be, something more than a mere miscellany or list of important topics of the sort to be found in some textbooks on metaphysics is required to constitute a system of categories. The categories in a system must mutually support and supplement each other in such fashion that they have a place for everything and so that no matter where you start, your analysis leads you to the other categories and sub-categories of the system. Thus in my own grouping of the contextualistic categories into textural and contextual ones we found that in one sense it was arbitrary which we started with, for full consideration of any one of them would bring in the others.

It seems to me, moreover, as I have indicated earlier, that a set of categories is built about a key insight, basic analogy, or root metaphor and that this key fact helps unify the system. When Whitehead, for example, indicates that his is the philosophy of organism or process, we may expect this basic fact to help constitute his categories a system; and to a certain extent this is the case. Curiously enough, however, he does not make as extensive use of this analogy as he might have, or, possibly more accurately, he goes about using it the hard way. In *Process and Reality,* at any rate, he builds his philosophy in good part by combining principles of several traditional philosophers I incline to think of as either antithetical to his organismic outlook—Locke, Hume, and Descartes—or ones not fully committed to it—like Kant—and has little or nothing to say about philosophers like, say, Hegel who might fit more naturally into the framework he has sketched. Thus the historical figures he quotes most put additional strain on his system in pointing in the direction of other basic analogies.

The late Professor Archie J. Bahm, one of the founders of this society, has devoted a great deal of ingenuity to developing techniques of grouping a large number of categories, and he has come up with some interesting ways of doing this—so interesting that for some years I have been thinking of devoting a paper to examining them at length. His organicism grows out of an emphasis upon wholes and organic interrelationships, and many of his expositions strongly suggest a development along the lines of Hegel or Bosanquet, but he demurs at various of the categories of their system—for example, those concerned with an absolute—and in his zeal to do justice to all the facts his categories proliferate into at least twenty-five or twenty-six pairs of polar opposites, each pair of which may be discussed in terms of his nine types: one-pole-ism, other-pole-ism, dualism, and aspectism, each in both extreme and modified forms, and organicism as the ninth and central type.[11] Thus his organicism is outlined in terms of its relations to eight other types of theories. It is interesting to note that Bahm uses contrast first to group his categories and then, since he has so many of these polar contrasts, groups the contrasts in terms of his nine types.

Others suggest that the categories should be organized and developed like a system of mathematical postulates. One starts with certain logical primitives—the categories—and goes on to deduce the system of facts. Spinoza, with substance as his fundamental category, comes to mind as one outstanding historical figure who attempted to develop his metaphysics in terms of this mathematical model. R. G. Collingwood is a recent figure who strongly objected to metaphysics as a deductive science.[12] He argued that metaphysics is a historical science rather than a mathematical one and held that mathematics would give a logical system without stresses or strains whereas, in point of fact, according to his view, it centers about a cluster of absolute presuppositions which are related like vector forces, full of stresses and strains. Not logic but dynamic forces shape the system. It seems to me, however, that historical events or processes constitute the basic fact for Collingwood and that they generate a logic or methodology of their own quite suggestive of the organicism of a Hegel or a Bosanquet.

## Conclusion

This, however, is another and fairly long story. Let me now, in conclusion, summarize very briefly what I have tried to say. This paper has treated all too sketchily of many things and of how they may be categorized in terms of the fundamental categories of a worldview; but mainly it has dealt with the categories themselves, attempting to explain how they may be characterized at least in part by showing the basic analogy or key fact about which they are grouped and noting that from my contextualistic point of view they are conceptual instruments for patterning, ordering, or interpreting facts. Their function, I maintained, is to help us make comprehensive sense of the full range of facts. I noted that they aim at universality—at being significant generic or pervasive traits of existence—and stressed their empirical relevance, touching on some of the ways of checking on their adequacy. I concluded with some remarks on the number of fundamental categories and how they may be grouped.

# 6

# Psychological Data and Philosophical Theory of Perception

A constructive pragmatic theory of perception, as contrasted with one mainly concerned with criticizing other views, has little chance of a hearing unless it be granted that the determination of the relevant psychological data in solving the problems of perception is the exclusive right of no metaphysical theory. A number of questions are involved in this point. First, does theory of perception rely upon psychological data? With reference to the first question, it seems clear that any empirical theory of perception must rely upon some data. In giving its answer to these problems, whatever its metaphysical outlook, no philosophical analysis which claims to be empirical can afford to ignore the relevant psychological data. Genuine philosophical problems arise in connection with difficulties in handling some subject matter. It is then possible, of course, to criticize and evaluate a philosopher's mode of handling this subject matter and later to criticize and evaluate this criticism and evaluation, and so on indefinitely. But the entire discussion is grounded in, or assumes, some background of facts. Theories of perception claim to offer interpretations of a certain range of facts, in this case a body of facts falling within the sphere of psychology.

With regard to the second question, whether this psychological material is simply neutral fact, it may not be out of order to indicate that many leading psychologists do not claim that such is the case within their field. According to one such psychologist, John A. McGeoch,[1] a concern for system-making is a major attribute of contemporary psychology, and facts, though important, have to be considered in connection with the interpretative framework in which they are given their place. The same set of facts or data may look vastly differ-

From *Journal of Philosophy* 39.11 (May 1942). Courtesy of *Journal of Philosophy.* The letter from John Dewey is reproduced by permission of the Center for Dewey Studies, Southern Illinois University Carbondale, and by permission of Special Collections, Morris Library, Southern Illinois University Carbondale, holder of proprietary rights for the John Dewey papers.

ent as interpreted by rival systems of psychology. In view of this, it is indeed a hardy, if not rash, philosopher who will insist upon the neutrality of his particular set of psychological data and demand that all other accounts of perception start with them.

But such philosophers are not lacking. As a matter of fact, some epistemologists are so convinced of the purity of their psychological data that they feel that they shouldn't even be regarded as psychological but rather simply as facts—plain or stubborn facts. They contend that (*a*) the psychological data as determined by their view are simply neutral facts which all views must take as the basis for further discussion and (*b*) views such as pragmatism which fail to accept these data are not concerned with philosophically significant questions; instead they are concerned, perhaps, with psychology—psychology which has been confused with philosophy.

Let us turn to (*a*). Those I am criticizing are probably ready for a word here. "There are," they will say, "at least two things drastically wrong with proposition (*a*) attributed to us: (1) we have never made any such statement; (2) speaking of psychological facts or data as being determined by any metaphysics, ours or anyone else's, is carrying metaphysical interpretation to the extreme and shows a misinterpretation of the character of facts. Facts are not mechanistic, idealistic, realistic, or pragmatic: they simply are. Of course we insist upon the facts; but the facts are not the result of our special interpretation. They are simply neutral indubitables which any philosophical theory must consider in making its analysis; and if the theory does not fit them, so much the worse for the theory, not the facts."

In answer to them I shall have to admit that they have never in so many words maintained that the psychological data as determined by their view are simply neutral facts which all views must take as the basis for further discussion. Presumably no one who realized that the data in question are such (that is, are data) as interpreted by their view would maintain this, but it is easy for all of us to mistake things as viewed from our point of view for unbiased fact. And this is what I think they have done. Their second charge in effect admits as much in its insistence upon stubborn, indubitable facts.

I do not wish to deny—in fact, I maintain—that wherever philosophical theories arise there is a region of common-sense facts to be explained or interpreted; and the theories must fit them in the sense of accounting for them or explaining them. If these facts were as clear and unquestionable as suggested, however, there would probably be a great deal less need for theorizing than seems to be the case. The philosophical theories arise precisely because this region of facts will not stand on its own but rather requires further refinement or clarification. This refinement or clarification is given in terms of certain other regions of fact or data, and determining which ones are relevant and in exactly what way is not something which can be left to stubborn, indubitable facts or neutral data; for there are facts and facts. Though this is not the place for a critique of all indubitables, it is significant that no data to be used as explanatory entities have ever been able to maintain indubitability in the face of all experts within the field of theory of knowledge. Indeed, insistence upon such indubitables has been found to be a fairly sure mark of some point of view at work—of some metaphysical theory being smuggled in without acknowledgment. In other words, so far as I can see, the *indubitable* facts or data needed to explain the admittedly troublesome common-sense situation simply do not exist; and maintaining that they do exist is tantamount to urging that if one accepts their point of view, the facts are—as indeed they probably are—perfectly evident; but nothing which depends upon accepting a point of view can claim unqualified indubitability.

At any rate, the ones who perhaps have been most troubled by the explicit introduction of psychological material into theory of knowledge and most insistent that theory of perception concern itself with indubitable, stubborn facts, presumably of a non-psychological character, have been either Platonic realists, whose whole view is colored by a very definite psychology based upon the dogma that all knowledge worthy of the name is immediate inspection, or mechanistic naturalists, who aver that primitive sense-data discovered by pure acts of sensing should, because of their indubitability, form the starting place for all theories of perception. That these views assume a psychological background is evident, I think, to anyone familiar with the field of psychology—or perhaps I should say with the history of psychology, for they are, for the time at least, somewhat outmoded. These writers, I am persuaded, lose sight of their own psychology, which is essential as a foundation for their theories of knowledge in general and of perception in particular. Their psychology, if they recognize it at all, is simply a part of the factual background which any theory must accept. Granting this background, which may indeed seem obvious if one accepts their metaphysics, one can go on to discuss the philosophical problems of theory of knowledge (and these, the pragmatist would add, are many and difficult, if not altogether insoluble).

Turning now to proposition (*b*)—that views such as pragmatism which fail to accept these data are not concerned with philosophically significant questions but rather with a form of psychology which has been confused with philosophy—there is, so far as I can tell, nothing peculiarly or distinctively philosophical, at least in a sense which would give one cause for congratulation, about the data of Platonic realism or mechanism as over against those of pragmatism unless it be their age. All views not completely a priori have to depend upon some empirical foundation; and there seems at present no convincing reason for retaining to the exclusion of all other interpretations the data as determined by any one traditional view. At any rate, the pragmatist has brought in psychological data selected in accordance with a different metaphysical outlook; and his data accordingly seem suspect. Taking a lesson from Lotze's criticism of his opponents, the critics of the pragmatist charge him with confusing psychology with logic or epistemology—that is, with confusing the history of the growth of knowledge with the theory of the character of knowledge. As philosophy what he says is not important. As psychology, granted that it can be freed from a confused philosophical admixture, it may be very good, though, of course, on psychological matters these philosophical critics do not wish to venture an opinion.

A better illustration of the dependence of the relevant psychological data upon the metaphysical outlook—the set of intellectual instruments involved in their selection—could hardly be had than in the pragmatists' own rejoinder to this type of criticism; for they have answered that it is really their critics who have been guilty of this confusion between psychology and theory of knowledge, as may in turn be sufficiently obvious from the pragmatic point of view. Dewey, for example, charges that some of the critics of pragmatism have been guilty of "a wholesale mistaking of logical determinations for facts of psychology."[2] The traditional mechanistic and realistic attempts to define true knowledge in terms of atomic sense-data have "treated a phase of the technique of inference as if it were a natural history of the growth of ideas and beliefs."[3] They have treated material discriminated for the sake of better inference—data worked out with great art to serve as the basis for inference—as if it were the primitive stuff from which all theories of perception should take their start. They have thought that perception actually starts from such data, though for the pragmatist this is obviously not the case. But if sincere, able philosophers differ thus radically concerning what data are relevant and how they are relevant, does it not seem likely that the intellectual instruments used in determining these matters are different?

My contention, then, is that the determination of the relevant psychological data in solving the problems of perception is the exclusive right of no metaphysical theory. What the relevant psychological facts are and just how they are interpreted are matters which different metaphysical theories may decide differently; and the proponents of no metaphysical theory are entitled to assume that the psychological facts as interpreted in terms of their categories are simply neutral facts which any and all other theories must accept as the basis for further philosophical discussion. Still less, of course, are they entitled to legislate out of the realm of the philosophically significant any discussion which makes use of other data than their own and which may therefore not have to deal with the problems arising from the facts as they interpret them.

From the beginning pragmatists have realized that any theory of knowledge which accepts the psychological theory of its rivals places itself at a tremendous disadvantage. If the psychological facts are to be interpreted by rival metaphysicians, the pragmatists have no chance of presenting their view; for what they find is ruled out, or may be ruled out, by opposing views on the basis of patent facts—patent facts on their mode of interpretation. The very facts for which they claim to be offering an interpretation may seem nonexistent or strangely distorted to the advocates of another view. This, the pragmatist maintains, is because their metaphysics and consequently their psychology are different. At any rate, without their determination of the psychological background, pragmatists would have no constructive case in theory of perception, for as Mead maintained, a behavioristic psychology which enables one to put intelligence within conduct and to state it in terms of the activity of the organism is basic to pragmatism.[4]

John Dewey
1 West 89th Street
New York City

June 7–42

Dear Mr. Hahn

Ever since I read your article in the May 21st issue of the *Journal,* I've been meaning to write you to tell you how much I enjoyed it, both for clarity of presentation and for the soundness of its point of view.

I have become more and more convinced that much contemporary epistemology—the whole "sensa" industry of Moore, etc, of Russell in part—depend upon assuming certain psychological conclusions as if they were data certain of themselves and independent of any psychology. The epistemologists who cry "psychology" as a decisive objection are likely to be those who rely most completely upon uncriticized psychological material.

I find it discouraging that opponents of such a position as you put forth go on repeating the same things, with no attempt to deal with objections to them which are put forward. Your article ought to call out a reply, but I doubt if it will. Maybe if you follow it with another one naming names and with citations, you will smoke some one out.

Sincerely yours,

John Dewey

# 7

## Neutral, Indubitable Sense-Data as the Starting Point for Theories of Perception

In this paper I should like to examine Professor H. H. Price's contention that all theories of perception should start with sense-data, since they are neutral and indubitable.[1] I shall maintain that these data as characterized by Mr. Price are neither neutral nor indubitable and that starting with them raises a number of difficult and, from the pragmatist's point of view, unnecessary problems as to how they are to be synthesized, combined, or otherwise related to give us things as we find them in actual experience.

By sense-data Mr. Price means that which is directly given to the senses, or that with which we are directly acquainted through the senses—not through the sense-organs (4). When he is in the situation called "seeing something," "touching it," "hearing it," "smelling it," and so forth, it seems to him indubitable that there is something directly given to him (or directly present to his consciousness)—a color patch, a pressure (or prement patch), a noise, a smell (3), or some other indubitable sense-datum. In speaking of them as "directly" present to consciousness he means that his "consciousness of them is not reached by inference, nor by any other intellectual process (such as abstraction or intuitive induction), nor by any passage from sign to significate" (3). They are a species of data *simpliciter* not data in a relative sense (4). Even though we doubt the existence of all material things, including our own body and its sense-organs, it is still "perfectly obvious that sense-data differ from other sorts of data" in that (1) they lead us "to conceive of and believe in the existence of material things, whether there are in fact such things or not" and (2) they possess the

From *Journal of Philosophy* 36.22 (Oct. 1939). Read before the Pacific Division of the American Philosophical Association at the University of California, Berkeley, Dec. 29, 1938. Courtesy of *Journal of Philosophy*.

obvious but indescribable characteristic of sensuousness (4). They are particular existents of a perfectly determinate nature, never vague, indefinite, or indeterminate (50). Though Mr. Price apparently thinks that metaphysical questions are of little import for theory of perception (105), he does indicate that sense-data are events which happen to nothing (136–37), that they are literally nowhere in physical space (252, 319), that they are dependent upon psycho-cerebral events for their origin, their persistence, and all their qualities (136), that they are in a non-spatial sense in the mind, though they do not inhere in it as a substance (124–25), and that they are immediately given, inefficacious events of a radically different order from material things (145–46).

One of the chief advantages of starting with sense-data, Mr. Price seems to feel, is that they are indubitable. His entire theory centers about indubitable sense-data. He constantly advises us to come back to that which is indubitable. For example, to quote a typical passage, he urges that "We must try to return to what is indubitable, putting all prepossessions . . . out of our mind. . . . We have to go back to the sense-data themselves: for they are what we are quite certain of " (37). The term *sense-datum* "is meant to stand for something whose existence is indubitable (however fleeting), something from which all theories of perception ought to start" (19).

But is the sense-datum really indubitable? If the doubts of other philosophers who have reflected long and carefully upon the matter are any criterion, it certainly is not. Mr. Dawes Hicks, for example, is so little convinced of the indubitability of sense-data—and remember that Messrs. G. E. Moore and Price propose that the term be applied to the given—that he maintains that the entities designated by this term "never are, as such, 'given.'"[2] Whether or not Mr. Dawes Hicks is right, it is hard to imagine a greater strain upon the indubitability of the sense-datum. Mr. Price's contention that sense-data *indubitably* exist seems passing strange, moreover, in view of his own statement that "it is certain that many philosophers do profess to doubt this and even to deny it" (5). In view of his further admission that these philosophers offer plausible, though not wholly acceptable, arguments for their position (6), these professions and denials should be enough to make one extremely hesitant about claiming indubitability for what these individuals are doubting.

Mr. Price's apparent refusal to believe that they can really be doubting the existence of sense-data may be based upon his conviction that they would see the indubitability of these data if they attempted to enter sympathetically into the prepossessions of his own view—as perhaps they would; but if a special set of prepossessions are required to give them credence, they can hardly claim indubitability. In this sense, moreover, they scarcely afford a neutral starting point for all theories of perception. This suggests that the sense in which every one could admit that there are sense-data is too vague to be of appreciable value in grounding any particular theory and that, at any rate, sense-data as characterized by Mr. Price are not likely to meet with such universal acceptance.

Time does not permit of a discussion of all the points which other philosophers have found doubtful in connection with the kind of data Mr. Price calls indubitable. Hence an examination of a few points must suffice. One of the first claims Mr. Price makes for sense-data is that they are particular existents characterized in various ways.[3] Though not existents of the same type as trees and chairs, they are none the less particular existents (116). They persist through time but do not change (114–16). Many have objected to the statement that sense-data are particular existents—Santayana,[4] Prall,[5] and Dawes Hicks,[6] to mention only a few. Mr. Price seems to think that most of the doubt concerning the fact that sense-data are particular existents is due to a failure to distinguish between substances and other particulars,[7] which may very well be the case with many doubters but which is equivalent again to saying that if they had a different point of view they would not doubt what he regards as indubitable. It seems highly doubtful, moreover, that the sole basis for the contention of a philosopher like Mr. Dawes Hicks that sense-data are characteristics, not entities having characteristics, is his possible failure to distinguish between substances and other existents; and whether he is right or wrong in this contention, the indubitability of the sense-datum is annihilated. But there is even more of doubtful character concerning these existents which are purported to persist in time. Professor Prall asserts that "time is itself only a postulate."[8] And for anyone who maintains this, sense-data which persist through time are far from indubitable. Once more, it may be added, whether he is right or wrong, Mr. Price's indubitables have been doubted.

Another characteristic of the sense-datum is that it does not admit of degree of definiteness. It is never vague. "It is of just exactly this shade of colour and has just this shape and no other. . . . The intensity of the sense-datum is always a perfectly determinate degree, be it great or small, and the same is true of the other characteristics" (50). Mr. Price admits that sense-data are sometimes said to be "dim" or "vague," but he declares that these adjectives are really inapplicable to sense-data. They belong rather to the perceptual act. The apparent vagueness of the datum is further explained away by saying that the sense-datum may be ineffective, but never vague. The faint intensity of a datum, the uniformity of its parts, and its slight difference from neighboring data may make it ineffective and thus lead to the mistaken idea that it is vague (150). But here again we find that another philosopher, Dr. Virgil C. Aldrich, after careful study and experimentation, doubts that there are no vague sense-data.[9] As a matter of fact, Dr. Aldrich goes even further. He offers certain data which seem to him vague, and he denies that they can be explained away after the fashion suggested above. The frontal shape of certain objects outside the stereoscopic zone, for example, seem to him, "after the closest scrutiny of which he is capable," not determinately flat, as Mr. Price says they are (32), but rather indeterminate—neither determinately flat nor bulgy.[10] Dr. Aldrich also maintains that he senses certain indeterminate distances in the non-stereoscopic zone.[11] Mr. Price himself maintains that if a sense-datum seems red, it is red; if it seems square, it is square; and so on—which is to say, he tells us, that the notions of seeming or appearing are inapplicable to sense-data (64–65). But when it comes to the apparent vagueness of some sense-data, this seems to be forgotten.[12] Apparently he should maintain, if he is to be consistent, that the notion of seeming or appearing is no more applicable in the case of sensory indeterminacy than in these other cases. If the data seem sensibly indeterminate to Mr. Aldrich, in terms of Mr. Price's logic, they are indeterminate; and yet another phase of the indubitability of the sense-datum has fallen suspect.

Mr. Price also maintains that he is directly conscious of sense-data in the sense that "his consciousness of them is not reached by inference, nor by any other intellectual process (such as abstraction or intuitive induction), nor by any passage from sign to significate" (3). But the pragmatists, among others, insist that this is not according to their findings. They argue that sense-data are "post-analytical data,"[13] products of analysis, abstracted from perceptually accepted objects for certain purposes, rather than entities of which we are directly conscious in perception.[14] Mr. Edward Strong, for example, declares that "the discrimination of sense-data is both perceptually derivative and analytically subsequent to the directly experienced."[15] And it has been easy for pragmatists to indicate how starting with these post-analytical data leads to problems of combining, joining, or otherwise relating them to give us things as we find them in actual experience—problems which are as difficult as they are unnecessary if one rejects the idea that we start with indubitable sense-data.

If one accepts the pragmatic contention that in perception we start, not with sense-data as described by Mr. Price, but rather with empirical things, perceptually accepted objects, moreover, it becomes clear that sense-data are not data *simpliciter,* but data abstracted out for a certain purpose.[16] In Mr. Price's case this purpose seems to be that of answering the question, What is there in this experience of which I cannot doubt?—a question which apparently he fails to distinguish from that as to what we start with in perception.

Enough has been said, I think, to show that if Mr. Price insists upon using sense-data as the basis of his theory, some other justification than their indubitability must be found. But we have by no means exhausted the features of sense-data and sensing which he regards as indubitable in spite of the doubts of other thinkers. For example, we have not taken up his contention that the having of sense-data constitutes knowledge, and presumably our most certain knowledge at that (344, 49, 147, 203), though Prall,[17] Dewey,[18] Lewis,[19] and many others deny that sensing is knowledge at all. We have not discussed the obvious sensuousness which is to distinguish sense-data from other data, such as memory images and the like (4), though Russell, among others, has found this far from obvious.[20] The only describable differentia Mr. Price seems to find for sense-data, namely, that they lead us to conceive of and believe in the existence of certain material things (4), is likewise unsatisfactory for Mr. Russell.[21]

Nor have we taken up his contention that intellectual activity (knowing, for example) does not alter that upon which it is directed. It is just obvious, it turns out, in a curious concealed sense for he admits that "though obvious, it is concealed for various reasons" (14). This admission comes in connection with his attempt to show that the view of the idealists, who maintain the opposite, is confused, extraordinary, and so on.[22] Nor have we discussed various other assumptions which would doubtless seem far from obvious to many philosophers. And please remember that in calling attention to these points, we are primarily concerned with the purported indubitability of sense-data as characterized by Mr. Price. Granted certain theoretical assumptions, certain ways of determining and viewing facts, what he says may be justifiable. But the claim of indubitability breaks down in view of the many philosophers who find sense-data as he characterizes them doubtful; and with it goes another reason for attempting to base a theory upon these data.

But our case against Mr. Price's neutral, indubitable sense-data is not yet complete. I should now like to indicate that another important argument against their indubitability centers about their lack of the neutrality claimed for them. I should think that Mr. Dawes Hicks is much more nearly correct in holding that it is impossible to find such a neutral term and should maintain, at any rate, that the term *sense-data* does not have the requisite freedom from theoretical implications.[23] In the first place, this term suggests that what is recognized through the senses is different in kind from objects presented by means of other organic structures (for example, those involved in memory), sense-data being characterized by a unique and indescribable "sensuousness."[24] It further tends to suggest a difference in kind between "sense objects" and "conceptual," or reflectively determined, objects. In the second place, this insistence upon these post-analytical data as fundamental seems to carry with it the notion that if you want what is basically real, you should go back to the elements. Once you have the elements, it is simply a matter of seeing how they are combined or related.

However justifiable these assumptions may be (and others might be mentioned), they hardly seem to be neutral. Both pragmatists (contextualists) and idealists find them seriously objectionable. Hence the assumptions seem to involve a great deal of controversial theory—which, I think, is just what we should expect. Any thoroughgoing analysis of perception is likely to have its roots in some metaphysical theory, and any claim to priority its conceptual instruments may have is due to the categories of its metaphysics. Each theory seems to select and interpret its data in terms of its categories. Hence the proper starting point for a theory of perception, it seems to me, is not ostensibly neutral indubitables but rather a statement of one's metaphysical bias, for otherwise the bias is likely to determine the "indubitable data" without the theorists ever realizing it.

With this in mind let us consider once again Mr. Price's starting point—the neutral, indubitable, sense-datum. He is asking us in effect to wipe the slate clean and start from the indubitably real—that which is directly present to my consciousness. Anything and everything of which there is the slightest doubt is thereby ruled out. The reality we have left—the indubitable sense-datum—is that which would exist even if there were no material things at all, even if we were living in a continual dream. This is not to say, of course, that we should not continue to accept the material world as real.[25] It is merely to say that in fact it is highly doubtful. If we were convinced of the very dubious character of the external world, we might try to order our dream-figments to form a phenomenalistic world of some sort. The relation of this sense-datum (or the entire present sense-field) to other data, past and future, would be dubious, though incomparably more certain than the relation of such a sense-datum to material things, which are never given. This, put quite baldly and stripped of Mr. Price's plausible rhetoric concerning ordinary macroscopic objects, is the sort of situation we should have if we really attempted to start with the indubitable sense-data he describes. But this, I submit, is not a neutral starting point. It is to start with the traditional mechanist's inner world of mind, as Mr. Price in effect admits on occasion,[26] and make the old attempt to show how we can have any knowledge of the external world. If we accept the mechanistic categories[27]—those of a Lucretius or a Descartes—this is the starting point we should expect; and it seems neutral to Mr. Price perhaps because we have had such a large body of philosophers since Descartes thinking in fundamentally mechanistic terms. Failing to accept the mechanistic world picture, however, we should hardly start with data of this sort and then attempt to gain knowledge of a dubiously real realm of material things.

That Mr. Price is concerned with this very problem comes out in his discussion of the criteria of sense-data. He rejects the most likely criterion of sense-data—namely, that they are data which come through the instrumentality of the sense-organs—in large part because the sense-organs are material things and because it seems likely that the term *material thing* cannot be defined apart from reference to sense-data, thus involving us, he thinks, in a vicious circle. Yet it does not trouble him to say that the only describable criterion of sense-data is that they lead us to believe in the existence of material things, "whether there are in fact any such things or not" (4). And when (in chapter 5) he comes to describe sense-data he finds it necessary to do so in terms of material things[28]—a fact which strongly suggests another starting point than the indubitable sense-data. Thus it is difficult to see that either criterion has the advantage on this score. But describing sense-data in terms of any set of material things is unfortunate, Mr. Price seems to think, since there may not be any material things. His procedure here suggests that he is trying to make a problem of the entire material world, as did another famous doubter long ago.

Descartes too thought that it was possible to doubt the existence of all material things, including his own body and its organs; and if one starts with a dualism of inner data and outer things, this might be expected; but if one starts from a truly neutral starting place, I fail to see how any one could become involved in the problem of a material world at large. Either Mr. Price simply forgets that he arrives at these data by considering what happens when he looks at a material thing such as a tomato, or he disregards the metaphysical foundation which would make possible starting in this way.

At any rate, once the problem is framed in this way, whether or not one calls the inner realm mind, there seems to be no good way out. If the entire material world is in fact doubtful, as Mr. Price's starting point assumes, how can we ever be sure that we are perceptually conscious of a material thing? If all that is ever given is sense-data, how should we know or even conjecture that there are material things at all? Mr. Price says that as a matter of fact we are conscious of material things, whether or not we succeed in explaining the fact (105). I agree with Mr. Price as to the fact. But starting as he does, how are we to account in natural terms for this type of consciousness? The basis of our beliefs about material things must be what is given, and he tells us from time to time that visual and tactual sense-data are obviously the basis of these beliefs (for example, 1, 21). But why should these indubitable sense-data be taken as evidence of the existence of a never-given external world? If we were ever acquainted with material things, there might be some hope. But on this theory we are never acquainted with things but only with sense-data which may or may not belong to material things. Mr. Price admits that sensing sense-data is not enough (21, 168–69).

But how, on this theory which makes so much of the indubitable data we start with, are we to account for the more? Mr. Price answers that it must be by finding certain relations among sense-data—by synthesizing (or syngnosing) them in certain ways. But how are we to suspect that they may be synthesized in these ways? And here Mr. Price reveals the desperateness of his situation by answering that it is simply an innate power of minds to make this passage (102, 168–69, 306 ff., and elsewhere). There are certain innate a priori ideas, that of material thinghood being one, and there are certain innate powers of expecting them to apply to sense-data; and this is how we come to pass from indubitable immediate data to dubiously real things with which we have never been acquainted. In other words, if indubitable data are not sufficient, bring in indubitable powers of extending the data; and presumably if they are not sufficient, yet other indubitables may be drawn in to justify our starting point. But what under high heaven is there which could not be justified by this kind of argument? No matter how we start, no matter how unsatisfactory the metaphysical presuppositions of our theory, we can always adjust everything by a priori machinery of this sort. Knowing the result we are heading for, ingenuity and sufficient use of this *deus ex machina* will enable us to synthesize satisfactorily any data we may start with. But this is a rather heavy price to pay for our indubitable data. It at least suggests the desirability of starting with other metaphysical presuppositions and attempting to account for the phenomena of perception in natural terms.

Thus not only are the data with which Mr. Price would have all theories of perception start neither neutral nor indubitable, but starting with them has the further disadvantage of launching us upon a series of extremely difficult, if not insoluble, problems which exist only for certain metaphysical points of view. Nor can he fall back upon the defense that, awkward as these problems of perception are, the other merits of his metaphysics compensate in some measure for these difficulties and thereby justify starting with these data, for he claims that they are neutral and indubitable.

# 8

# A Contextualistic View of Experience
# and Ecological Responsibility

In developing a contextualistic view of experience and ecological responsibility, I should like to begin by sketching the main features of contextualism. I think of this view as a pragmatic naturalism shared by such American philosophers as C. S. Peirce, William James, John Dewey, George H. Mead,
Stephen C. Pepper, Henry N. Wieman, S. Morris Eames, and myself. As a group
pragmatists are known for their diversity, and many of them—for example,
Peirce, Dewey, and Pepper—have been reluctant to call themselves pragmatists
lest this appear to commit them to some doctrines they do not hold. Even
William James, who early on did most to bring the movement to the attention of the philosophic world and who was one of the more ecumenically
minded pragmatists, disliked "pragmatism" as a name for the collection of tendencies but indicated in 1907 in the Preface to *Pragmatism* that it was probably
too late to change it.

One of the main unifying factors in this body of doctrines, however, at least
since James, has been the attempt to take seriously time as passage, ongoing
processes, or felt durations. Most pragmatists since James, accordingly, have been
concerned with changing realities, things in time or process, patterned events;
and with James they have maintained that truly empirical philosophers focus
not on static eternal realities but on things in the making or in the process of
becoming, for no concrete things exist apart from change. With the process
philosophers, some of whom are not pragmatists, what we find is not endur-
ing substances and attributes but things in process, histories in relation to other histories, changing events, with their mixture of novelty, contingency, and

Paper presented originally for the Highlands Institute for American Religious Thought Second
International Conference on Philosophical Theology, University of St. Andrews, Scotland, Aug.
5, 1993. Published in *Religious Experience and Ecological Responsibility*, ed. Donald A. Crosby and
Charley D. Hardwick (New York: Peter Lang, 1996), 173–87.

stability. These patterned events have within them movements from and toward other events, and they always occur in contexts and have reference to other events within these contexts.

Such patterned events or happenings, in Pepper's terms, constitute the root metaphor of contextualism as a worldview. And these events do not have to be ones of the magnitude of a world war or of the significance of current crises of acid rain, or air pollution, the disappearance of our rain forests, the developing hole in the ozone layer in the Antarctic, or the war on drugs. They may be everyday ones like talking to a friend on the telephone, crossing a crowded street, or reading a newspaper. If we understand the structure and quality of simple happenings like these, we may be on the way to a better understanding of the world and our place in it, for the main traits of these events comprise the categories of this world hypothesis and, we contextualists hold, may be used to characterize or shed light on any set of problematic facts.[1]

Although there are various alternative accounts of these categorial features,[2] I find it convenient to divide them into (1) a set of textural traits which indicate the nature or "stuff" of an event, and (2) a group of contextual or environmental traits which denote the place of the event in relation to other events. The textural categories include *texture, strand, quality, fusion,* and *reference* (direction-distance values), whereas perhaps the most important contextual ones are *environment, initiations, means* or *instruments, terminations, consummations,* and *frustrations* (blocking).

As I put it in another study of pragmatism some years ago:[3]

> The patterned event or affair with which the contextualist starts is not a discrete atomic unit but rather a complex interrelationship of tendencies all interwoven into an integral whole with its own individual character or quality. As the term *texture* (borrowed from the weaver's art) suggests, each historical event is a web or network of happenings (strands), a focal center into which features of other histories somehow enter. Textures may be analyzed into constituent strands, and texture, strand, and context are relative to each other. What is strand or detail in a larger context may become texture in another. As a detail of a texture a strand reaches out into the context and brings some of the quality of the latter into the texture. Since the character of a texture is a fusion of the qualities of its strands and the latter are partly from its context, analysis of a texture takes us into the texture of other events.
>
> References are both part of the character or nature of an event and links with its context. Strands reach out or refer to other textures. They move from initiations through means-objects or instruments to frustrations or consummations, and to control the direction of affairs we must direct our attention to the means.

Pragmatists have long recognized that every event has a certain internal organization or structure. Both James and Dewey, for example, saw that experienced events do not have to have relations superimposed on them from another realm. The diverse factors and qualities constituting an event hang together to form a connective or relational pattern describable as we noted above in terms of textures and strands. The latter term helps make clear that the constituent factors are relative to the pattern or whole and not "elements," detachable or independent "entities," "essences," "simples," or "realities" occurring in isolation from equally detachable "relations."

A new notion of analysis which recognizes the importance for many purposes of a genetic account of events goes with this view. Analysis is not a matter of reducing a complex to permanent or fixed elements. It is rather an affair of exhibiting the texture of an event through tracing patterns of change. This involves discrimination of its strands, but they derive part of their quality from the event's context and have a way of leading off into it. So analysis becomes an affair of following references from one texture to another, and how far we follow them or which ones we trace depends on the problem which occasions our analytic inquiry. If, for example, an officer is investigating a possible homicide, there are at least as many analyses as there are possible causes of the death, and these lead from indications in the present texture into different environing textures depending upon whether it is death by food poisoning, strangulation, a stab to the heart, a blow to the head, or something else. Accordingly, depending upon which referential strand we follow and which environmental texture or textures we trace it into, we may have many analyses, each of which may be more or less adequate for its purpose. But we never reach ultimate elements, and there is no such thing as *the* analysis of anything, for the texture of an event may be exhibited in any number of different ways, depending upon the purpose of the analysis or the nature of the problem generating it.

The contextual categories are important for analysis as well as for felt qualities. Indeed, it is difficult to exaggerate the importance of context for any area of philosophy, and yet as John Dewey saw it, "the most pervasive fallacy of philosophic thinking goes back to neglect of context."[4] Placing a texture in a different context changes its felt quality, and whether this change is significant for a given purpose may depend on the purpose or the context. With a suitable context virtually any event may have the enhanced quality of beauty; and by setting up appropriate instruments and control textures we can tackle our practical and theoretical problems.

Any given event is characterized by a certain "from which" and a particular "toward which," and these make it the distinctive affair it is, showing its special thrust or vector quality. For that matter, we may ask of any event: When and where is it? Whence is it? Whither does it go? How does it go? or What means or instruments move it toward its termination? And we answer these questions in terms of references or means and context. To indicate the context of an event we specify (1) its environment, (2) the initiations from which it started, and (3) the means or instruments through which it moves toward (4) consummations or (5) frustrations, blocks, breaks, or hitches. Each event involves an environment of other affairs which support, block, or condition its quality, but it is not in its environment like a marble in a box or Newtonian container. It is rather in it in the sense that event and environment jointly participate in various transactions, interactions, or ventures in common. Indeed, it may be more illuminating to say of a live creature that it lives by means of its environment than that it is in it.

One important set of transactions between live creature and environment is what may be called from the point of view of the former, problem-solving activities and experimentation. It is perhaps better known as pragmatism's empirical method, sometimes called by Dewey the scientific method, but I think more aptly designated as the method of reflective inquiry. In any event, it is central for Dewey's Instrumentalism. Pragmatism's concern with consequences and an empirical method for dealing with them fits in with the Jamesian and Deweyan conception of an unfinished universe, one still in process of becoming, in which ideas as hypotheses can make a difference; and this concern also seems to me highly relevant for some of our ecological problems.

Dewey sets forth this method in terms of the steps in a complete act of reflective thinking in several different books: for example, in *How We Think* (1910, 1933) and in *Logic: The Theory of Inquiry* (1938). Reflective thinking, in these accounts, differs from such other modes of thinking as daydreaming and trial and error or fumble and success thinking in at least two ways: (1) it is occasioned by some question, problem, or difficulty; and (2) it results not merely in a solution for the problem but also in some descriptive or explanatory statements about how it was solved. On this general view, reflective inquiry starts with problems or difficulties, sometimes only a vague sense of something having gone wrong, clarifies them in terms of observation and analysis, seeks hypotheses for solving the problems, reasons out the implications of these suggested solutions, and verifies or disconfirms them through observation and experimentation. Some such general procedure has been followed successfully in the sciences, but contextualists are convinced that it may be at least equally important to apply some such method in the more difficult area of our value problems.

Accompanying this method has been a different psychology from the traditional introspective psychology of, say, Locke, Berkeley, and Hume, for contextualists have long seen that one's interpretation of people and their environment is closely tied up with the psychology one adopts. If we start with the above introspective psychology and its accompanying metaphysics which describe experience in terms of relatively distinct impressions and ideas somehow related by association, we may well be faced with a dualism which places people and their environment in separate and opposed metaphysical realms; but if we adopt a newer psychology which draws on developments in physiological and experimental psychology and describes experience in terms of ongoing courses of purposive behavior, it becomes apparent that people are parts of nature and that the biological matrix is central. Of course, contemporary proponents of something like the Lockean view may charge that we contextualists are confusing psychology and theory of knowledge, and we consider that they are the guilty ones, for we see that both of us are making use of psychology and that refusing to acknowledge this does not convert psychology into simple neutral fact.

The behavioristic psychology of G. H. Mead and E. C. Tolman adopted by contextualists, however, should be distinguished from Watsonian behaviorism, which is fundamentally individual, mechanistic, and antithetical to introspection. In contrast to this view, we hold a purposive behaviorism which starts with behavior on a molar rather than a molecular level and finds a place equally for the usual observational material and for that which is open more readily to the observation of the acting individual. As I noted in an earlier treatment of this topic,[5]

> Behavior, on Mead's account, is basically social, and language as an instrument of socialization is a form of interaction within a social group rather than something to be explained simply in terms of movements within the larynx of the individual. Mind or consciousness, according to Mead, instead of being something to be ruled out of account, is something to be explained in relation to conduct; and the distinction between inner and outer, instead of being one between disparate metaphysical realms, is one made within experience.

The biological matrix of experience comes out clearly in E. C. Tolman's *Purposive Behavior in Animals and Men,* which offers an excellent systematic formulation of a purposive behaviorism of this general type and summarizes a wealth of experimental material which both fits in with and uses the contextualistic categories. It needs supplementation, however, in terms of social and cultural considerations in view of the fact that the demands of adult human beings are far richer and more varied than the core of fundamental physiological drives might suggest.

It is perhaps clear that the contextualistic idea of textures and their contexts, with strands or threads of reference running from one to the other, does not accord with the Cartesian presumption of two insulated realms of self and world or mind and matter or mind and body. Neither the conception of a private inner mind-set over against an external material world nor the idea of a self-contained subject which somehow knows an equally self-contained but alien object is acceptable contextualistically. The notion of segregated compartments or dualisms is foreign to the contextualistic worldview both in terms of contextualistic and naturalistic considerations. Also, as might be expected from their contention that it is possible to account for natural events, with their beginnings and endings, in terms of natural principles without going outside the system, contextualists reject the concept of a deity who intervenes arbitrarily through supernatural measures, and they question the supernatural doctrines of special creation, miracles, and revelation. They are concerned with questions growing out of affairs within nature rather than with attempts to discover a divine design for the totality of things. They try to focus on investigating ways in which one set of changes serves concrete purposes and another works against them.

Although contextualists forthrightly reject supernaturalism, some of them use the term *God,* but in each case the term has been reinterpreted in naturalistic fashion, usually in terms of values and frequently with the assertion that the ideas with which they are concerned can be formulated without the term. Dewey, for example, in *A Common Faith,* writes of God as an active relation between the ideal and the actual rather than as an eternal, completed Being. And another contextualistically oriented philosopher, Henry Wieman, speaks of God as the source of human good, the complex of forces making for creativity.

In any event, with their naturalism, contextualists conceptually place people in nature and find a basic continuity and intimate intercourse between them and their environment, natural, social, and cultural. We human beings interact with our environment in multitudinous ways, and it is not too much to say that we and our lifestyles are in large part constituted by these transactions, just as our environment is similarly constituted. What we do, we do with our natural, social, and cultural environment, and we live, move, and have our being in it. We enter into more or less stable integrations with our environment and form uneasy equilibriums requiring frequent adjustments or modifications, with our very survival depending on making some of them. As Dewey remarks in *Logic: The Theory of Inquiry,* an environment is "primarily the scene of actions performed and of consequences undergone in processes of interaction," and its "constituents are first of all objects of use and enjoyment-suffering, not of knowledge." It functions in connection with the maintenance of life as a continuous affair.[6] Such activities as breathing, swimming, skiing, walking, crawling, and flying require environmental support; and nature provides a mixture of support and frustration of our plans. Where support is lacking we have a problem and need to make use of reflective inquiry to find instruments for solving it or to modify our behavior patterns.

What we have discussed so far in connection with the environment as the total range of transactions or interactions between things and live creatures already gets us into the contextualistic view of experience. Traditionally, Dewey and various other pragmatists argued, philosophers have thought of experience mainly as an act of experiencing quite apart from what is experienced, but Dewey and contemporary contextualists agree with William James that experience is a double-barreled fact which includes both what is experienced and the act of experiencing, and they have their own account of both: a purposive behavioral psychology which has a place for introspection for the experiencing and the contextualistic worldview for the experienced and how it is related to the experiencing.

The distinctive character of the contextualistic view of experience may be clearer from Dewey's admirably succinct summary in "The Need for a Recovery of Philosophy" of the main points of contrast between it and the position shared by both the traditional empiricists and their rationalistic opponents.[7] In the first place, according to the contextualists, whereas the traditional or orthodox account mistakenly treats experience as basically a way of getting good, poor, or mediocre knowledge, as we have seen above, it is primarily intercourse with one's environment or with nature at large; an affair of had qualities; a transaction of enjoying and suffering, of doing and undergoing, of employing direct environmental supports in order indirectly to help effect changes favorable to our further functioning. It is the special mixture of support and frustration of a living creature by nature. In the second place, as over against the orthodox version of experience as a peculiarly psychical or invidiously subjective activity, contextualists think of it as something which flows in and through its objective environment, which supports or blocks it and is in turn modified by it. It is of a piece with an objective world in which and by means of which we live, move, and have our being. Again, in keeping with their emphasis on experience as cognitive, proponents of the traditional theory have been preoccupied with what is or has been "given" in a bare present whereas for contextualists the salient mark of experience is its connection with a future, not what has been or is given but rather what may be done to change what is given or taken to advance human purposes.

Or to mention yet another contrast, as opposed to the particularism of traditional empiricists who concentrate on more or less disconnected sense data, impressions, and ideas and neglect or minimize connections, relations, and continuities of experience, contextualists stress the contextual, situational, transactional, and field character of experience and see experience as adaptive courses of action, connections of doing and undergoing. Finally, instead of holding with the orthodox account that experience and thought in the sense of inference are antithetical, contextualists see experience as full of inference and anticipation. For them it is loaded with references which trace directions and relations and pregnant with imaginative forecasts of future trends and movements. For that matter, how could it be otherwise when we try to maintain conditions favorable to our future life activity and modify or remove ones deemed unfavorable to it? What else should we expect if we seek to enrich and enhance the qualities of experience and to share their enjoyment?

In what has been said up to now about the contextualistic view of experience I have emphasized the problem solving aspects of experience as perhaps more focal for ecological problems, but experience exhibits itself more fully and in greater detail in terms of aesthetics. For contextualists the aesthetic field may be defined either in terms of vivid experience or enhanced quality. Irwin Edman and Dewey write of the aesthetic as experience vivified, intensified, clarified, and unified whereas Stephen C. Pepper and I use the language of enhanced quality. But for the most part we are all in substantial agreement on the aesthetic field.[8] We also agree that there is something of quality in every event even though, for successful habitual responses, there is often no time to take it in, but artists help us take it in and share it. In expressing our feelings, poets and other artists socialize our appreciations and help provide sympathetic understanding of both us and the community sharing our feelings.

On the score of ecological responsibility, there are, of course, many questions about global environmental problems not yet adequately answered, but we do have enough answers to show more than amply that we have a disturbing set of critical global ecological problems; and Al Gore, in his *Earth in the Balance: Ecology and the Human Spirit,* has admirably summarized a number of them.[9] Especially impressive are his accounts of the clusters concerning global air pollution and the earth's water system and the way these problems are exacerbated by our greatly expanding population. One of his main thrusts, however, is that "Our increasingly aggressive encroachment into the natural world and the resulting damage to the ecological systems of the earth have weakened the resilience of the global environment itself and threatened its very ability to maintain its equilibrium."[10] That of all earthlings we humans pose the gravest threat to the environment may be easier to comprehend than that anything any person or group of persons can do actually imperils it. And one of the reasons why we do not see the devastating damage our aggressive encroachment is doing to the earth's ecological systems is that we and our modern industrial civilization have lost our feeling of connectedness to the rest of nature,[11] our sense of connection to our world and its future. One's personal experience may help overcome this, as may reflection on nature and environment from the perspective of other worldviews or cultures with a closer bond between people and nature.

For example, as a native Texan familiar with declining water tables and what happened to farms and the total economy during the Dust Bowl Era, I am well aware of the regional ecological ills caused by improper agricultural techniques coupled with drought, and the contextualistic worldview makes it easy to understand our global ecological crisis, for in its stress upon the intimate interrelationship between organism and environment this view provides a general theory of ecology. It also brings a sense of connection with our world and its future.

A similar sense of the close relationship between people and nature existed among the native American Indians, and Chief Seattle's response to the United States president who offered to buy his tribe's land puts it very well.

> How can you buy or sell the sky? The land? . . . we do not own the freshness of the air and the sparkle of the water. . . . The earth does not belong to man, man belongs to the earth. All things are connected like the blood that unites us all. Man did not weave the web of life, he is merely a strand in it. Whatever he does to the web, he does to himself.[12]

The ancient Chinese Taoists and Confucians more than twenty-four thousand years ago also shared the wisdom of believing in a basic continuity and intimate intercourse between people and their environment.

But what can we do to prevent loss of the earth's balance? Granted that grave damage has occurred, how can we get sufficient consensus early enough to save the earth? One encouraging note is that we have made great progress in reducing the threat of nuclear omnicide. What can we do about the present unparalleled global environmental crisis? The method, I think, should be an application on a vast cooperative scale of the method of reflective inquiry, an empirical method turning about looking into antecedents and consequences of proposed modes of action. This method is not infallible but it is self-correcting. Much of our crisis stems from the fact that success in reaching some of our earlier stated goals has carried with it unforeseen disastrous consequences for our environment. But we have to do better in taking into account environmental consequences.

Our project is one requiring cooperation on a vast scale between geographical regions, political agencies, and individuals, and getting this cooperation will be slowed by the fact that too few of us understand the intimate intercourse between people and their natural environment and the ways in which unconsidered or improperly considered actions can cause great damage to the environment. But the stakes are high enough to justify sharing this knowledge as widely as possible so that bold decisive action to rescue the environment can be undertaken. And, incidentally, a word of appreciation is due the organizers of this conference for their part in helping focus attention on ecological responsibility.

I find it encouraging that a professional politician with a long-term interest in ecological problems like Al Gore thinks a politically feasible unified global program can be devised for meeting the crisis; and something on the order of his Global Environmental Marshall Plan may offer a start toward this end. The original Marshall Plan, of course, serves as both a model and an inspiration for his program. He outlines five strategic goals to direct and inform efforts to save the global environment: (1) stabilizing world population, with policies designed to create in every nation the so-called demographic transition from an uneasy equilibrium of high birth and death rates to a stable equilibrium of low birth and death rates; (2) the rapid creation and development of environmentally appropriate technologies; (3) a comprehensive and ubiquitous change in the economic systems of accounting by which we measure the impact of our decisions on the environment; (4) the negotiation and approval of a new generation of international agreements necessary to make the plan work; and (5) the establishment of a cooperative plan for educating the world's citizens about our global environment. Additionally, the plan should have as its more general, integrating goal the establishment, especially in the developing world, of the social and political conditions most conducive to the emergence of sustainable societies.[13]

Admittedly, any such plan faces great hurdles in being accepted and put into place, but our world is in the balance, and there is need for help from every interested person. Gore, moreover, is convinced that "political measures to protect the global atmosphere will one day surge when the meaning of the word 'backyard' expands to encompass each person's share of the air we all breathe."[14]

In summary, then, in this paper I have sketched the main features of contextualism as a form of pragmatic naturalism, stressing its emphasis on change and things in process. In light of this I have outlined the contextualistic view of experience as a double-barreled fact which includes both what is experienced and the act of experiencing and have indicated how intimately experience is related to its environment. In terms of this account I concluded by commenting on our global environmental crisis and made some suggestions concerning what we can do about it.

# 9

# Creating: Solving Problems
# and Experiencing Afresh

What do we do when we create? In answering this question contextualistic philosophers of creativity from Dewey to Wieman and beyond take their cue from the fact that the Indo-European base for our word *create* is one meaning "to grow or to cause to grow" *(Webster's New World Dictionary of the American Language)* and hold that to create is to grow and help others to grow. Thus for contextualists creation aims at human growth. People grow in many ways, but the two important ones on which I shall focus tonight are growing through using reflective inquiry to solve problems and taking in the qualities of things, or experiencing afresh.

It may be objected, however, that the term *human growth* can embrace the pathological and the reprehensible as well as the praiseworthy. It may include cancerous growths, furtherance of cruelty, proliferation of destructive antisocial forces of drug gangs, and expansion of evil tendencies of one sort or another. Shouldn't I make clear what I wish the term to cover? Perhaps the late Professor George Axtelle's marks of growth will help point in the right direction here; but, of course, there is no guarantee that creative forces in the sense of more efficient or skilled ones will not be used for socially unacceptable purposes; and the merits of a given course of action have to be checked out in specific situations. According to Axtelle, the marks of genuine growth are "flexibility, openness to new insights, new possibilities, hospitality to novelty, to the imaginative and to the creative." To grow one needs also "integrity, balance,

Invited paper for the Annual Meeting of the Society for Philosophy of Creativity, Central Division, Riverfront Hilton Hotel, New Orleans, Apr. 26, 1990, under the title "Creating: Inquiring Reflectively and Taking in Qualities." I am grateful to the Society for Philosophy of Creativity and the Foundation for Philosophy of Creativity for permission to use it here, and also to Special Collections, Morris Library, Southern Illinois University Carbondale. The papers are with the Philosophy Collections, Special Collections, Morris Library, Southern Illinois University Carbondale.

proportion, dynamic equilibrium, a unified wholeness of character . . . the integral expression of all the resources and powers of the self."[1] Or in the words of Axtelle and Burnett, *growth* as we are using the term, is not neutral or amoral development but rather "is life guided with an eye to the enrichment of present and future development."[2] At least the first of our two approaches, moreover, is self-corrective.

Now, however, before continuing with our two main approaches to growth, I should like to indicate where I am coming from by describing contextualism, a worldview which stems from such pragmatic philosophers as C. S. Peirce, William James, F. C. S. Schiller, John Dewey, George H. Mead, and Stephen C. Pepper. Contextualists agree that context is very important for all areas of philosophy. Place a texture in a different context, and you change its quality. Whether this change is significant for a given purpose, however, may depend on the purpose or the context. And to achieve constancy from one context to another is likely to require planning and setting up appropriate control textures. In any event, to take things out of context is to risk distortion or loss of meaning. Dewey puts it even more strongly in his 1931 University of California Howison Lecture on "Context and Thought," declaring that "neglect of context is the greatest single disaster which philosophic thinking can incur" and adding that "the most pervasive fallacy of philosophic thinking goes back to neglect of context."[3]

I think of contextualism as a form of pragmatic naturalism which takes as its root metaphor or key experience historical events, happenings, or occurrences, viewed not as something past and done with but rather as dynamic, concrete presences. And these events do not have to be ones of the magnitude of World War I or II or of the significance of the current crises of acid rain, the recent oil spills, the disappearance of our rain forests, the developing hole in the ozone layer in the Antarctic, or the war on drugs. They may be everyday ones like talking to a friend on the telephone, crossing a street, or reading a newspaper. If we understand the structure of simple happenings like these, we may be on our way to a better understanding of the world and our place in it, for the main traits of such historical events constitute the categories of my brand of contextualism.[4]

For contextualists the salient feature of our world is change; and nature is a scene of incessant beginnings and endings. All things in nature, including persons, begin, undergo qualitative change, and finally come to an end, making way for other individuals. Although many philosophers and members of the public at large are convinced that permanence is the touchstone of the real and the perfect, I go with John Dewey in stressing change as a pervasive trait of what we find in experience. Some things change more slowly than others and thus give a relative stability, but no concrete things exist apart from temporal process. The things that seem to "exclude movement and change," as Dewey has it, are only "phases of things," perhaps legitimate abstractions but not concrete things.[5] Things in process, histories, with their mixture of contingency and stability, are what we find empirically, and the contextualistic worldview takes them as basic. Each event is a web or texture of strands with its own distinctive fused quality, a quality enriched by features of other histories which somehow enter its focal net. This happening has beginnings and referential movements through means-objects or instruments toward blockings, consummations, or terminations. It contains movements from and toward other events, and it always occurs in certain contexts and refers (has direction-distance values) to other events within these contexts. Moreover, textures, strands, and contexts are relative to each other. What is strand in one context may be texture in another, and vice versa; and what is texture in one perspective may be context in a different one. And, of course, in a world of change, if we wish to effect desired changes or block harmful ones, we seek appropriate instruments; for it is through them that good things may be made more stable and bad ones less persistent.

In terms of their naturalism, contextualists maintain that it is possible to account for natural events, with their beginnings and endings, in terms of natural principles, without going outside the system; and their concerns are with affairs within nature rather than with attempts to discover some divinely imposed design for the totality of things. They reject the notion of a deity who intervenes arbitrarily through special measures; and they question the supernatural doctrines of special creation, miracles, and revelation. Perhaps I should add, however, that denial of supernatural purpose or intent, for the contextualists, does not mean that the natural order is purposeless, for people are parts of nature; and there is a basic continuity between them and their environment, natural, social, and cultural. Contextualists, with their purposive behaviorism, find purposiveness to be an outstanding feature of the interaction of both the lower animals and people with their environment.[6] The organism, which is motivated by some drive or purpose, experiences or has commerce with its environment in indefinitely numerous ways and enters into multiple interactions or transactions with it, some of them so integral to the events related that the distinction between organism and environment becomes a functional one which may be drawn differently depending on the context. The environment supports some transactions and fails to support others so that organism and environment form more or less uneasy equilibriums sometimes requiring frequent adjustments, with the organism's survival depending on how some of them are made. At any rate, the natural order within which the contingent and uncertain, the incomplete and the broken, the novel and the precarious are no less genuine than the relatively well established, complete, routine, and stable, affords not merely challenges to seek intelligent ways of redirecting ongoing affairs but also much of the time welcomes support and on occasion welcomes also a world rich in quality to be enjoyed. A world of this sort, as William James was fond of reiterating, is one shot through with unexpected novelties and risks, struggles, real losses, and genuine gains. It is not one whose evolution is finished and done for but rather a world "in the making," one still in process of becoming, and, accordingly, one in which there is room for constructive, creative endeavors to make portions of the world other than what they would have been without our efforts.[7]

It may be added that contextualists, with their acceptance of continuity and intimate intercourse between organism and environment, reject such sharp metaphysical dualisms as those between the self and the world, mind and matter, and subject and object. The conception of two insulated domains of self and world or mind and matter does not accord with the contextualistic idea of textures and their contexts, with strands of reference running from one to the other in open and aboveboard fashion.

The contextualistic world hypothesis with its emphasis on change also carries with it a new interpretation of analysis and what it means to understand things. How one conceives analysis, of course, depends on what we think is involved in understanding or interpreting a whole and its parts; and the dominant position in Western philosophy from Plato to Russell has been that analysis exhaustively and finally reduces a complex phenomenon to fixed and permanent elements. But if contextualists are right about the prevalence of change, this commonplace won't do. Contextualists deny that a whole can be broken down into irreducible constituents and insist that understanding or interpreting a situation means, above all, placing it in an appropriate context. For them analysis means distinguishing temporal patterns rather than timeless distinctions. To analyze is to disentangle or sort strands, remembering that the latter are relative to textures and contexts. Analysis exhibits the texture or structure of an event, and this requires discrimination of constituent strands and relevant contextual references, for the strands derive part of their quality from environing textures and have a way of leading off into them. So analysis becomes a process of following references from one texture to another, and how far we follow them or which ones we trace depends on the problem occasioning our analytic inquiry. But we never arrive at ultimate elements immune to further analysis and with no variation from one context to another.

Contextualistic analysis takes various forms, depending on the problem. We may, for example in situations demanding maximum uniformity or stability, trace the strands of a given texture into convenient control textures (schematic textures or schemes) such as the color cone or a musical scale, and these in turn may be traced into schemes of light wave or air vibrations. These latter schemes are tied in with the system of schemes constituting physics and are interknit in various ways with the schematic structures of the other sciences. But for many problems tracing the genetic career of an event through the various phases of its history to its terminus, noting its conditions and consequences, proves more illuminating than alternative explanations. And this mode of analysis has been fruitfully applied in many different fields to such varied items as stars and galactic systems, the constituents of matter, plant and animal species, field crops, linguistics, economic institutions, and cultural patterns.

But perhaps a somewhat more detailed example developed in another of my essays will further clarify this mode of analysis, especially if some of you share my liking for detective stories.[8] It is one of my favorite illustrations. In it I analyze the death of JB and maintain that something more than timeless distinctions is needed to exhibit the texture of an event with temporal spread such as an act of dying. The latter is not a knife-edge instant; it takes some time, sometimes very little and sometimes a fairly long time. And what happens within that span varies with the cause of death. So it will not do to say that whatever the cause, he is nonetheless dead, and no considerations of attendant circumstances or of anything before or after the instant of death are needed. Which circumstances are relevant will depend, of course, on the purpose of the analysis; but if homicide is suspected, the attendant circumstances may be crucially important for the police investigation. Hence, although to be sure, after the fact JB is equally dead whatever the cause, the analysis made by the police will differ in significant ways depending on whether the cause is asphyxiation, strangulation, food poisoning, a blow on the head, a stab in the heart, arsenic poisoning, an electric shock, cancer, or something else. Death from any one of these causes will involve different control textures, observations, means-objects, laboratory reports, and so on. And an adequate analysis of JB's death for the purpose cited needs to exhibit the distinctive features of the total texture stemming from whichever cause or complex of causes may be involved, along with, of course, pertinent ramifications in more or less distant environing textures; for a different genetic pattern is involved in each of these cases. But there is no such thing as *the* analysis of anything, whether the death of JB or something more pleasant like the flavor of lemonade. There are as many analyses of these things as there are problems or purposes associated with JB's death or the flavor of lemonade.

But to return to our main theme and the first of the two types of growth I mentioned at the beginning, using reflective inquiry to solve problems, pragmatists since Peirce's "How to Make Our Ideas Clear" (1878) and Dewey's *How We Think* (1910, 1933) and *Logic: The Theory of Inquiry* (1938) have been concerned with a method for resolving doubts or solving problems. They recognized that if we seek a greater measure of security in a changing world, we need something better than authoritarianism, a priori formulas, plain guesswork, or merely allowing events to run their course. They also saw that attempts to base this method on indubitables, Descartes to the contrary notwithstanding, are likely to lead to skepticism or despair. Fortunately, however, we neither find nor need to find indubitable axioms for starting points. If we can base our account on a number of converging lines of evidence even if each of them considered separately is only probable, we can arrive at beliefs that are highly probable and, accordingly, much better guides to action than so-called indubitables.

What we need, as these earlier philosophers and contemporary contextualists agree, is an intelligently guided experimental procedure for discovering what changes need to be made in a situation to bring about appropriate resolutions of difficulties, and this program of action for bringing intelligence into a situation has been variously called the method of reflective or critical inquiry or the scientific method.

What, then, is reflective or critical inquiry? It is a way of solving problems or resolving doubts or indeterminacies, and we contextualists are convinced that the pattern exemplified in it is applicable, with appropriate modifications, to the full range of perplexities and difficulties facing us in our changing world. These problems, as we see them, are specific and concrete, or can be made so; and to the extent that we can formulate them in these terms, we can work at overcoming them. If, however, we try to make a problem of everything at once or the cosmos at large, we have no way of solving or getting a handle on it; and the response is likely to be utter frustration or escape. Descartes's universal doubt, according to Peirce and his fellow pragmatists, was spurious: we do not doubt in general or wholesale fashion. Genuine doubt is a piecemeal affair. Doubt about specific items is possible because, for the moment, we accept without question a context of beliefs. This is not to say, of course, that these beliefs are indubitable, for they too may be questioned, given a different context and problem, but once more only within a framework of accepted beliefs.

Or alternatively stated, in coping with the multiplicity and diversity of our world, we develop routines or habits, and our drives are carried largely by these habits. Were it not so, and we made a problem of each segment of a given course of action, we should not have enough time to perform simple acts like getting up and leaving the room, for they owe their simplicity to the multiplicity of means-end articulations fused or telescoped into them. The complex diversities of our environment would overwhelm us. But recognition of objects for use in connection with our practical drives in some instances enables us to tie in a whole battery of habits and thus react or interact expeditiously and aptly to or with our environment. It is only when something goes wrong with our routines that a problem arises.

Where things do not go as expected, a problem develops; and to solve it we make use of critical inquiry, or reflective thinking, a widely helpful method but one conspicuously successful in the natural sciences. Because of this, Dewey frequently referred to it as the scientific method; but since effective use has also been made of it in fields not commonly designated as scientific and in principle it is applicable to any problematic situation, I prefer to speak of it as reflective or critical inquiry. At any rate, this method, long advocated by Dewey, who stressed its applicability to values, starts with problems or difficulties, initially more or less vague feelings of something amiss, defines them in terms of observation and analysis, suggests hypotheses for solving the problems, reasons out the implications of these suggested solutions, and verifies them through observation and experimentation. There is room for creativity at every step of a complete act of reflective inquiry. In the stage of clarification or definition of the problem, for example, alert, apt observation is crucial, as is imagination in determining which patterns to trace in contextualistic analysis. In the sciences investigators who are fertile in making suggestions for solving problems are likely to be leaders in the field. Nor should we underestimate the importance of seeing clearly the implications of a proposed solution or of skill in developing experimental procedures for confirming or disconfirming hypotheses. Contextualistically speaking, experiments are programs to determine consequences and thus ways of introducing intelligence into situations. In short, on this approach a significant measure of growth is increased ability to recognize and solve problems.

Perhaps an example I have sometimes used in classes to illustrate reflective inquiry and solving problems and, incidentally, to suggest my preference for having students write their examination papers for me in ink may clarify the steps involved. Suppose one is writing answers to questions and notes that one's pen is not making visible marks on the sheet of paper. A problem appears. To clarify it one may shake one's fountain pen to check whether it is clogged or out of ink or turn one's ballpoint pen from side to side to ascertain whether the point is simply covered with something. But not to spin out the example at greater length, let us assume that the observations show that the pen is out of ink. The problem may then be how, in view of the fact that one has run out of ink, is one to complete the examination in satisfactory fashion. Various possible solutions occur to one: (1) simply turn in the paper; (2) continue with a pencil; (3) look through pockets and accompanying possessions for another pen; (4) get ink or pen from instructor; (5) borrow ink or a pen from a classmate; and so on. In terms of the implications of the proposed solutions, (1) is not likely to look at all attractive unless it is near the end of the examination period and one has already written all one knows about the questions, for otherwise it would mean a lower grade. (2) If one continues with a hard-lead pencil, it will be difficult to read one's answer, and the harder it is to read, the more searching the instructor's scrutiny of it; if it is a soft-lead pencil, by the time one's paper has rubbed against other papers in the instructor's brief case for a while it may look messy, thus putting one at a psychological disadvantage. (3) Looking through one's things may arouse suspicions in the instructor that one is looking for notes. In connection with (4) one may not remember ever seeing the instructor with a bottle of ink or any other writing tool than a red pencil. (5) If one leans over to inquire about an extra pen, the instructor may think one is trying to get the answer to a question. Considerations of these implications may lead one to go back to the stage of suggesting solutions and advance a sixth one of simply holding up a hand and inquiring aloud whether anyone has an extra pen. This may cause minor disturbance but is unlikely to arouse suspicion that one is trying to get information on the quiz from others. So (6) may look more promising than the alternatives, and if we act on it, by the time our paper is returned we should know whether this was a satisfactory solution for our difficulty.

The above pattern is somewhat oversimplified, and the stages do not always come in the order in which I list them. On easy problems especially, moreover, there may be telescoping of stages. But in spite of its simplicity, the above account seems to me basically accurate.

An immense amount of the world's work depends upon how creative we are in solving problems and how widely we apply the method of reflective inquiry. Most commentators agree that natural scientists have made more effective use of the method than have social scientists, but surely the need for applying it to problems in interpersonal and international relations is compelling. With questions of war, peace, and nuclear omnicide at stake in addition to that of devising ways of working cooperatively for our common well-being, we cannot afford to rely on appeals to authority or coercion, or take our chances on things working out without our assistance, or simply pin our hopes on muddling through with no attempt to foresee consequences. The method of reflective inquiry is admittedly fallible but self-correcting, it encourages dialogue rather than confrontation, and it is a better bet than its alternatives for helping create conditions favorable to growth. In point of fact, our changing world is full of problems, and we live in a time when change, both within ourselves and our environment, is accelerating at an incredibly rapid rate. At the very least, this means that an educational program which prepares people for only one specific set of conditions virtually guarantees that the knowledge and skills acquired will be outdated before they have a chance to use them. Accordingly, to paraphrase and quote from the pedagogic creed of an eminent apostle of change, John Dewey, to prepare people for a changing world means to give them command of themselves; it means so to train them that they will have the full and ready use of all their capacities; that their eyes and ears and hands may be tools ready to command, that their "judgment may be capable of grasping the conditions under which it has to work, and the executive forces be trained to act economically and efficiently."[9]

Our first approach to growth in terms of reflective inquiry and problem solving is one which leans heavily on the sciences, both in terms of their methods and their findings, but our second, emphasizing the qualities which characterize events or getting the feel of things, draws heavily on literature and the arts, on the humanities broadly conceived. Its primary stress is not upon instruments, identifying for use, and solving problems but rather upon perception and appreciation of the qualities characterizing things, or aesthetic perception. The former make operable the habits that make our practical activities efficient and keep us alive, but we look to the latter for reasons why executing efficiently and living are important.

It should be remembered that for contextualists the aesthetic field may be defined either in terms of vivified experience or enhanced quality. Irwin Edman and Dewey think of the aesthetic as experience vivified, intensified, clarified, and organized (unified). Stephen C. Pepper and I use the language of enhanced quality, but for the most part we are all in substantial agreement on the aesthetic field.[10] Since I first wrote this I discovered Thomas M. Alexander's immensely illuminative and suggestive volume on Dewey's worldview and aesthetics. Although quite different in major ways, it seems to me clearly contextualistic with an emphasis on the pervasively qualitative. One of his most important and fruitful ideas is that of *Experience and Nature* as a sustained inquiry into Dewey's principle of continuity as well as an application of it.[11]

At the opposite pole from practical drive perception is what I call diffusion or primitive aesthetic perception. In practical drive perception the perceived object tends to be accepted exclusively for the sake of this, that, or the other end; but in diffusion perception it becomes a center of interest, a qualitative complex to be enjoyed. In this kind of perception, instead of perceptually accepting the texture solely as a means to a practical end, the percipient takes in its quality. In diffusion perception the rush and the restricting influence of the practical drive are lacking, and we have time to linger over the object and thus make more interesting discriminations than an efficient practical drive would permit. In successful habitual responses it may be necessary to discriminate only one cue or set of cues, and most of the other quality is lost or slurred over. Diffusion perception is thus perceptual experience which has preceded or escaped the numbing effect of habit and convention. But perhaps a few examples will help clarify what is involved.

One of my favorite illustrations contrasts two kinds of perception of clouds on a hot summer day. For farmers who are trying to haul the hay to the barn before it rains, the clouds are signs of more or less imminent rain and of the need to make haste. For me stretched out on my back under the shade of a tree with no pressing drives directing my attention, the clouds may be interesting in their own right. The clouds change in form and shape, presenting moving figures, appearing now like giant faces in the sky, now like great mountains, some perhaps with huge partially hidden castles on them, another time like snowy landscapes, or perhaps like billowing mounds of flour. The changing forms of the clouds, the smell of new-mown hay, fresh vegetation, and the warm earth, and sounds of birds, cicadas, and rustling leaves may absorb our attention for an indefinite period of time just taking in what's sensibly present.

Or to take another illustration, in driving a car over familiar routes we are likely to be more concerned with getting wherever we are going with minimum expenditure of time and effort than with taking in the sights. We probably note efficiently enough road signs, traffic, and possible obstructions while carrying on a conversation with others in the car. Contrast this with the experience of a small youngster you have sent on a simple errand to the corner store or a house a few blocks away, only to find what seems to be an inordinate amount of time go by before the child returns with a report of the many re-markable things found on the way—an ant hill, some new flowers blooming, some bumblebees, a mud puddle with wiggle-tails, a butterfly, a bird's nest with four eggs, a broken toy, something the dog was barking at, and so on through such a list that it is a wonder the errand was accomplished at all.

But not to expand this example further, diffusion perception comes in wherever the percipient takes in more of the quality of an event or set of events than the demands of a practical drive require: for instance, the smell of some-thing mildly pleasant, say a flower, the feel of a material like satin or velvet, the glow of coals in the fireplace when the lights are out, or even the sound of snoring before it becomes annoying.

Between the polar extremes of practical drive perception and diffusion per-ception, however, there is a third type, aesthetic drive perception, which com-bines the driving power and direction of the former with the qualitative glow of the latter. Artists build up or set up imaginatively in the percipient a certain drive (hunger, love, jealousy, fear, hate, ambition, or the like), and the perceiver tends to accept the qualities of the event or set of events in the light of this drive. To prevent the percipient from moving on the fulfillment too fast to take in the quality of the events, artists provide means of holding back the percip-ient to dwell on the quality by interposing obstacles or interludes, like Shakes-peare's grave diggers scene in *Hamlet,* which help insure that the quality is sa-vored. The obstacles lead to conflict and the generation of added quality, and not merely novelists and playwrights but artists in general are masters at build-ing up and controlling the conflicts which generate quality.

Novelty, conflict, and emotion are primary ways of enhancing quality, and, Croce to the contrary notwithstanding, quality is maximized not by eliminat-ing conflict, analysis, and regularity but rather by using them properly. Con-flicts generate quality and emotion, but if the qualities are not to be drained off in practical action, controls are required for the conflicts. Analysis and reg-ularity contribute to organization, which increases the spread of quality and helps overcome a confusing multiplicity.

If scientists can help with problem solving, poets and other artists can help make the qualities of things come alive for us. I suspect that many of us in look-ing back on our childhood share Wordsworth's recollection when he wrote in "Intimations of Immortality":

> There was a time when meadow, grove, and stream
> The earth, and every common sight
> > To me did seem
> > Apparel'd in celestial light,
> The glory and the freshness of a dream.
> It is not now as it has been of yore;—
> > Turn wheresoe'er I may,

By night or day,
The things which I have seen I now can see no more!

The development of efficient habit patterns has come at the cost of losing sight of the glory about us; and here is where poets and other artists come to the rescue. For illustration I shall speak primarily of poetry, but what I say about poets is equally applicable to other artists. They make it their business, as I have noted elsewhere,[12] to realize, take in, or create quality in events, and they have systematic ways of sharing their realization with us in poems, novels, plays, songs, dances, paintings, and other works of art, producing vivid, clear, intense, and unified experiences. To enter appreciatively into the realm of qualities, however, as to enter the kingdom of heaven, we may need to become as little children and devote ourselves wholeheartedly to the qualities of events.

Contextualists are convinced that there is something of interest and value in every event, but we routinely neglect or pass over the quality of most events. As one poet put it, we casually measure the world. Development of smoothly functioning, efficient habits sometimes produces in us a kind of functional blindness, deafness, or insensitivity to the qualities of things around us. Poets, however, cultivate sensitivity to sights, sounds, and feelings; and they have developed techniques for breaking up our habits, or putting them in a context which helps us see, feel, and experience the qualities of our world, and presenting objects in fresh fashion—the footworn stone or wayside flower, as Edwin Markham puts it. The poet-philosopher Emerson suggested that something as slight as viewing things from a different point of view, say, bending over and looking back through one's legs, gives everyday objects a novel pictorial quality, and poets through a felicitous use of language in many ways help us achieve a fresh look.

Everyday things take on special significance through a poet's art. Wordsworth writes: "My heart leaps up when I behold / A rainbow in the sky," and our hearts leap with him. Common daffodils acquire vividness and freshness when Wordsworth tells us:

> I wander'd lonely as a cloud
> That floats on high o'er vales and hills,
> When all at once I saw a crowd,
> A host, of golden daffodils;
> Beside the lake, beneath the trees,
> Fluttering and dancing in the breeze.

What can be more monotonous than the succession of faces seen at a subway station from the train? But in "In a Station of the Metro," when Ezra Pound characterizes "[t]he apparition of these faces in the crowd" as "[p]etals on a wet, black bough," a fresh turn has been given to them.

Our habits may cause us to focus almost exclusively on our well worn ruts and restrict our outlook, but poets open up and broaden our world, giving us a sense of largeness of spirit, a feeling of aliveness or vitality. A Parmenides, a Lucretius, a Dante, or a Goethe may give us insight into what our world is like and why things are as they are in it; and whether or not we agree with their interpretations, such features as change or apparent change will take on new meaning in light of their explanations. Such poets, moreover, present ethical reactions or ideals in far more lively and concrete fashion than our textbook accounts.

In this connection I read recently some very apt and suggestive comments by another philosopher-poet, David Lee Miller:

> Peircian firstness and Heideggerian presencing
> eliminate the grip of tedium and habit
> offering being back to maybe.[13]

Poets also help us overcome our inarticulateness and incoherence in expressing our feelings and our visions. By a relevant choice of imagery and the right words they give appropriate expression to what we may have felt dimly but stated clumsily. And in another field like music or painting, a Chopin étude or Van Gogh painting may evoke or express feelings for which we have no precise verbal equivalent.

Poets perform yet another important function: namely, that of helping release us from a certain loneliness (or aloneness) and providing a basis for communion and community. Through the help of the poets we discover that we are not alone in having thought such thoughts and felt such feelings. Others share our appreciations. In expressing our feelings, poets and other artists socialize our appreciations and help provide sympathetic understanding of both us and those sharing our feelings.

If, then, creation aims at human growth, there are at least two important avenues to it. The first, as we have seen, develops out of reflective inquiry and problem solving. And Larry Hickman reminds us that with Dewey such inquiry is not limited to the nonartistic or nonaesthetic but can be expanded to apply to experiences of making and enjoying artistic artifacts as well as presumably to discovering and appreciating events of natural beauty.[14] The second is aesthetic perception. Poets and artists use it to help cure our functional sensory and spiritual blindness, help us see and feel the glories around us, aid us in overcoming our inarticulateness and incoherence in expressing our feelings and visions, open up and broaden our world and give us a sense of largeness of spirit, and assist us toward communion and community through shared values.

If, moreover, we follow the root meaning of what it is to create and think of creating as growing or causing to grow, both increased ability to recognize and solve problems and enhanced capacity to see, feel, and otherwise experience the qualities of things are creative. Thus, contextualistically speaking, one need not be a genius to be creative. Each of us perceives and experiences things from a uniquely different vantage point and therefore has something distinctive to report, and the more we can learn from poets and artists, the better we can express our distinctive insights.

I have sketched two major forms of creativity or growth, but it may be asked how we can encourage people to inquire reflectively and take in the qualities of things. For a view in which instruments are categorial, what are the instruments for developing in individuals habits of inquiring reflectively in coping with value problems and in seeking reflectively approved values? Or in societies, how can we develop institutional procedures for responding intelligently to value conflicts? And, of course, similar questions may be put in connection with fostering habits of taking in the qualities of things and of broadening and deepening our heritage of values and making it more widely accessible. Answering these questions with the care they merit would require another paper at least as long as this one; but tonight I should like to suggest a contextualistic approach to them.

That approach is one in terms of education and democracy, and once more, John Dewey has been an eloquent spokesman for it. Both education and democracy are at once instruments for developing habits and procedures of the sort referred to above and themselves modes of growth in their own right. So, what do we do when we educate a person, whether one's self or another? The answer clearly is that we help that person to grow, and we do this within a social setting through the great socializing agency of communication, the heart of education. Through communication we learn and teach how to make and remake ourselves and our environment. Small wonder that of all affairs, Dewey declares that "communication is the most wonderful" in lifting us from our isolation and enabling us to share in a communion of meanings. It is indeed a natural "wonder by the side of which transubstantiation pales."[15]

If we accept this Deweyan conception of education as growth, there are important consequences for education. It is valuable for its own sake and not simply as preparation. The test of social institutions is whether they make for continued education and growth. Education is not something exclusively for the young and dependent but rather is something for all of us, regardless of age. It must continue throughout our lives and vary with our current condition. We never get too old to learn. Education should start with a person where that person now is, with that individual's present stock of interests, knowledge, and appreciations, and strive to expand and deepen all three of them so that one may grow as a person in one's community and one's society and work for conditions which will make possible growth for all members of society. Further, education is not primarily a spectator activity but rather one of participation. We learn by doing. Education in this sense, Dewey saw clearly, is crucially important for democracy both as a form of government and as a way of life. Democracy offers one of the better ways of sharing values, and education is an essential means of making its procedures effective. Dewey's essay as part of the celebration of his eightieth birthday admirably sums up democracy as belief in "the ability of human experience to generate the aims and methods by which further experience will grow in ordered richness." He added that since "the process of experience is capable of being educative, faith in democracy is all one with faith in experience and education."[16]

In conclusion, then, in this essay I have outlined a contextualistic account of creation as growth and focused on growing through taking in the qualities of things and using reflective inquiry to solve problems. To shed further light on this topic I have summarized contextualism as a pragmatic naturalistic worldview which finds change to be the salient feature of our heterogeneous and diverse world and holds that analysis is an affair of tracing patterns of change. And at the last I have suggested that education and democracy are at once major modes of growth and important instruments for fostering habits of experiencing things afresh and using reflective inquiry to solve individual and social problems. Although reflective inquiry is fallible, it is self-corrective and far and away our most promising method for coping with our many specific problems. With a measure of good fortune and effective use of methods of fostering habits and procedures for taking in qualities and using reflective inquiry to solve our problems we can both enhance our capacity to experience the qualities of things and remake ourselves and our environment into something better.

# 10

# Coping with Change:
# A Philosophy of Life

I am happy to be with you once more, this time holding forth on the importance of one's philosophy of life and how a particular philosophy of life attempts to cope with change. For I agree with Lord Chesterton that one of the most practical and important things about a person is that person's view of the universe. With him I think that "for a landlady considering a lodger it is important to know his income, but still more important to know his philosophy" and that "for a general about to fight an enemy it is important to know the enemy's numbers, but still more important to know the enemy's philosophy."

With William James, moreover, I maintain that the philosophy which is so important for each of us is something only partly learned from books: "it's our individual way of just seeing and feeling the total push and pressure of the cosmos," and these seeings and feelings each of us has, whether or not we happen to be professional philosophers. Philosophy is everybody's business, and each of us needs to think as clearly as we can about the world and our place in it.

A philosophy of life involves both a worldview and a way of estimating what is worth seeking, doing, or being in the world outlined by our outlook; and this point may be clearer if we turn to a problem with which each of us must try to cope, namely, the problem of change. Is there anything in our world which does not change? Some hold with Parmenides that nothing real changes, others with Lucretius and Bertrand Russell that there is an eternal realm of matter but that man is mortal, and still others maintain as does traditional Christianity that there is a transcendent eternal order in which immortal man has a place. But in our day with the writings of Charles Darwin and John Dewey another view has come to the fore which maintains that all things change. Since I happen to share this view, I'd like to explore it with you today and ask what is worth seeking, doing, or being in a world of change.

---

Address for Unitarian Fellowship of Waco, Texas, Feb. 24, 1980.

Many, however, find this view shocking. They view change with alarm and seek the certainty of the fixed and permanent. And, indeed, the notion that change is the single most distinctive feature of the real world is in sharp opposition to most traditional Western philosophers, for the latter hold with Plato that the touchstone of the real is permanence, and the permanent and the perfect they tend to equate. What changes, they say, is subject to decay and thus at best is a lower order of reality if not definitely unreal. But, of course, changes are not limited to decay and disintegration but include growth and integration as well, and the more closely we scrutinize allegedly unchanging things, the more evident is change. Although some things like granite and iron change at a slower rate than ice cream, paper, and the weather, nothing is free from change; and why should we think that sneezes or flashes of lightning are somehow less real than chemical elements or blocks of marble? The things that seem to involve no movement or change are likely to be only phases of things, perhaps legitimate abstractions for certain purposes but not concrete things. All things in nature, including human beings, have their beginnings, undergo qualitative changes, and finally come to an end, making way for other individuals. Hence nature is a great complex of transactions and histories, marked by incessant beginnings and endings.

Within this complex the incomplete and the unstable, the contingent and uncertain, the novel and precarious are as real as the relatively complete, stable, and well established. Indeed, our world is a mixture of all these qualities, and to meet its challenges we must seek not an illusory permanence but rather intelligent ways of redirecting ongoing affairs. Permanence we cannot find, but stabilities and continuities we may. We can find patterns of change and constant or invariant relations between changes. Accordingly, we need to stabilize patterns we find good, seek ways of averting or reconstructing, if possible, patterns we find bad, and develop ways of living acceptably with unavoidable evils.

So, whether we wish to understand our world or to do something about some aspect of it, the central fact is one of change. The fixed and the permanent, accordingly, far from being marks of perfection, are much more likely to be illusory expressions of something past and outmoded; and insistence on the unchanging, one fears, will far more probably guarantee botching a current enterprise than guide us to a higher reality.

It may be argued, however, that at least God must be permanent and therefore an exception to the pervasiveness of change, but on the contextualistic philosophy I am espousing, if there be a God, the deity also changes and is to be understood in natural rather than supernatural terms. However one interprets God on this view, whether with Henry Nelson Wieman as the set of forces making for creative interchange and constituting the source of human good, or with John Dewey as an active relation between the ideal and the actual, or in some other terms, one may be sure that the deity will not be one who intervenes in arbitrary fashion through special supernatural measures. My approach is rather a naturalistic one which tries to account for natural events wholly in terms of other natural events without going outside the system. I am more concerned with questions growing out of affairs within nature than with any attempt to discover some divine design for the totality of things.

But what about values? What should we mortals seek, do, or be in a changing world? It seems to me that change presents us with two main sets or types of value experiences, one concerned with coping as intelligently as we can with problems, or the work of the world, and the other with taking in, perceiving, the diverse qualitative richness of the world around us. Because of new developments we are never without problems, and yet through intelligently guided procedures or critical inquiry we can discover what further changes need to be made in a situation to meet its difficulties and ward off future ills or secure goods. And because of change our surroundings vary from moment to moment in light and color, pattern, sound, and a host of other ways, and we have all the more unique opportunities for the realization of quality. An artist friend assures me that any natural setting changes throughout the day and that, accordingly, its pictorial quality is never quite the same. Not merely, then, is the world full of problems we strive to solve, it is also alive with unique vivid qualities which are worth having and sharing for their own sake. What we do, see, hear, smell, feel, taste, or otherwise experience in realizing quality, what we enjoy or suffer, all these add to our store of values. And if we are indebted to scientists for furthering the method of critical inquiry, we likewise owe a tremendous debt to artists who help us strip away the blankets with which practically efficient habits and routines have covered qualities so that we may experience them in all their freshness and vividness. A George Crumb may lead us to hear sounds we've never before experienced or a Renoir may help us see flesh colors we previously had not recognized as such.

In short, then, if we would make the most of this life, what we seek for ourselves and the human community is a life rich in enhanced qualities, amply supplied with opportunities for bettering our world, and increasingly capable of coping with our problems. Basic for this outlook are the enjoyments and sufferings, the prizings and aversions of individual human agents who function in natural social contexts. For values in the full sense, however, these immediate valuings are not kept in their raw form but rather are transmuted into reflectively approved values through a critical review of their conditions and consequences and a survey of alternative possibilities. For example, a love of lobster clearly becomes less compelling if every time we eat it we become violently ill.

Perhaps, however, a review of a sampling of five erroneous notions about values will do more in brief compass to clarify my basic value attitude than further efforts at summarizing it. Accordingly, let us examine in turn the following misconceptions: 1. To make sense of values there must be a single fixed end or goal for all values, *the* good; 2. The basic determiner of values is possession of material goods; 3. There is nothing good or bad but thinking makes it so; 4. Values are just matters of taste about which disputing is pointless; and 5. Values are strictly an individual affair.

1. Making sense of values does not require a single fixed end or goal for all values, *the* good. There are indefinitely numerous values, as many unique goods as there are specific problematic situations; and if one is to speak in terms of the good, one does well to interpret it with Dewey as growth or problem-solving. The basic value notion on my view, however, is "better" rather than "good," and one determines which course of action in a given situation is better by applying the method of critical inquiry with its weighing of conditions and consequences.

2. Nor is it true that the basic determiner of values is possession of material goods; for our moral, aesthetic, and spiritual needs stand in no one-to-one relation to such possessions, and many of our most important problems turn about other values. This of course, is not to deny the tremendous importance of food, shelter, clothing, and a certain degree of material well-being. Without them the distinctively human level of living in our time would not be possible; but it is not the case that the more money we have, the happier and better off we are. Far more important for our total system of values is ability to forecast in the imagination the consequences of alternative lines of action and to use these forecasts in choosing what we shall do or become.

3. To those misguided persons who argue that there is nothing good or bad but thinking makes it so, suffice it to say that it takes more than thinking something is a good solution for a problem to solve it, and a course of actions which has disastrous consequences is none the less ruinous because we do not think it bad.

4. The contention that moral, aesthetic, and spiritual values are just matters of taste about which disputing is pointless is, I hold, a misleading oversimplification which is often advanced as a way of closing off discussion and blocking further inquiry. The world is interesting because tastes and needs differ—the lion does not share the horse's taste for grain; and I quite agree that imposing our standard of taste on others is undesirable, but are there any more interesting or significant topics to discuss than matters of taste? Where differences of taste occur we may go into great detail to explain why we like what we do, and on occasion as a result of such discussion we may come to discern features we had not previously noted in, say, a particular work of art and in consequence re-appraise it. I dare say that it is a rare individual who has never come through later hearings to appreciate some musical composition which was first experienced as distasteful. Do we not normally assume, moreover, that our tastes can be improved in the sense of becoming broader and more discriminating and think that we have evidence in regard to ourselves that such is the case? And those who claim that to say something is good or right is merely to say that we like it seem to overlook the fact that at least some of our likes and dislikes,

fortunately, can be modified through a reflective consideration of conditions and consequences.

5. The declaration that values are strictly an individual affair, a matter of individual likes and dislikes, seems to me clearly an overstatement. The very language the individual uses to make the assertion brings in the community with whom we share the language even when we are alone. It neglects the importance of cooperation, joint efforts, and shared experiences and minimizes the attitudes, appreciations, and aspirations we have in common. Without the human community, past and present, and its interactions with nature, moreover, we should not have the values we prize most. As humans, we are social creatures, and our spiritual values like most of our other values gain from being shared. Even scarce material goods cannot be fully enjoyed in the presence of those who need and lack them. In community, then, we find our highest values; and in our common pursuit of the better we reinforce each other and enhance our values.

In conclusion, then, today I have maintained that one of the most practical and important things about a person is that person's philosophy of life. Such a philosophy, I further claimed, involves both a worldview and an attitude toward values. And in this friendly group I have attempted to sketch my own philosophy of life, my particular way of coping with change, with the hope that it will encourage each of you to do likewise.

# Part Two

## Modern American Philosophers

# 11

# John Dewey and Our Time

John Dewey has had greater impact on philosophy and education than any other philosopher this country has produced, and he put his philosophy to the service of society on a scale unsurpassed by any other modern philosopher. He had an unusually long and productive career. Born in 1859, the year in which Darwin's *Origin of Species* appeared, he lived for more than ninety-two years and had an active career of teaching and writing of more than seventy years. Every year from 1882 to the year of his death in 1952 he published at least one article, and in only two of the early years of this long period did he publish as few as a single article. Indeed, for most of those years he published from ten to thirty items, including major books; and his writings have been translated into some thirty-five languages. His teaching ranged from high school teaching in Oil City, Pennsylvania, and a rural area near Charlotte, Vermont, to university level work at the Universities of Michigan, Minnesota, Chicago, and Columbia, among others. He also lectured extensively in various parts of the world.

When John D. Rockefeller's millions made it possible to start the University of Chicago, the founders sought outstanding individuals to head their various programs, and the thirty-five year old Dewey was their choice in 1894 to head the Department of Philosophy and Psychology, the Department of Pedagogy, and the Experimental School. The work of Dewey and his associates there from 1894 to 1904 made the fledgling University of Chicago a world center for Philosophy and Education. From Chicago he moved on to Columbia University in 1904 and finished out his career there.

About ten years after Dewey's death the Center for Dewey Studies of Southern Illinois University Carbondale, under the direction of Dr. George E. Axtelle, mounted a massive project to collect, edit, and publish the collected works of John Dewey in some thirty-seven or thirty-eight volumes. Upon the death

From *Baylor Educator* (Spring 1978): 1–7, 14. Reprinted by permission of Baylor University, publisher of *Baylor Educator*.

of Dewey's widow, the John Dewey Foundation she established in his memory gave Southern Illinois University Carbondale his personal library and the unpublished manuscript materials he left at the time of his death, some sixty-seven boxes of them. As Chairman of the Center's Editorial Board for some years, I have been gratified to see Southern Illinois University Carbondale develop the best collection of material by and about John Dewey in the world. It is our hope that through the efforts of the Dewey Center, first under the direction of Dr. Jo Ann Boydston and now under the leadership of Dr. Larry Hickman, Dewey's writings will become more accessible and his work better known throughout the world. Incidentally, Dr. Boydston in 1977 edited a volume of Dewey's poems.

Dewey's Instrumentalism or Pragmatism was recognized by William James as early as 1903 as a new school of thought. Here was a philosophical approach that would test ideas and proposals by their fruits or consequences, and the products of this school seemed to James to be, in his words, "splendid stuff." Needless to say, however, not all philosophers received the school so favorably, but what with the numerous attacks on it and the counterattacks on its behalf, its doctrines were the occasion for a large portion of the philosophical writing of the early decades of the twentieth century and Dewey became known worldwide as the philosophic spokesman of America. Since those decades, however, other movements have come to occupy the center of the philosophical stage, and it may be questioned whether Instrumentalism or Pragmatism in Dewey's sense remains as a philosophical movement. To be sure, it may be conceded, certain of Dewey's ideas have been absorbed and continued in other movements; but are his views of anything more than antiquarian interest now?

I am indeed convinced that his views both were important for his time and are relevant for ours. Whether or not we can accept precisely his answer to the questions he raised is less important than whether the issues he raised are ones we still must reckon with. Accordingly, I should like to explore four central clusters of his ideas: (1) a new worldview with emphasis on change and with it a new conception of analysis; (2) a new method of critical inquiry; (3) a new view of experience and a different conception of the role of philosophy; and (4) a conception of human growth as both the moral end and the goal of education. In connection with these notions I shall raise two questions: (1) What was new about them? and (2) Are they significant for our time?

So what was new about Dewey's Instrumentalism or Pragmatism? First, implicit at least in his writings was a new worldview which took change to be the salient mark of our world at a time when most people, both philosophers and general public, were still convinced that permanence was the touchstone of reality and perfection, and that change was a sign of the unreal or at best of a lower level of reality. John Dewey, taking his cue from Charles Darwin, stressed change as a pervasive trait of the real. In Dewey's words, for the pragmatist "every existence is an event"—a history.[1] Although some things change at a slower rate and thus give a relative stability, no concrete thing exists apart from temporal process. The things that seem to "exclude movement and change," according to the pragmatist, are only "phases of things," perhaps legitimate abstractions but not concrete things.[2] Things in process, changing events, with their mixture of contingency and stability, are what we find empirically, and they are thus basic for any adequate metaphysics or worldview. These patterned events have within them movements from and toward other events, and they always occur in certain contexts and have reference to other events within these contexts. Nature, accordingly, is a scene of incessant beginnings and endings; and initiations, consummations, blockings, with connecting references and intervening means-objects or instruments operating within a certain context, are basic features of the temporal process. In such a setting, if we wish to effect desired changes or block harmful ones, attention to instruments, Dewey saw, was crucial. This was a natural means of rendering good things more stable and bad ones less persistent. Because he hammered at this fact his view became known as Instrumentalism.

At any rate, whether we wish to understand our world or to do something about it, according to Dewey, the central fact is one of change. This led Dewey to suspect that the fixed and the permanent, far from being signs of perfection, were expressions of the dead and the outmoded; and insistence on the unchanging, instead of guiding us to a higher reality, confirmed the suspicion that we were in a rut.

Accompanying this new worldview with its emphasis on change was a new interpretation of the nature of analysis and what it means to understand something. What do we do when we analyze something? What is it to understand or interpret something? The traditional answer has been that analysis is an affair of reducing a complex to fixed and permanent elements; but if Dewey is right about the prevalence of change, this won't do. His view denies the possibility of element analysis in the sense of breaking a whole down into atomic units or irreducible constituents of some sort. Analysis, on this new view, becomes an affair of distinguishing temporal patterns rather than one of unveiling timeless distinctions. Analysis exhibits the texture or structure of an event, and this requires discrimination of strands, but the strands derive part of their quality from the event's context and have a way of leading off into it. So analysis becomes a matter of following references from one texture to another, and how far we follow them or which ones we trace depends on the problem which occasions our analytic inquiry. But we never reach ultimate elements. For many problems, moreover, tracing the genetic career of an event from its beginnings through the various phases of its history to its ending or conclusion proves more illuminating than any other type of analysis or explanation of an event.

If, for example, we are analyzing the death of JB, something more than timeless distinctions of ultimate elements are needed. It won't do, as all of us detective story buffs know, to say that whatever the cause, he is none the less dead, and no considerations of attendant circumstances or of anything before or after the instant of death are needed. Which considerations of this sort are relevant will depend, of course, on the purpose of the analysis. If homicide is suspected, the attendant circumstances may be crucially important for the police investigation. Hence, although to be sure, after the fact JB is equally dead whatever the cause, the police investigator's analysis of his death will be different in significant ways depending on whether the cause is asphyxiation, cyanide poisoning, food poisoning, strangulation, a stab in the heart, a blow on the head, cancer, or something else. Death from one of these causes will lead into different environing textures from another cause and will involve different control textures, observations, laboratory reports, and so on. And an adequate analysis of JB's death for the purpose cited needs to exhibit the distinctive features of the total texture stemming from whichever cause or complex of causes may be involved, along with, of course, pertinent ramifications in more or less distant environing textures; for a different genetic pattern is involved in each of these cases. But there is no such thing as *the* analysis of anything, whether the death of JB or the flavor of lemonade. There are as many analyses of these things as there are problems or purposes connected with JB's death or the flavor of lemonade.

Where, then, does this leave us with respect to the idea of the primacy of change and its implications for analysis? I think we may safely say that this idea was sufficiently revolutionary that, Bergson, the existentialists, and the pragmatists notwithstanding, we have not yet fully developed the implications of the primacy of change. The philosopher of change, moreover, whether or not we can go all the way with him, has shaken up the traditional notion of analysis and opened up new possibilities. And more and more explanations are being given in terms of origin and development, in terms of phases of a career or history, whether with reference to the stars and galactic systems, or to the constituents of matter, or to plants and animals, or to linguistics, or to economic and educational institutions, or to religion and cultural patterns. Increasingly, that is to say, the genetic emphasis has entered into the analyses of investigators in such fields as experimental physiology, experimental psychology, ecology, physical and cultural anthropology, social psychology, sociology, comparative religion, institutional and historical economics, linguistics, and a host of new social sciences appearing in the last seventy-five or eighty years.

The change-centered worldview is important for each of the other clusters of ideas I wish to sketch, but space does not permit following out these relations. Accordingly, let us turn to our second cluster of Dewey's key ideas, the ones concerned with his method of critical inquiry. He sets forth this method in terms of the steps in a complete act of reflective thinking in a variety of different books: e.g., in *How We Think* (1910, 1933) and in *Logic: The Theory of Inquiry* (1938). So central is this method for all Dewey's thinking that each of his major works may be outlined in terms of it. Reflective thinking, on his view, differs from such other modes of thinking as daydreaming and trial and error or fumble and success thinking in at least two ways: (1) it is occasioned by some question, problem, or difficulty; and (2) it results not merely in a solution for the problem but also in some descriptive or explanatory statements about how it was solved. According to his general account, critical thinking starts with problems or difficulties, defines them in terms of observation and analysis, seeks hypotheses for solving the problems, reasons out the implications of these suggested solutions, and verifies them through observation and experimentation. Since Dewey thought that this experimental method had been used with conspicuous success by the natural sciences, he frequently referred to it as the scientific method. I prefer the term *critical thinking,* however, in view of the fact that this method has been used effectively also in various other areas of investigation not commonly designated as scientific.

If, for example, while attending a philosophy convention, I am reading some philosophy papers in my fourth floor hotel room and smell smoke, this may mark the appearance of a problem, the more especially since I do not smoke. Further observation may indeed show that smoke is pouring under the bottom of the door, and opening it a crack may reveal that the hall is in flames. How, then, can I get out of the building safely? With the problem thus formulated, various possible solutions occur: (1) I can telephone the hotel operator for information and instructions. (2) I can jump from the window. (3) I can try crawling out on the ledge just outside my window. (4) I can wet sheets or a blanket, wrap them about my head and body, and try crawling along the floor to an exit from the building. (5) I can fashion a rope from the sheets, tie one end to something solid, and lower myself nearer the ground. And so on.

By reasoning out the implications of the different hypotheses and considering them in relation to the relevant facts, I may decide which looks most promising, which appears to be most worth putting into practice. If, say, I act on Hypothesis 1, I should be able to secure helpful information. This looks so promising that I may forthwith dial the operator; but if on doing this I get no answer and the telephone appears to be dead, instead of a solution I have a heightening of my problem. What, then, about Hypothesis 2, jumping out the window? The window appears to be at least 30 feet above the ground, and the ground looks hard. If I jump that far, I am fairly sure to be injured in the fall, perhaps seriously. So I table this possibility. What about Hypothesis 3, crawling out on the ledge? The ledge looks very narrow and there doesn't seem to be much of anything to hold on to. Accordingly, if I act on this possibility, the chances of falling are very likely. So I'll explore other possibilities.

What about Hypothesis 4, wrapping a wet blanket or sheet about me, opening the door, and crawling to an exit? This hypothesis will look more or less promising, depending on how far my room is from an exit, how thick the smoke or how hot the flames. If, say, I remember that my room is near the middle of a long corridor, this possibility will not look attractive.

Accordingly, I might turn to Hypothesis 5, fashioning a rope out of the sheets and blanket and dropping the mattress out the window to afford a cushion for whatever drop may be involved. This hypothesis will look more promising if there is something solid or stable to which to secure one end of the rope, for lacking this I may be worse off than jumping from the window. If I take this possibility, there will still be some drop and some risk; but it may appear more promising than the other alternatives.

Obviously, this simple example might be elaborated at greater length, but this is perhaps enough to suggest the five steps Dewey found in a complete act of reflective thinking: (1) appearance of a problem; (2) clarification and definition of the problem; (3) suggested solutions for it; (4) deductive elaboration of these hypotheses; and (5) verification of one or more of them. He was convinced that this method could be applied to any problematic situation. What was mainly novel about his approach was his plea for applying this method to values, both individual and social. Its applicability to scientific problems was generally accepted in his time, but questions were raised about its appropriateness for values. Can we apply critical inquiry to the solution of our value problems? Or are values and value problems so different from the materials and problems of the sciences that a method which works very well with them is inapplicable to values, to questions of better or worse in human conduct? This remains, however, a crucial challenge for our times, perhaps Dewey's greatest challenge for us. What are the alternatives to the Deweyan method? Whatever its limitations, is there any more promising way of meeting our value problems?

So much, then, for Dewey's critical method. Let us turn now to our third cluster of key ideas: namely, to Dewey's new view of experience and an accompanying different conception of the role of philosophy. Traditionally, Dewey argued, philosophers have thought of experience mainly as the act of experiencing quite apart from what is experienced, but for Dewey as for William James experience is a double-barreled fact which includes both what is experienced and the experiencing of it. Indeed, his pragmatic outlook led him to think of it primarily as intercourse with one's environment, both physical and social; a transaction of enjoying and suffering, of doing and undergoing. For Dewey, experience constitutes the entire range of a person's transactions with nature at large or the universe. It is the peculiar mixture of support and frustration of a person by nature. Whereas the traditional view of experience saw it as a peculiarly psychical or invidiously subjective activity, Dewey thought of it as something which flows in and through its objective environment, which supports or blocks it and is in turn modified by it. Again, according to Dewey in "The Need for a Recovery of Philosophy"[3] the proponents of the traditional view have been preoccupied with what is or has been "given" in a bare present whereas for Dewey the salient trait of experience is its connection with a future, not what has been or is given but rather what may be done to change what is given to advance human purposes.

Or to mention another contrast, the traditionalist was committed to particularism, to more or less atomic sense data, isolated impressions and ideas of the sort Hume and the British Empiricists claimed to find; but Dewey thought this view neglected the relations, connections, and continuities of experience and prevented the traditionalist from seeing experience as adaptive courses of action, connections of doing and undergoing. Finally, the supporters of the orthodox view oppose experience to thought in the sense of inference, but for Dewey experience is full of inference and anticipation.

This view of experience Dewey presents in many different works, but it is perhaps most clearly and fully presented in *Art as Experience*.

If, then, experience is thought of as a way of interacting with our environment, what are the implications for one's conception of the role of philosophy? According to Dewey, once one adopts this view of experience, philosophy ceases to be "a device for dealing with the problems of philosophers and becomes a method, cultivated by philosophers, for dealing with the problems of men."[4] It becomes "a revelation of the predicaments, protests and aspirations of humanity,"[5] a way of shedding fresh light on the role of intelligence and the urgent, deep-seated social and human problems of our time. In a time when a basic tendency of our century has been to define the function of philosophy very, very narrowly, Dewey made a plea for a broad conception which stressed the social relevance of philosophy. The problem of the proper function of philosophical thinking was a debatable one in Dewey's time, and it remains a fundamental problem of our time.

Fourth and last of our clusters of Dewey's central ideas is his conception of human growth as both the moral end and the goal of education. This is one of his most challenging theses. For fixed notions of the good Dewey substituted the idea of growth or problem-solving. Not "good," but "better" was his central concept. The good person is the one who is improving, whatever the person's place on some absolute scale. If this notion be accepted, there are important consequences for education. Education *is* growth and is valuable not simply as preparation but for its own sake. The test of social institutions is whether they make for continued education and growth. Education is not something exclusively for the young and dependent but rather is something for all of us. Thus Dewey is an apostle of continuing education. Further, education is not a spectator activity but rather one for participants. We learn by doing. For Dewey, moreover, education is of crucial importance for democracy. Indeed, democracy is belief in "the ability of human experience to generate the aims and methods by which further experience will grow in ordered richness."[6]

Dewey in his time was a recognized educational leader. Many praised him for making education meaningful and relevant. Others damned him for moving the schools away from the traditional in anti-intellectual directions. On this score much depends on whether one reads Dewey's own writings or some of his followers. When some of the misconceptions of progressive education and the distortions of Dewey's views have been removed and his teachings are placed in perspective through reading what he has to say and not simply what others have said about him, I am convinced that he will be established as one of the great educational leaders of all time, one who has much of the wisdom needed to guide future educational programs.

In conclusion, then, John Dewey has presented us with an impressive array of ideas important both for his day and ours. His views are definitely of more than antiquarian interest today. Whether or not we agree completely with him, these ideas present challenges we must meet. To summarize what we have seen, (1) in the first place, Dewey has sketched a change-centered worldview and provided the background for a new conception of analysis, a different account of what it means to explain or understand anything. (2) Secondly, he has developed in impressive detail a new method of critical inquiry and made a forceful plea for its application to our value problems. (3) Thirdly, he has set forth a new view of experience and, as a corollary to it, a new conception of the role of philosophy as critical intelligence applied to basic human predicaments, protests, and aspirations. (4) Finally, he has expounded human growth as both the moral end and the goal of education. His message is that through critical inquiry, making use of modern science and technology, we can remake ourselves and our world into something better.

# 12

# Dewey's View of
# Experience and Culture

Experience is a focal concept for Dewey's philosophy, and he labored long
and diligently to clarify it. Such major works as his *Art as Experience,
Experience and Education,* and *Experience and Nature* deal with it; and some
of his last writings, for example, his unpublished drafts of a new introduction
for *Experience and Nature,* show his continuing concern for this key notion.[1]

For Dewey as for William James experience is a double-barreled fact which
includes both the experien*ced* and the experien*cing,* both what is experienced
and the ways in which it is experienced. It is *of* as well as *in* nature. It constitutes the entire range of man's relations to, or transactions with, nature at large
or the universe. It is "something at least as wide and deep and full as all history
on this earth, a history which . . . includes the earth and the physical relatives
of man."[2] It is an affair of intercourse, mutual adaptation, between a living organism and its physical, social, and cultural environment, a matter of simulta-
neous doings and sufferings. It is "the peculiar intermixture of support and
frustration of man by nature."[3] It carries principles of connection and order
within itself. It is experimental and self-corrective.

Although Dewey offers an empirical approach, it is not the traditional empiricism; and to understand his view of experience one must take it within the
context of a new worldview which stresses change, becoming, and innovation,
rather than the immutable or permanent. It is not enough, I fear, simply to follow
the Dewey-Bentley program of returning the term to its idiomatic usages
without the interpretive guidance of the worldview. At any rate, Dewey calls
this view empirical naturalism, naturalistic empiricism, or naturalistic humanism. I prefer to call it contextualism, and I have discussed this view at length

Originally presented for the Bicentennial Symposium of Philosophy, Oct. 7–10, 1976. Published
in *Two Centuries of Philosophy in America,* ed. Peter Caws, American Philosophical Quarterly Library of Philosophy (Oxford: Basil Blackwell, 1980), 167–73. Reprinted from *Philosophy in the
Life of a Nation.*

elsewhere.[4] In these other discussions I hold that in a contextualistic world-view we find existence characterized not merely by change but also by such other generic traits as diversity, interaction or transaction, continuity, texture, strands, quality, fusion, reference or connection, and context. Analysis on this view is an affair of tracing patterns of change rather than one of reducing wholes to eternal elements.

One of the major advantages of this view for Dewey's account of experience, moreover, is that a Lockean or Cartesian dualism of an inner subjective realm as over against an outer objective world does not arise in it. Although for Dewey experience is the human side of reality and nature the non-human, they are not separate but continuous. In a draft for a new introduction to *Experience and Nature* Dewey speaks of the intimate connections and outstanding differences or distinctions between human achievements, failures, and strivings, "the subject matter collectively named by the word *Experience*," and "what is marked off on the other hand as the non-human to which as such the name *nature* applies." Experience is the method for getting at nature, and nature empirically disclosed deepens, enriches, and directs the further development of experience.[5]

Some of the major differences between Dewey's empiricism and the traditional empiricism turn about their respective interpretations of experience; and in "The Need for a Recovery of Philosophy" Dewey offers five points of contrast between his interpretation and what he calls the orthodox view, that accepted by both the traditional empiricists and their opponents.[6] In the first place, whereas on the orthodox view experience is primarily a knowledge affair, on Dewey's it is centrally intercourse between a living organism and its physical and social environment, an affair of had qualities, a transaction of enjoying and suffering, of doing and undergoing. Although any experience may become an object of knowledge or reflection, the knowing is always part of a larger basically non-cognitive interaction.

In the second place, for the traditionalist, experience is a psychical thing, infected throughout by subjectivity, an inner private collection of mental states set over against an outer physical world. For Dewey, on the other hand, experience flows in and through its objective environment, which supports or blocks it and is in turn modified by it. Experience is of a piece with the objective world which surrounds, maintains, and supports it—a situation significantly different from the traditionalist's picture of two separate and disparate realms separated by a cosmic chasm. Dewey repeatedly complains that his critics attribute to him the view he is criticizing; they forget or overlook the more "vital, concrete, and pregnant sense" in which he uses the term *experience* and substitute a kind of psychological abstract.

Thirdly, the proponents of the traditional view have been preoccupied with what is or has been "given" in a bare present, whereas for Dewey the salient trait of experience is its connection with a future. What is important, as he sees it, is not what has been or is given but rather what might be done to change what is given to further human purposes. An experimental form of experience requires a forward look, with emphasis on anticipation rather than recollection.

A fourth major point of difference between the two versions of experience turns about the traditionalist's commitment to particularism, to discrete sense data or more or less isolated states of consciousness, sensations, impressions, or ideas. This view, according to Dewey, neglects connections, relations, and continuities, supposing them to be either foreign to experience or dubious by-products of it. Dewey, like James, stressed relations and held that experience carries principles of connection and organization within itself. He emphasized the contextual, situational, transactional, or field character of experience. It was for him, as he repeatedly noted, "a matter of functions and habits, of active adjustments and re-adjustments, of co-ordinations and activities, rather than of states of consciousness," isolated impressions or ideas.[7] As he declared in *Reconstruction in Philosophy,* adaptive courses of action, connections of doing and undergoing, and not discrete sensations, are the "stuff" of experience.[8]

Fifth and finally, the supporters of the orthodox view oppose experience to thought in the sense of inference, but for Dewey experience is full of inference, as might be expected from his relational emphasis. For him, moreover, inference is not a mere recall of the past or a desperate and probably invalid leap beyond experience, but rather is an essential part of it. If one is to employ the direct support of the environment to effect indirectly changes that would not otherwise occur, to avoid the hostile and make more secure the favorable incidents, an imaginative forecast of the future, inference, is needed for guidance.

The nature of experience, on Dewey's view, however, is exhibited most clearly in aesthetic experience. In it, according to *Art as Experience,* we find experiences in their fullness and singularity, vivified, clarified, intensified, and integrated. In them the interactive character of experience comes out with special clarity. In Dewey's words, "In an experience, things and events belonging to the world, physical and social, are transformed through the human context they enter, while the live creature is changed and developed through its intercourse with things previously external to it."[9] There is an "intrinsic connection of the self with the world through reciprocity of undergoing and doing," and "all distinctions which analysis can introduce into the psychological factor are but different aspects and phases of a continuous, though varied, interaction of self and environment."[10]

As late as 1951 Dewey could still say that he did not feel the need to take back any of the things he said about experience in the earlier text of *Experience and Nature;* but this statement was coupled with the declaration that "were the book that was published with the title *Experience and Nature* being written today, its caption would be *Culture and Nature* and the treatment of specific subject matters would be correspondingly modified."[11] Although in theory he could still see justification for his previous use of the terms *experience* and *expe-*

*riential,* it seemed to him that there were both negative and positive grounds for changing to the term *culture.*

He mentions at least four lines of justification for his earlier usage. In the first place, as over against the dualisms of subjective and objective, mind and the world, psychological and physical which have tended to dominate the systems and doctrines of modern philosophy, "there is much to be said in favor of using 'experience' and 'experiential' (as distinct from 'empirical') to designate the *inclusive* subject matter in which *what* is experienced is taken systematically into account as well as the *ways* in which it is experienced." Secondly, the appeal to experience seemed to him a wholesome and "much needed aspiration to get philosophy away from desiccated abstraction into an area that is vitally concrete."

A third justification has to do with the office or role of philosophy in its comprehensive aim, in its claim to make comprehensive sense of the full range of experienced facts. Since the comprehensiveness of its subject matter is what distinguishes philosophy from other intellectual or cognitive undertakings, "a linguistic expression is needed which specifically designates that property," and "experience" in its inclusive sense is one way of meeting this need. Somewhat differently stated, nature when viewed and treated as material of and for human experience seems "to satisfy the historic claim of philosophy to be concerned with what is comprehensive in scope and abundant and intense in content."

Fourthly, the appeal to experience was a commendable "protest against the attempt of previously accepted philosophies to neglect, to slight and slur over the possibilities of human life in locating what is comprehensive and basic in what was taken to be eternal, above time, immutable, far above change, and universal . . . ." Dewey was convinced that the rational ground and justification as well as the practical and factual base of the newer and more promising movements in modern philosophy were to be found in the "systematic recognition of *Process* as providing *the* comprehensive point of view from which to survey and report the natural world to which man belongs."

From these lines of justification it seems clear that Dewey had not changed his substantive views of experience. Why, then, was he considering abandoning the terms *experience* and *experiential*? A primary reason was the negative consideration that "the course of *historical* events within and outside of developments in philosophy formed an effective and solid obstruction to the words being understood in the sense intended—one namely in which . . . they named *what* is *experienced* in full conjunction with the ways of experiencing that are involved in the very structure and constitution of *what* is experienced." In the course of history experience had become effectively identified with experiencing in the psychological sense, and the psychological had come to be thought of as the exclusively individual or the "intrinsically psychical, mental, private," the subjective as set over against the objective. In short, the course of history had resulted in what he had called in "The Need for a Recovery of Philosophy" the orthodox view of experience, a view against which he had been arguing all these years. But this account of experience has no place in the worldview of empirical naturalism or contextualism.

There was, however, something new in the situation, and this constituted the positive ground for the proposed change from "experience" to "culture." Other historical developments in anthropology had conferred upon "culture" just the range and depth of significance of which "experience" had been progressively and effectively deprived. Dewey, therefore, concluded that

> as a matter of historical fact the only sense in which "experience" could be understood to designate the vast range of things experienced in an indefinite variety of ways is by identifying its import or significance with that of the whole range of considerations to which the name "culture" in its anthropological (not its Matthew Arnold) sense is now applied. It possesses as a name just that body of substantial references of which . . . "experience" as a name has been emptied. In addition "culture" names a whole set of considerations which are of utmost significance in and for the enterprise of philosophy as intellectually inclusive.

These include material artifacts and technologies, beliefs and practices, moral attitudes and scientific dispositions, the material and ideal in their reciprocal relations each upon the other. In addition "culture" also designates, "also in their reciprocal connections with one another, that immense diversity of human affairs, interests, concerns, values, which when specified piecemeal are designated *religious, moral, aesthetic, political, economic,* et cetera, et cetera, thereby holding them together in their human and humanistic unity—a service which . . . if philosophy is to fulfill its ambition to be comprehensive, is of utmost importance for its status and development."

In short, then, "culture" is to do what Dewey previously had hoped "experience" would do. This is a very suggestive idea, but whether the new term can perform this function any better than the old remains to be seen. The new term may help emphasize the social side of experience. Many found the older term slanted toward individuals in a biological matrix. Perhaps, moreover, substituting "culture" for "experience" will enable some readers to better understand Dewey's interpretation of experience and thus possibly make it more acceptable, but it does not seem to me that any substantive change in his outlook is involved. Accordingly, I think it unlikely that the new terminology will change the attitude of those who have been most critical of the old. As I see it, then, a basic defense or critique of his account of experience would still need to be offered in terms of an examination of this account in relation to the relevant facts and his comprehensive philosophy; and the case for it turns largely, not on the terminology used, but rather on how well one finds these facts illuminated by this worldview. Since I find this view quite illuminating, it seems to me that we should be the poorer without his account of experience.

# *13*

# Wieman's Empiricism

Henry Nelson Wieman (1884–1975), prophet, philosopher, theologian, and concerned person, had a fresh vision of God as creative interchange, a strong sense of urgency, and a zeal for making his vision operative in a changing world. He reworked the traditional religious problems and concepts in terms of a naturalistic, empirical approach, and in some ways he learned as much from the views he opposed as he did from ones closer to his own outlook. Thus the sources of his empirical theology are many and varied, but two of the most important clusters of strands in his view are a contextualistic metaphysics and an empirical attitude and method. In what follows I should like to comment on these emphases.

## Empiricism and Metaphysics

Some interpreters of Wieman's view wonder whether there is any place in it for any metaphysics, much less a contextualistic one with which he has said on occasion it would be a mistake to identify his view.[1] But does his empiricism exclude metaphysics? I think not, but it must be admitted that his statements on metaphysics do show some ambivalence. On the one hand, he says that metaphysical vision can be a precious value and, on the other, he declares that "religious inquiry should seek no metaphysical system but rather, a better understanding of the creativity which transforms all such systems to meet the demands of human existence as it undergoes transformation."[2]

In part, this turns about which metaphysical system or what kind of metaphysics one is talking about; but there seems to be a fairly strong suggestion in his writings that metaphysical inquiry is a risky, dubious venture and that metaphysics or worldviews are less important than what operates more directly in

Reprinted with the permission of the Foundation for Philosophy of Creativity from *Creative Interchange*, ed. John A. Broyer and William S. Minor (Carbondale: Southern Illinois University Press, 1982), 97–106. My thanks go to the Foundation for Philosophy of Creativity for permission to reprint it here.

human life to promote creativity.[3] He has considerable suspicion of views which stress the ultimate nature or mystery of being or the universe at large. Such views, as he sees it, are a mixture of illusion and of the empirically unjustifiable. Ones which claim to give us the ultimate, final structure of being in a form which cannot be improved upon by any further inquiry are illusory. As he puts it, if metaphysics "is thought to give us the ultimate and comprehensive structure of all being, beyond which no further inquiry can reach, then metaphysics in that sense is an illusion."[4]

On Wieman's interpretation no metaphysics can comprehend the fullness of being for all time because, even if its categories should comprehend all being so far as it is knowable at a given time, as human existence undergoes creative transformation our knowledge systems and categories will need to be different (Religious Inquiry, 188–89). In other words, the facts of change may make a view which was an illuminating one for one time or epoch no longer valid for a new age. Even what was a good metaphysical system for one time, moreover, may become a great evil if, "instead of being committed to creative interchange with other systems, it is dogmatically and coercively imposed on others who live for values expressed by a different metaphysical system" (Religious Inquiry, 189).

In view of this situation one can understand Wieman's impatience with the proponents of some forms of metaphysics and why he might for a moment think we should avoid metaphysical systems altogether and seek in other ways a better understanding of the creativity which transforms all such systems. But what is involved in this search or this understanding? Must not our inquiry be guided by theory?[5] Wieman agrees that for this understanding "we must have a coherent and intelligible understanding of the ontology of human existence" (Religious Inquiry, 190), and this would seem to involve a worldview. Accordingly, the choice is not between metaphysics and no metaphysics. Instead, the contrast would appear to be between different ways of viewing or understanding the things of the world rather than between having a metaphysics and not having any. If, moreover, the search for understanding of creativity is not guided explicitly by some worldview, it may have to depend on an implicit view or views; and an explicitly recognized worldview, contextualistically speaking, is likely to afford better guidance and is more readily correctable than one operating only implicitly. The question then becomes one of whether Wieman's metaphysics of creativity can more fully do justice to the range of facts in a changing world than any of the alternative possibilities can or whether a creative interchange between various of them is needed.

But how does one check on the adequacy of a worldview? To what extent is the empirical method applicable to it? These are difficult questions, but each worldview provides its criteria for answering them. Stephen C. Pepper, in World Hypotheses: A Study in Evidence, suggests that scope and precision are the two most important general criteria.[6] The more facts which can be given a precise characterization in terms of the categories of a view, the better it looks. Wieman's general tests of truth are observation, agreement among observers, and coherence (*Human Good*, 211), but he asks that a metaphysics be able to explain everything in terms of its key fact and that it afford guidance for action (*Human Good*, 301).

In terms of his criticism of some traditional views for their dogmatism, the remoteness of their categories from experience, and their claims to exclusive possession of truth, we might have expected him to hold, as indeed he does, that there are more ways than one to reach truth; and if worldviews are treated as hypotheses rather than dogmatic claims to certitude, this removes part of the basis for his suspicion of metaphysics. One might say of reality, as Wieman does say of value, that there are at least as many ways to take hold of it as there are ways to take hold of a cat (*Human Good*, 3), but experience shows that some ways of taking hold of it work out better than others. Wieman has had less to say on the choice of a metaphysics than on the choice of a value theory, but in both cases he is interested in how they work out operationally. He does not claim that only his metaphysics of creativity is true. Rather he maintains that there are several true metaphysics, because for him "a metaphysics is true if it selects some element necessarily involved in all human existence and explains everything in terms of it" (*Human Good*, 301), and there are several of these generic traits of human existence. He prefers the metaphysics of creativity, or creative interchange, because he believes "it provides a better guide to action than any other" (*Human Good*, 301).

In the postscript to *The Source of Human Good* Wieman concedes that the metaphysics of contextualism is a recurrent theme in this book even though he has misgivings about having his view identified with contextualism (*Human Good*, 297). In view of various of his fresh insights and the fact that he has developed his view in significantly different ways from such contextualists as Dewey, James, C. I. Lewis, Mead, and Pepper, a case can be made for not calling him a contextualist; but when one notes the basic points of agreement between his general approach and theirs it seems clear that in the main he belongs with this group. As Pepper notes in his essay on "Wieman's Contextual Metaphysics," "There is little question that Wieman's mode of thought conforms most closely to the group of philosophers who have come to be known as contextualists" (*Empirical Theology*, 142). Accordingly, in recognition of both the differences and the basic similarities, we might say that the metaphysics of creativity, or creative interchange, belongs to the family of contextualism.

Both Wieman and contextualism are naturalistic in holding that we need not go outside the natural order of objects and processes to explain problematic features of the world. Both reject supernaturalism. Wieman maintains, however, that human salvation depends on something beyond the power of persons but not on something outside the natural order. He espouses a form of theism rather than the humanism accepted by most other contextualists; but both make value central for their accounts of God.

Both are committed to the method of reflective inquiry as the basic method of investigation for our problems, whether practical, scientific, religious, or metaphysical. Thus Wieman is committed to inquiry as the guide to creative interchange. The basic approach of both is broadly empirical. Metaphysical theories are hypotheses, not dogmatic pronouncements concerning reality. They are to be judged in terms of what light they shed on the basic problems of human existence.

For both, human experience has a crucial role. Problems and possible solutions in the matter of fact realm need to be defined in terms drawn from experience. It constitutes the entire range of people's relations to, or transactions with, their environment, both physical and social. It is not something invidiously mental or inner but rather is of a piece with the environment which supports or blocks our strivings. There is nothing more fundamental than experience in terms of which it is to be explained. Accordingly, as Wieman sees it, "we cannot go beyond human experience. What we experience is ultimate reality" (*Human Good,* 304).

Wieman takes as his key fact creative interchange rather than the historical event or patterned event of the contextualists, but most of the basic categories of contextualism have prominent roles in his metaphysics. Such concepts as change, diversity, interaction or transaction, continuity, quality, fusion or funding, context, texture, strands, and reference or connection loom large in both sets of views. Wieman handles with exceptional felicity such concepts as felt quality, fusion, and funding.

Both Wieman and the contextualists make change basic. Things in process, historical events, happenings, things temporal rather than eternal are central for them. In Wieman's words, "Quality changes continuously in our experience,"[7] or "Diversity of kinds and nuances of change in the quality of events as they occur are infinite in their complexity" (*Human Good,* 302). He criticizes some traditional metaphysical systems for treating what becomes as unreal and for insisting that only the timeless is real. As we have noted earlier, he argues that no metaphysics can comprehend the fullness of being for all time because human existence undergoes creative transformation and requires new knowledge systems and categories (*Religious Inquiry,* 188–89).

But on Wieman's view the contextualists go too far on change. They hold that "nothing is immune to change; no structure, order, or form is permanent" (*Human Good,* 298). Accordingly, "there is no basic unity; unities come and go, integrate and disintegrate, but nothing continues forever" (*Human Good,* 298). As over against this Wieman claims that there are two distinguishable aspects of any change: (1) something changing, and (2) a law or order to which the process of change conforms (*Man's Ultimate Commitment,* 79). The law or order does not change; it is a changeless form. One structure may be replaced by another, but this is not change for Wieman. For a table to change it must maintain its identity, and the form of change of the table gives this. In like fashion the universe as a whole is "a universe only because throughout all its changes there is a constitutive structure whereby we can call it a universe" (*Man's Ultimate Commitment,* 81). This unchanging form of the universe presupposed in all change Wieman identifies with creativity,[8] and the creative event itself he identifies with God (*Human Good,* 305–9). Thus the creative event as a concrete whole changes, but not the form of its change, creativity.

This interesting speculation about God has some parallels with Whitehead's primordial and consequent natures of God although, of course, there are also significant differences. The notion of a divine unchanging form of the universe is also reminiscent of Aristotle's argument for the existence of God in terms of the necessity for keeping the world and its processes going. Unhappily, however, time does not permit the development of significant points of agreement and difference here. The hint of Aristotelian formism, however, is enough to raise some questions for the contextualist about this aspect of Wieman's argument.

So far as the contention that there is something free from change, namely, the law of change, is concerned, moreover, most contextualists would be dubious of this rationalistic line of reasoning and would want to know whether it was submitted as a hypothesis, a definition, or an analysis of what is necessarily involved in all experience, or what; and in any event some justification would be needed. In principle, of course, one might discover stable patterns among changes, but the suggestion that there is *always* one is an overstatement. C. I. Lewis with his sharp contrast between eternal a priori concepts and given immediacy would appear to be the contextualist closest to Wieman in this regard.

A 1943 article, "Can God Be Perceived?," shows another aspect of Wieman's efforts to marshal evidence to show that God can be perceived or that, granted certain conditions, He may reveal Himself to us. Although his conclusions apart from his supporting evidence may seem surprising, this argument proceeds along contextualistic lines, and he notes that his theory of perception "is derived most directly from Lewis, Pepper, Hahn, Mead, and Dewey. Whitehead's work has been very influential but more indirectly."[9]

But to bring this section to a close, as Pepper notes in his essay on "Wieman's Contextual Metaphysics," Wieman has provided an essentially contextualistic description of human experience and in his religious interpretation has correlated "the central features of religious experience with features of the world as empirically grounded and described by this contextualistic world view" (*Empirical Theology,* 147). To the extent that he is successful in this "he brings the full weight of the empirical evidence supporting the world theory to the support of his interpretation of basic religious concepts" (*Empirical Theology,* 147). His penetrating analysis of religious experience in terms of his metaphysics, moreover, provides a type of corroboration for the metaphysics.

## Empirical Attitude and Method

In general Wieman's empirical method and attitude and his metaphysics are mutually supportive. So we do not need to ask which comes first, his metaphysics or his empirical method. They are distinguishable, and on occasion there may be tensions between them, but for the most part they form a relatively well unified package. Openness to empirical evidence, indeed, zeal to get it, is characteristic of his outlook. He had an abiding fear of allowing one's hopes, prejudices, or biases to distort the evidence, and it seemed to him, if not at least spiritual arrogance, a manifestation of sinful pride to claim to have knowledge unsupported by empirical evidence (*Empirical Theology*, 369). Where the subject matter is God and other religious concepts this sin is all the greater. James's pragmatic theory of truth as he interpreted it, with its suggestion that believing something, say, in religion or metaphysics, might help make it true, caused him such misgivings that he demanded more conventional evidence of truth before considering the usefulness of a belief. At any rate, he held that a metaphysics must meet other empirical tests of truth before its utility may properly enter the picture (*Human Good*, 301).

Apparently, however, he did share James's idea that the only things debatable among philosophers should be things definable in terms drawn from experience. I think he would probably have granted James's supplementary remark on the postulate of radical empiricism that "things of an unexperienceable nature may exist ad libitum, but they form no part of the material for philosophic debate,"[10] and asserting their existence would be irresponsible. At any rate, he insisted on an experiential base for his claims concerning matters of fact.

What, then, is experience? It may be well to note first that it is not what the traditional view of the British empiricists says it is. It is not something peculiarly and invidiously psychical, subjective, or inner to be set over against a real, objective, external world. It is not a set of more or less discrete atomic sense data, impressions, or ideas but is, rather, something manifesting continuity and relations. It has or is a situational quality. By experience, declares Wieman, "we mean the sensuous qualities in the temporal and spatial structure that goes to make up nature."[11] And there is nothing more fundamental back of this experience: "There is nothing back of experience except more experience."[12] It is ultimate reality. "Immediate experience is the flowing together of self and world and other selves, out of which we develop the structures of self, of world, and of other selves" (*Empirical Theology*, 71). This immediate felt quality is, according to Wieman, noncognitive experience. Dewey calls it "having." In any event, quality so felt or experienced "is objective fact. It is ultimate reality" (*Human Good*, 303). And when we refer something back to experience, this is what we are talking about.

To have knowledge, however, we must conceptualize experience and formulate it in statements which can be verified. Thus, though, on Wieman's view, immediate experience is not knowledge, all knowledge is based on it. To know that a statement is true we must apply what Dewey calls the method of reflective inquiry or what Wieman calls the tests of reason: namely, the method of analysis, observation, inference, prediction, experiment, and logical coherence (*Man's Ultimate Commitment,* 138). Wieman summarizes what it means to have knowledge as follows:

> A statement is an instance of knowledge if, and only if, we (1) have an insight variously called "hypothesis," "theory," or "innovating suggestion"; (2) have put this suggestion into the form of a statement with terms unambiguously defined; (3) have developed the implications of this statement into a logical structure of such sort that some of the propositions specify what must be observed under required conditions if the statement is to be accepted as knowledge; and (4) have made the observations under the specified conditions to discover if the data do appear in the order required to warrant accepting the statement as having met the tests of probability.[13]

For an empirical account of religion our theology must be translated into operational terms along the lines suggested above. Religious inquiry must be a passionate commitment to "casting our lives in devotion under guidance of the best knowledge we can discover,"[14] for "[k]nowledge, fallible as it may be, is the best guide we have in making decisions and in the ultimate commitment of faith."[15] Does this mean then that one is not justified in holding that one's "*ultimate* commitment is to what, in truth, does create, sustain, renew, and transform, even when it is more than, and in some respects different from, the beliefs about it which" one "now holds" (*Empirical Theology,* 156–57)? No, according to Wieman. Although "blind commitment is never justifiable" and "commitment is justifiable only on the basis of the most nearly justified belief when one is forced to act," one must consider the total body of available evidence bearing on the case, including evidence that one's beliefs are limited and fallible (*Empirical Theology,* 157). In terms of these considerations we may have to risk acting on the basis of a commitment to what is unknown with respect to its specific character.

Fortunately, however, something less than logical certainty may well justify belief and action. In a manuscript in the Wieman Archives on "The Empirical Method in Religion," possibly delivered as a Phi Beta Kappa address in 1958, Wieman notes that philosophers sometimes confuse two entirely different things: (1) the kind of evidence required for logical certainty, and (2) the kind of evidence which justifies the attitude of doubt. "The logical procedures by which evidence is gathered to support a statement about existing things," he declares, "always end with some kind of probability rather than absolute logical certainty. But that has nothing to do with justifiable doubt."[16]

# *14*

# Stephen C. Pepper's World Hypotheses

Stephen C. Pepper (1891–1972) is one of the most original and suggestive philosophers of our time. And one of his most interesting theses is
that we can study factually and describe metaphysical theories or, as he
preferred to call them, world hypotheses as objects in their own right as a scientist studies his particular specialty and do this without lapsing into the position of some one of the worldviews. In his metaphilosophy such views are ways
of giving a general account of what is and how we come to know it. Whereas
other theories have a restricted range of application, worldviews are unrestricted:
they claim to provide knowledge of the total range of facts or experiences. They
are integrated explanatory or interpretive accounts of the order and meaning of
the totality of things, events, or happenings and their values or significances.

In what follows I should like to sketch some of the basic features of Pepper's metaphilosophy, note some of his contributions to various worldviews,
and comment on the import of his views for creative interchange.

## 1. Pepper's Metaphilosophy

Pepper's most extended treatment of world hypotheses is in his book *World
Hypotheses: A Study in Evidence*,[1] which along with *Basis of Criticism in the Arts*[2]
and a shorter version of *Aesthetic Quality*[3] was originally part of "The Philosophy of Criticism,"[4] a much longer unpublished manuscript on aesthetics and
world hypotheses. In this work, as he tells us in his unpublished autobiography, "History of Stephen C. Pepper, A Philosopher,"[5] he was concerned to give
the world hypothesis that serves as the empirical support of each major type

Invited paper for the Annual Meeting of the Society for Philosophy of Creativity, American
Philosophical Association, Eastern Division, Sheraton Boston Hotel, Dec. 28, 1983. I am grateful
to the Society for Philosophy of Creativity and the Foundation for Philosophy of Creativity for
permission to use it here, and also to Special Collections, Morris Library, Southern Illinois University Carbondale. The papers are with the Philosophy Collections, Special Collections, Morris
Library, Southern Illinois University Carbondale.

of aesthetic criticism. Although at the time he had been working on it for three or four years, my first acquaintance with the content of "The Philosophy of Criticism" was in a year-long seminar on aesthetics in 1931–32 at the University of California, Berkeley. At the beginning of the seminar Pepper noted that philosophers had tended to approach worldviews too exclusively from the point of view of traditional epistemology and the sciences and had slighted cognitive grounds based on aesthetics and the arts. Accordingly, there is ample justification for A. J. Reck's suspicion that Pepper's metaphilosophy was engendered and nurtured in an aesthetic context[6] or, as Pepper liked to say, in an empirical aesthetic context.

Most metaphysical theories, as Pepper saw them, claimed certainty for their position; but he spends the first part of *World Hypotheses* arguing against claims to certainty, whether in the form of infallible authority, self-evident principles, or indubitable facts. These claims block investigation. The "certainly" in, say, the statement "I *certainly* perceive a tomato" or "I *certainly* think I perceive a tomato," according to Pepper, "has only one effect, and that is to forbid us to question the assertion or to seek other evidence for its truth" (*World Hypotheses,* 38). Like Peirce he thought that theoretical certainty was neither necessary nor desirable for any view, and claims to such certainty were fairly sure to be forms of dogmatism, which he defined as believing or disbelieving in excess of what the evidence calls for (*World Hypotheses,* 11). What we should seek is not certainty but converging lines of evidence, and we frame our hypotheses in terms of these convergences. Our beliefs should steer a course between utter skepticism and dogmatism, both of which extremes go beyond the available evidence.

Evidence as he saw it was of two main kinds: namely, uncriticized, and criticized or refined evidence (*World Hypotheses,* 39). The latter is critical knowledge—definite, consistent, reasoned, and responsible, but sometimes thin and abstract. The former is Plato's "opinion," the domain of common sense, "middle-sized facts," "preanalytical data," or "dubitanda," and it is with this sort of precritical evidence rather than with some alleged certainty that knowledge begins. No refined theory is fully happy with common sense, and yet with all its shortcomings it is something which each theory must come back to. To make it definite and clear is to pass beyond it. But what we find in common sense calls for corroboration, and for Pepper the two main forms of this are multiplicative and structural corroboration.

The former consists largely of checking one person's observations against another's. The latter is an affair of checking fact against fact, and it is predominantly the method of hypothesis (*World Hypotheses,* 47–49). Pepper referred to the products of the former as "data" and the fruit of the latter as "danda" and illustrated the two kinds of corroboration by the example of how we may determine whether a chair is strong enough to support a man's weight. We can try sitting in it and ask some of our friends to do likewise, and if we all agree, the strength of the chair is confirmed by multiplicative corroboration. Or, alternatively, through structural corroboration we can examine the way the chair is constructed, its present condition, and the materials of which it is made—wood, nails, glue, and so on—and infer that it is strong enough.

Refined data are of two main kinds, empirical and logical; and nearly ideal exemplifications of them are, respectively, pointer readings and such logical or mathematical rules as those of substitution, adjunction, and inference. The best illustrations of danda are products of world hypotheses, for it is in hypotheses of unrestricted scope that we get the most extended corroboration of fact by fact. Both empirical and logical data are elements of invariant evidence, but danda vary with the hypothesis, and in a world hypothesis fact and interpretation tend to merge in a dandum. Accordingly, the force of data comes mainly from their invariancy, and the persuasiveness of danda derives from the mass of converging evidence upon the same point of fact.

The most extreme opponents of the epistemology Pepper used to support metaphysics were the positivists. As he saw it, in their opposition to metaphysics they sought to reject structural corroboration and held that ideally knowledge consists only of refined data. Pepper argued, however, that this effort falls into either dogmatism or inconsistency. The undogmatic positivist must advance a structural theory of his own, for to defend his position he must show that both common sense and danda can be interpreted in terms of data, and to maintain refined data as the sole norm of evidence he must assemble his data in such fashion as to drive out the claims of danda derived from various structural worldviews. And more than multiplicative corroboration is needed for this.

The process of structural corroboration sets up a drive for hypotheses of unlimited scope and maximum precision, for "in terms of the corroboration of fact with fact one can never be quite assured that a hypothesis is precisely adequate to a fact under consideration unless he believes that no fact would fail to corroborate it" (*World Hypotheses,* 77). By being precisely adequate Pepper means having the hypothesis exactly fit, conform to, apply to, describe, or strictly refer to the facts under consideration (*World Hypotheses,* 76). Specialists may hold for practical purposes that only facts within a certain area are relevant for the purpose in hand, but this tentative or provisional conclusion is contingent on there being no disturbing facts outside the area in question. And the contingency of unexamined irrelevant facts is not open to world hypotheses, or ones that all facts will corroborate. It is perhaps needless to add that worldviews draw data within their scope as well as dubitanda and danda.

Pepper's general account of corroboration acquires impressive support and added pointedness from his original root metaphor theory concerning the origin and development of world hypotheses. This theory sheds fresh light on the nature of worldviews and their categories, shows their relation to common sense, and provides a basis for describing, classifying, and criticizing world hypotheses. In view of the low esteem many logicians have for analogical reasoning, however, it is perhaps noteworthy that a philosopher with a rich background in the arts who sought in worldviews a means of grounding art criticism should find in metaphor a key to understanding world hypotheses both historically and epistemologically. For that matter, Pepper suggests, most of us are not aware of the metaphorical nature of our philosophical interpretations because we lack the necessary cognitive "distance," if we may take a cue from the "aesthetic distance," required in the arts to appreciate the realism of a play or a novel or a picture.[7]

Once we see that deriving philosophical systems from instances of alleged certainty is unreliable, we may be ready to accept methods for seeking probable knowledge through hypotheses supported by corroboration. And this, of course, is where Pepper's root metaphor theory comes in. World hypotheses get started in much the same way as everyday specialized hypotheses framed to solve some practical problem. We look back over our past experience for some analogous situation which might be applicable to our present problem. In this case we are puzzled about the nature of the universe and cast about "for some pregnant experience that appears to be a good sample of the nature of things." This is our root metaphor or basic analogy. If we analyze this sample, discriminate its structural features, and generalize them as guiding concepts for a world hypothesis, we have the categories of a worldview ("Metaphor in Philosophy," 199). Thus, with Pepper as with Whitehead, we start with a restricted area of common sense experience and see if its structure can be generalized to apply significantly to the interpretation of other areas, perhaps to any other area.

The root metaphor theory also provides a method of classifying the hundreds of worldviews proposed by philosophers. If a worldview is determined by its root metaphor (World Hypotheses, 96), basically there are no more and no fewer hypotheses of unrestricted scope than there are sets of structural lines of corroboration or development from root metaphors. Accordingly, this theory puts the emphasis on the lines of corroboration rather than on the particular philosophers espousing the views and maintains that there are only so many major world hypotheses as there are fruitful root metaphors. This number, according to Pepper, is probably ten or under, and the number of relatively adequate worldviews turns out to be even smaller. In World Hypotheses Pepper describes at some length only four: Platonic and Aristotelian formism from the root metaphor of similarity of form; mechanism of Democritus, Lucretius, Descartes, Locke, and Newton from the root metaphor of the machine; organicism, or absolute idealism, of Schelling, Hegel, Bradley, Bosanquet, Royce, and Blanshard from the root metaphor of the organism; and contextualism, or pragmatism, of Peirce, James, Bergson, Dewey, and Mead from the root metaphor of the historical event. Later, in his Carus Lectures, Concept and Quality,[8] Pepper elaborates in great detail a fifth relatively adequate worldview, selectivism of Pepper and Whitehead, which stems from the root metaphor of the purposive act as a selective system.

But how do we check on the adequacy of a worldview? Pepper answers this question in three different contexts: (1) in terms of his general metaphilosophy; (2) in terms of his root metaphor theory, which is a part of the metaphilosophy; and (3) in terms of relatively adequate worldviews.

(1) His standard answer from his metaphilosophy is in terms of maximum scope and precision. A view is not a world hypothesis unless it aims at unlimited scope, but Pepper concedes that this "is more a matter of intent and accepted responsibility than a matter of actual test" (*World Hypotheses,* 97) although we can check on a view's ability to handle traditional philosophical problems and on how extensively it uses the label "unreal." If most items of common sense are ruled out as unreal by the worldview, this raises questions about its scope. Precision, as we noted above, is a matter of fitting, conforming to, applying to, describing, or strictly referring to the facts under consideration.

In Pepper's metaphilosophy scope is fairly clear, but at times precision seems to include consistency, coherence, variety, fruitfulness, clear derivation from the categories, and whatever else may serve to differentiate an item or set of items. And for a discussion at the level of common sense or rough danda this perhaps overly simple account in terms of scope and precision may be as much as we should expect; but Donald S. Lee maintains that clearly Pepper makes use of more criteria of adequacy of worldviews than scope and precision; and he reconstructs in impressive fashion Pepper's criteria in the spirit of the latter's enterprise and comes out with five basic criteria arranged in ascending order plus a set of derived criteria.[9] Each of Lee's criteria after the first builds on and presumes the one preceding it. His reconstructed criteria are: (a) consistency, (b) coherence, (c) scope, (d) precision, and (e) corroboration. I think contextualism and the other relatively adequate worldviews identified by Pepper would find Lee's reconstruction a desirable refinement of Pepper's criteria, assuming that coherence is interpreted in such fashion as not to rule out discontinuities; but mysticism at least among the other major views would not accept it. Pepper might very well have preferred to let the major worldviews work out the criteria for themselves although I think he might have agreed that for the relatively adequate hypotheses the expected outcome would be something close to Lee's version.

(2) Within the context of the root metaphor theory Pepper's explicit criteria of adequacy are still unlimited scope and maximum precision, but the latter is stated in terms of keeping the basic analogy in view and making applications in terms of the categorial development from it. A view which gets out of touch with its root metaphor loses precision. One which tries to combine two or more root metaphors is fairly sure to be confusing. The two are bound to interfere with each other. Since each aims at unlimited scope and seeks out its own distinct lines of structural corroboration, trying to use one hypothesis for one problematic area and the other for another does not work, and two bad

things methodologically occur: we do not give either view a chance to show what it can do on a world-wide basis, and there is great loss in clarity.

Pepper's negative reaction to eclecticism at the system-building stage apparently grew out of his early problems in trying to develop a neutral theory of art criticism. In this connection he found that unless he kept his worldviews distinct confusion rather than neutrality was the outcome. At any rate, the place for eclecticism, he insisted, was after each major view has been given an opportunity to make its distinctive contributions. Such postrational eclecticism is highly prudent, but the earlier eclecticism which interferes with the processes of structural corroboration is irrational (*World Hypotheses,* 341). In taking this position, however, Pepper had to admit that the literature of philosophy is full of eclecticism and that nearly all of the great philosophers were in some degree eclectic in a dynamic, accidental way; but he argued that their greatness is due to their scent for new facts, to their creativity, rather than to their eclecticism, which obstructed full realization of the cognitive potentialities of their new ideas (*World Hypotheses,* 106–7).

But is there no way in which a worldview can make use of the strengths of the other views? In this connection Paul Kuntz would probably maintain that by making use of the principle of order one might combine the best of the various worldviews in one. And to the extent that each relatively adequate worldview must find a place in its conceptual framework for alternative hypotheses and their insights, this is possible although, of course, certain of these strengths may not appear to be strengths at all under different categories. This, however, is not the eclecticism Pepper opposed and may not be what Kuntz has in mind. This procedure is not one of using one world hypothesis for one set of facts and another for a different set but rather is an affair of how each world hypothesis interprets and perhaps adapts to its own use the insights of the other views. For example, in *Concept and Quality* Pepper for the most part does an admirable job of interpreting and giving appropriate places to the insights of the other worldviews in the ordered selective systems of selectivism; but proponents of alternative views can hardly be expected to agree with these interpretations of their positions and findings. At most they are likely to say that from a selectivistic perspective this may well be how things look.

(3) Our most assured cognitive judgment on criteria of adequacy of worldviews, then, comes in our best worldviews themselves. According to Pepper, each relatively adequate world hypothesis is autonomous and develops its own tests of adequacy. Each has its theory of truth and/or adequacy, and it is by means of its own structural lines of corroboration that it evaluates its adequacy and points to its own shortcomings. As suggested above, each relatively adequate worldview must have its account of other world hypotheses and their danda, of course, as well as its description of the root metaphor theory and the general theory about world hypotheses. These two theories are not unrestricted world

theories in competition with the relatively adequate worldviews. Rather in view of the inadequacies shown by the latter, these other two theories are make-shifts, ways of helping fill in the gaps, and, if accepted, function as rough danda to be refined by the various worldviews (*World Hypotheses,* 86).

In terms of the principle of autonomy no world hypothesis can rule out as unworthy of consideration the findings of another equally adequate view. It is, moreover, a mistake to think that one can establish one's own view by citing the shortcomings of the other views, for the best available have shortcomings. One establishes the adequacy of one's view by showing that its lines of cor-roboration can develop an integrated explanatory account of the full range of experiences in consistent, coherent, precise, and fruitful fashion.

To conclude the first and main section of this paper, however, I should like to comment on the question of whether Richard Rorty's brilliant critique of epistemology and systematic philosophy in various writings but most succinctly in his 1979 presidential address for the Eastern Division of the American Philo-sophical Association, "Pragmatism, Relativism, and Irrationalism,"[10] does not show that traditional epistemology and systematic philosophy are hopeless and that, therefore, Pepper's philosophy becomes unworkable. Taking his start from James and Dewey, Rorty in good pragmatic or contextualistic fashion calls into question the correspondence theory of truth of Plato and Descartes and the Kantian method of grounding all forms of knowledge in immutable princi-ples in an all-embracing ahistorical framework of some sort. He argues that the only support for our culture, or purpose, or intuitions is through conversation ("Pragmatism," 728) and maintains that talking about "the facts" or "the way the world is" is not a very informative way of trying to find objects with which our knowledge can correspond ("Pragmatism," 723). Incidentally, he charac-terizes mainstream Anglo-American analytic philosophy as a watered-down Kantianism ("Pragmatism," 725), and in his book *Philosophy and the Mirror of Nature,*[11] drawing on the writings of Wilfrid Sellars, W. V. Quine, Hilary Put-nam, Thomas Kuhn, and others, he offers a devastating critique of the episte-mological foundationalism of this movement. Rorty admits that "it would be good to hook up our views about democracy, mathematics, physics, God, and everything else, into a coherent story about how everything hangs together" and that getting such a synoptic view often requires us to change radically our views on particular subjects. But this holistic process of readjustment, this "mud-dling through on a large scale," he argues, "has nothing to do with the Platonic-Kantian notion of grounding," which "involves finding constraints, demonstrat-ing necessities, finding immutable principles to which to subordinate oneself" ("Pragmatism," 730).

Rorty does indeed raise serious questions about traditional epistemology and systematic philosophy, as did James and Dewey before him. But Pepper's account differs significantly from the views criticized by Rorty in that, for example, he offers hypotheses rather than claims to certainty and accepts the contingency of starting points. Rorty's critical strictures and claims, moreover, may well be too sweeping, and there may be much more to consider hypothetically than he suggests. Because indubitable givens cannot be provided, shall we forego resort to immediate experience and common sense objects? Shall we say that nothing more than consensus with enlightened colleagues is possible without taking into account James's and Dewey's views on experience, human interactions with their environment, and action since these might suggest more supports for our intuitions or culture than conversation? Can we not learn by doing? Because pragmatists are not convinced that necessary truths and immutable principles can be had, shall we say that converging lines of structural corroboration are of little worth? If Rorty does care about "alternative, concrete, detailed, cosmologies" ("Pragmatism," 729), wouldn't Pepper's relatively adequate world hypotheses with their root metaphors, categories, and structural corroboration be well worth trying? And, finally, although for a contextualist who starts with historical events finding the ahistorical may be a dubious venture, might we not on occasion transcend our time in a measure and at least with other cognitive spectacles find insights and ways of viewing things which held in earlier times and may hold in future ones?

## 2. Pepper's Contributions to Various Worldviews

It may be maintained, however, that it is all very well to speak of Pepper's metaphilosophy and his criteria of adequacy of the world hypotheses of other philosophers but that the key questions are: What is Pepper's own worldview? What is the root metaphor of the root metaphor theory? And Pepper took some satisfaction in noting that each of his relatively adequate worldviews in turn had been attributed to him by various critics. His standard response, however, was that the root metaphor hypothesis was not one more unrestricted worldview to add to the others. It has no root metaphor. It is a restricted hypothesis concerning a particular kind of fact: namely, unrestricted hypotheses.

It is possible, nevertheless, to cite certain contributions Pepper made to various of the most adequate worldviews and to mention some features in his metaphilosophy which were probably suggested to him by proponents of different ones of these hypotheses. For that matter, although he had studied with Hoernlé and Palmer at Harvard, the evidential force of the idealistic or organistic view did not come through for him for years, and James, though a masterful writer, was not to be taken seriously as a metaphysician. So he came out of Harvard a self-characterized dogmatic atomic naturalist or materialist; but, as he tells us in the preface to *World Hypotheses,* the impact of Gestalt psychology and pragmatic doctrines shook his dogmatism.

His autobiography, "History of Stephen C. Pepper, A Philosopher,"[12] provides a fuller account of the effect of these ideas on him and in particular tells of a Chicago evening in 1924 with George Herbert Mead that, he declared, "awakened me from my particular sort of dogmatic slumber. And my *World Hypotheses* of fifteen years later was the culminating result of this evening with Mead." It came as quite a surprise to Pepper to find that pragmatism, at least in the hands of a Mead, was definitely not a weak hypothesis but one of the best and that Mead, operating within its categories, could offer a plausible interpretation of any experienced facts Pepper brought up. Consequently, the latter eventually concluded that much of what he had taken to be simple fact was fact as viewed through "atomistic spectacles" and that the pragmatic position was as well based as his own atomic naturalism or mechanism.

Mead's impact was all the greater because the preceding year Pepper and E. C. Tolman had had extensive discussions in Giessen, Germany, with the Gestalt psychologist Kurt Koffka, and in terms of his element analysis Pepper had opposed Koffka's thesis that there are important complex patterns or Gestalts that cannot be analyzed without residue into elements. But in light of his session with Mead, Pepper came to see that with another kind of cognitive spectacles Koffka's way of viewing things disclosed significant features of experience that would be lost through atomistic spectacles. And if even pragmatism proved to be relatively adequate, another look at the idealistic organicism of Hegel, Hoernlé, and Palmer was in order, not to mention a fresh look at the worldview of Plato and Aristotle.

Pepper's most extensive contributions to the literature of the various worldviews were to contextualism and selectivism, which at times he thought of as a drastic revision of contextualism. He engaged in numerous contextualistic studies, one of the most important of which was his contextualistic interpretation of aesthetics in *Aesthetic Quality*. His most elaborate study of any worldview was his Carus Lectures, *Concept and Quality*. His *Digest of Purposive Values*[13] and *The Sources of Value*[14] retrospectively fit in better with the selectivism of *Concept and Quality* than with any other worldview although when I first read them before the latter was published the *Digest* seemed to me mechanistic and *The Sources of Value* to have strong mechanistic overtones. Pepper's *Principles of Art Appreciation*[15] is a mechanistic interpretation of aesthetics.

To mention only a few features of Pepper's metaphilosophy that are reminiscent of one or more of his worldviews, his claim that there are five relatively adequate worldviews rather than only one is a notion that goes better with contextualism and possibly selectivism than with the other worldviews. The organicist would think of the other four as approximations to adequacy, and both the typical mechanist and formist would probably have greater reservations.

Pepper's rejection of self-evident principles and indubitable facts may be more suggestive categorially of contextualism and organicism than of formism and mechanism. The pragmatists have traditionally questioned claims to certainty. The idea of converging lines of evidence, fact checked against fact, is one that both the contextualists and the organicists have stressed, but the insistence that adequacy of a world hypothesis requires that no fact would fail to corroborate it is reminiscent of Hegel, Blanshard, and the organicists.

## 3. Import of Pepper's Views for Creative Interchange

If one asks what factors in philosophy are most conducive to promoting a wholesome creativity and creative interchange, the answers would include such items as improving our understanding of the world, encouraging dialogue, removing blockages to investigation and keeping the paths to inquiry open, openness to evidence, developing trustworthy procedures for marshalling evidence, recognizing that there are more good ways than one of understanding and interpreting the world and learning to place ourselves sympathetically within the conceptual framework of worldviews other than our own, becoming aware of the categories of our own world hypothesis, maintaining links with the major philosophical traditions of the past and with the principal philosophical movements of our day, developing appropriate critical criteria and evaluative procedures, sharing and deepening our appreciation of values, and doing what we can to better the human condition. And a case can be made for Pepper having something significant to contribute to each of them, but making this case would require more time and space than are at my disposal.

Accordingly, I shall select for comment four features of Pepper's views particularly important for creative interchange: (1) Pepper's Pluralism; (2) Root Metaphors; (3) Structural Corroboration; and (4) Values and Worldviews.

(1) Pepper's pluralism furthers creative interchange in a number of ways. In the first place, on Pepper's view we have not one but at least five accounts of creativity and creative interchange; and it would be worth our while to explore what each of the relatively adequate world hypotheses has to offer on these topics. Secondly, the more good sources of light we have, the greater our chances of better illumination of our world. Thirdly, this pluralism increases the links between diverse inquirers and major philosophical traditions of the past and principal philosophical movements of the present. Fourthly, having more than one worldview helps give us the distance needed to recognize and appreciate our own view. Finally, Pepper's ability to enter sympathetically and creatively into the conceptual framework of major opposing views provides a fine model for us and helps encourage fruitful dialogue between proponents of different world hypotheses.

(2) Pepper's root metaphors help give us a better understanding of what the world is like. They offer several ways of seeing how everything hangs together; and to the extent that we can enter into another's worldview we have a better background for understanding that person's decisions. Our problem solving goes better to the extent that we can find similarities between our present situation and other experienced states of affairs, and a root metaphor gives us the widest possible basis for noting these similarities. Besides what we gain from en-

tering sympathetically into the categorial structure of well established root metaphors, moreover, there is the challenge of possibly discovering or creating a new root metaphor of great potential.

(3) If we decline to claim certainty for our findings, we need as much corroboration as possible for our hypotheses, and structural corroboration is Pepper's method of checking fact against fact to obtain converging lines of evidence on a world-wide basis. Since a world hypothesis has unlimited scope, every type of experience is included, and finding that the categories of a particular world hypothesis interpret in illuminating fashion different types of evidence corroborates the hypothesis. Although this type of corroboration makes use of the multiplicative corroboration which checks one person's observation of a particular reading, say, against another's, it mainly adduces different types of evidence after the fashion of circumstantial evidence in, say, a murder trial. To work well it requires openness to evidence and keeping the paths to inquiry open; and once more, Pepper's practice in these regards provides an excellent model.

(4) For Pepper how well worldviews can handle values is a primary consideration; and he wrote several books on empirical aesthetics, ethics, and general theory of value. For that matter, he developed his world hypotheses as a means of grounding theories of art criticism. This support is not of the Kantian type which aims at necessary immutable principles transcending the empirical but is rather the empirical structural corroboration commented on above. It is part of what must hang together if a world hypothesis is to be relatively adequate. Contextualists, among others, of course, tend to be skeptical of the need for a Kantian grounding of values in a worldview, but perhaps even they would find it passing strange if value decisions and theories had no relation to worldviews or the kind of world the decision-makers and theorists think they live in. At any rate, few enterprises, if any, afford greater opportunity for creativity and creative interchange than do empirical attempts to make sense of values.

# 15

# Brand Blanshard's Worldview

Although Brand Blanshard (1892–1987) has been more concerned to apply his general philosophy or worldview to problems of knowledge and moral conduct than to set it forth explicitly and systematically, it is clear that he offers a fresh and lucid version of Absolute or Objective Idealism, a view exemplified also by Hegel, Bradley, Bosanquet, and Royce. The main thrust of this view is toward integrating experienced material in larger and larger wholes, each more inclusive, more determinate, and more coherent than the level before, until the Absolute is reached; and then it turns out that in a sense the Absolute has been present all along guiding the movement of thought or reason toward fulfillment in a comprehensive intelligible system of necessarily related parts. The features of any organic or integrative process and its achievement, on this view as one commentator puts it, are:

> (1) fragments of experience which appear with (2) *nexuses* or connections or implications, which spontaneously lead as a result of the aggravation of (3) *contradictions,* gaps, oppositions, or counteractions to resolution in (4) an *organic whole,* which is found to have been (5) *implicit* in the fragments, and to (6) *transcend* the previous contradictions by means of a coherent totality, which (7) *economizes,* saves, preserves all the original fragments of experience without any loss.[1]

Blanshard does not set forth this system as demonstrably true. Rather he insists that it is a hypothetical or postulational affair, something to be judged in terms of empirical consequences. He suggests that it is neither self-evident nor certain; but if we do accept it provisionally, we can then see how well the facts fall into illuminating order and how far the exercise of reason goes toward justifying our postulate.[2] Proceeding on this assumption, we may be sur-

Reprinted by permission from *The Philosophy of Brand Blanshard,* ed. Paul Arthur Schilpp, vol. 15 (La Salle, Ill.: Open Court, 1980), 878–91. Copyright © 1980 Library of Living Philosophers.

prised at how well things fall into place. This is not to say that his worldview is without its problems, but which of its alternatives is free from difficulties?

Blanshard has developed this position with resourcefulness and verve and with such attention to details, problems, and relations that one may be sure the difficulties have not escaped his attention. Accordingly, if he has nevertheless maintained his position, he undoubtedly has his reasons and good ones, growing out of the logic of the materials and ideas involved; and our questions will come as no surprise to him. But, hopefully, they may afford him an opportunity to shed further light on some aspects of his worldview and to direct our attention to the lines of evidence pointing toward, perhaps even necessitating his conclusions.

My questions fall into four main groups: first, some queries concerning Blanshard's explanatory ideal and his account of explanation; second, some misgivings concerning the place of change and novelty in his view; third, some questions concerning his treatment of the many finite individuals; and fourth, some inquiries as to values and the relation between the intelligible and the valuable for him.

## 1. Cosmic Geography: Islands, Continents, and Central Mass of Experience

Before turning to these questions I should like to outline in somewhat greater detail some key features of his view, beginning with his account of the integrative process. For Blanshard this process is developed in large part in terms of thought, not surprisingly for an idealist; but if we remember that for him thought is in process of identifying itself with or becoming its object and is already this object *in posse,*[3] we see that he is talking about the full range of facts and experiences in the world and not simply about the psychological as opposed to or apart from things. On his view, as we have noted earlier, thought moves in the direction of increasing comprehensiveness, determinateness, and coherence.

For Blanshard, the ultimate reason why thought moves is "because the system of ideas which at any moment *is* the mind on its intellectual side is incomplete and fragmentary, and because that completed system which is immanent and operative within it impels to explicit fulfilment" (*Nature of Thought,* 2:45). The course of thinking in any given case begins with a shock to the present system of thought. What we find conflicts with the system. "Something is offered so alien to the present circle of ideas, so inassimilable by it, so tantalizingly isolated from it, that the impulse toward integration is stung into action" (2:47).

Typically in any given situation thought starts in the following way:

> There comes, as in Macbeth, a knocking at the door by something that the mind is not prepared to receive, but must find a place for. The unity of thought is shattered; outside the continent that forms

its mainland—to use a very useful figure—there appears an island that ought to be attached to it and yet is not; and this disunion on the surface sets in motion a force below, which by upheavals and rearrangements seeks to unite the fragments to the mainland. (*Nature of Thought,* 2:48)

These fragments have connections, implications, or "logical filaments" which lead on toward a complete whole or totality. Nothing is irrelevant to anything else. Everything has relevance for something. Everything has referential strands pointing beyond itself toward something else. As Blanshard and Bosanquet agree, a "nisus toward wholeness," or a "nisus toward completion," is everywhere the spring of thought (*Nature of Thought,* 2:129). The aim of understanding "is to achieve systematic vision, so to apprehend what is now unknown to us as to relate it, and relate it necessarily, to what we know already" (2:261).

The dynamics of the world situation are such that there is no stopping short of the Absolute. So long as any possible unattached island remains in thought there is a restless surge toward tying it firmly to the mainland. The drive toward necessary intelligible system, as Blanshard interprets it, struggles against the unstable, the incoherent, the incomplete, the inarticulate, the indeterminate, the partial, the contingent, and the changing. The presence of any one of these—and some would hold that they are present throughout our world—is a sign of the need for greater logical stability, more coherence with more inclusiveness. The goal of the theoretic impulse "is nothing short of a system perfect and all-embracing" (*Nature of Thought,* 2:438). It "cannot rest while anything in the universe is outside the web of necessity" (1:654).

The drive toward completeness and necessary coherence culminates in an absolute organic whole, "a system which, because subject to no further conditions, can alone be self-subsistently real" (*Nature of Thought,* 2:427). This intelligible whole or system, "as all-comprehensive, is logically stable, and, as perfectly integrated, leaves no loose ends" (2:428). It is "a system at once perfect and all-embracing" (2:449), fully determinate, and fully real. As something beyond the potential, it is also beyond time and thus unchanging. Or to take Blanshard's phrasing in his *Encyclopaedia Britannica* article on "The Absolute," the Absolute "is timeless or eternal," "not subject to change."[4] It is the one and only true particular (*Nature of Thought,* 1:639). In short, then, for both Blanshard and Bosanquet, "the world is a single individual whose parts are connected with each other by a necessity so intimate and so organic that the nature of the part" depends "on its place in the Absolute" (*Reason and Analysis,* 145).

Once the Absolute is reached it is seen to have been implicit in the fragments, in the islands, of experience from the beginning. It has been "there" all along (*Nature of Thought,* 1:516). Although our comprehension of it may change from time to time, the Absolute is unchanging. So in spite of all the talk of development, growth, fulfillment, realization, advancing, and the like, in reality the Absolute does not need to have developed; it has been there throughout in its perfection, in its completeness, of necessity, guiding our search for the all-comprehensive, coherent system. Blanshard, however, describes the search in terms of two major ends of thought, "one immanent, one transcendent. On the one hand it [thought] seeks fulfilment in a special kind of satisfaction, the satisfaction of systematic vision. On the other hand it seeks fulfilment in its object ... these ends are one" (2:262). The more fully we realize the immanent end, the more adequately we characterize the transcendent reality.

All the contradictions, fragments, incoherencies, and contingencies are transcended in the Absolute, and the various fragments are preserved without loss in the totality, the system of systems. All the parts or lesser wholes are combined and integrated into an intelligible structure, a coherent totality, without omitting what is distinctive in each (*Nature of Thought*, 2:442). In superseding lesser systems the Absolute as the perfect and all-embracing system absorbs and extends their gains (2:438). It is "an all-inclusive system in which everything is related internally to everything else" (2:453), which is to say that everything is so integral a part of its context "that it can neither be nor be truly conceived apart from that context" (2:452). Blanshard explains that a relation "is internal to a term when in its absence the term would be different; it is external when its addition or withdrawal would make *no* difference to the term" (2:451). Thus the parts are fully coherent in the double sense of being consistent throughout and mutually entailing each other.[5] Every part coheres perfectly with every other and is thus necessarily related to every other (*Nature of Thought*, 2:429).

## 2. Knowing, Understanding, and Explaining

What is it to know something? To understand something? To explain it? To render it intelligible? To analyze it? These are questions which, understandably, may be answered differently by representatives of different worldviews. These notions, as Blanshard and I agree (*Reason and Analysis*, 382), may well be interpreted differently in terms of their different conceptual frameworks. Accordingly, an Aristotle, a Peirce, or a James may answer the questions differently from a Blanshard. Whereas for Blanshard any deviation from the notion that everything in the universe is logically necessary and intelligible marks a retreat from rationalism (81–82), an Aristotelian may argue that there is in nature a material surd factor which it is only reasonable to recognize. Or again, though Blanshard conceives of reason as "the power and function of grasping necessary connections" (382), a Peirce or a James would find it eminently reasonable to emphasize contingency in our world. For the latter pair there is a place in the real world for the almost, the not quite, the imprecise, the aleatory, and the maybe so. But not so for Blanshard. And we might well ask how much evidence or what kind of evidence, if any, he would need to shift these from the realm of appearances into the real world. Perhaps nothing short of a radical transformation of his conceptions of reason or the intelligible and the real would do.

Blanshard's explanatory ideal is based on the Absolute. It is not until we see things in their necessary place in the Absolute that we understand them and they become intelligible. Understanding means "apprehending something in a system which renders it necessary" (*Nature of Thought,* 2:24). Something becomes intelligible "only when it is seen in context, and seen as required by that context."[6] Stopping with a limited context, moreover, will not satisfy Blanshard's version of reason or the theoretic impulse. Accepting the rational postulate "commits us to the view that the world is rational in the specific sense that every fact and event is connected with its context, and ultimately with every other fact and event, in a way that is logically necessary." This, in turn, "implies that every fact and event is ultimately connected with all others by internal relations" ("Internal Relations," 228).

For Blanshard there are many types and degrees of necessity or required-ness—causal, means-end relation, logical, and so on; and as a contextualist I can see, with Dewey, that the needs or requirements of different problematic situations are varied. The types of explanation may vary accordingly, and although the philosopher may use all types, as Blanshard sees it,

> only the logical type seems wholly satisfactory. For only when a proposition is self-evidently true, or is seen to follow from something else that is, can the question Why? be so conclusively answered that it is meaningless to raise it again. When one sees that a proposition, thing, or event *must* be what it is, it is idle to ask Why? again, for one already holds in one's hands the clearest and most conclusive answer that is possible. ("Internal Relations," 227–28)

If only the logical type of explanation or necessity seems wholly satisfactory, is the reason cited above the appropriate one for an objective idealist? Is self-evidence the reason why? This seems contrary to Blanshard's usual emphasis on a coherent, comprehensive system and to the basic categories of objective idealism. I should think that for him the reasons would have to be given, if possible, in terms of the requirements of the Absolute as a comprehensive system of necessarily related parts.

There are, however, some problems with this too. Our experience is with far more restricted contexts than that of the Absolute. Our problems are many and varied and grow out of specific situations and contexts, and their solutions require something far short of the totality of things. Although it may be possible to trace connections between any two things one may happen to mention, with many or few intermediary links, the degree of relevance for any given problem may vary from crucial to practically insignificant; and to hold that all things are parts of the absolute web of necessity may go beyond both our evidence and our needs for any given problem.

The vision of a tidy universe with no litter, no loose ends, and no contingencies may have a certain aesthetic appeal, but is it required by reason or the intellectual impulse? And if our world is shot through and through with change and contingency, do we understand it better by calling these features unreal? Do we understand the imperfect better by treating it as perfect? Does not understanding anything involve seeing it as it is, both in actuality and in potential, rather than converting it into what would be crystal clear for human reason?

Will nothing short of perfect all-embracing totality satisfy the theoretic drive and the requirements of reason for Blanshard? And if the answer is that only the Absolute will do, is this so by stipulation or definition? For that matter, is a counsel of perfection required by or even in accord with what he sometimes refers to as the good gray virtue of reasonableness? Are we identifying the theoretic end with a partial system which, though "informed by the genuine theoretic aim, still falls so far short of the end as to present this only in abortive form" (*Nature of Thought,* 2:440–41) if we suggest as a whole appropriate for the theoretic interest anything short of the Absolute? Is a system or whole partial if it is sufficient for the purpose in hand but not all-embracing?

It seems clear that for Blanshard a nisus toward wholeness is central for the theoretic interest and that this involves both inclusion of appropriate materials and organic interrelatedness of parts. The intellectual impulse is always one to integrate (*Nature of Thought,* 2:49), to apprehend things in a system or whole. But how extensive must the system or whole be? The normal requirements of action become manifest in and apply to relatively specific situations, a fact which, according to Blanshard, has blinded pragmatists like Dewey and James to the important truth that "the drive of reason ... presses ... far beyond the point at which utility ceases ..." (*Philosophical Interrogations,* 257). Thought, "even when in the service of action, has an interest or aim of its own," namely, that of understanding the nature of things, apprehending them in a system (*Nature of Thought,* 2:33).

If we carry the intellectual drive to the cosmic context, there are at least two ways of developing worldviews or attempting to do justice to all there is. One of these is the way of the objective idealist who attempts to advance from fragments, or lesser wholes, to more inclusive wholes to the Absolute, the all-embracing totality of necessarily interrelated parts. This has the disadvantage that the finite knower never arrives at the absolute view of things, never achieves the world as seen by the Absolute. It would seem to go beyond the kinds of systems we finite humans have experienced. It also makes the world in which we find ourselves a vast domain of appearances, perhaps pointing toward reality, perhaps constituting from the Absolute's view a fragmentary, distorted version of the real. But if it is valid, it has everything wrapped up in one great system.

A second way of developing a world hypothesis is to attempt to provide a set of categories which will apply to each and every thing or situation. It is an effort to achieve a distributive comprehension of the full range of things rather than to apprehend everything at once as an all-embracing totality or whole.

As William James suggested, reality may exist as a strung-along, incomplete, or unfinished world in time, not as a totality of internally related parts but rather as an indefinitely numerous set of *eaches,* coherent in all sorts of ways and degrees but with a large measure of contingency. There is obviously an element of risk in such a world. Even if its categories seem to apply in illuminating fashion to everything so far, who can be sure what tomorrow will bring? But it has the advantage of doing less violence to common sense than the totalistic view. There may be as much connection as one finds between things, but there is no commitment to the notion that everything is connected by strands of necessity with everything else. Indeed, we may find more and more connections, referential strands, between things; and each and every situation will doubtless have connections with others; but from this, as James saw it, it does not follow that all of them are necessarily interconnected in an Absolute.

One may wonder, for that matter, whether some one of the innumerable forms of chaos is the only alternative to Blanshard's version of logical unity or system as the appropriate object of the drive for understanding. But granted that the notion of organic wholes is crucially significant for his worldview, is the way of the Absolute the only fruitful one which can satisfy the theoretic interest? Are there not at least two different ways of making significant use of the notion, one emphasizing wholes and the other *the* whole? In Aristotle's philosophy, for example, there is a place for many organic wholes; in Hegel's there is but one. But in aesthetics both of them, along with Bosanquet and A. C. Bradley, make use of many wholes, each work of art constituting such a whole and exemplifying balance, order, and harmony of parts. The degree of integration and the amount of material integrated are significant for the work.

Blanshard, however, warns us that we must distinguish between the aesthetic and the logical or intellectual interest (*Nature of Thought,* 2:438–40), and the fact that idealistic aestheticians commonly agree that we can have not one but many organically related wholes or systems fully satisfying aesthetically does not show that the theoretic interest can be satisfied in this way. It may be enough, nevertheless, to raise some question as to the necessity of a single all-embracing whole for reason. What human context requires this? For understanding? Understanding for what? Does apprehending the nature of things require that we comprehend not simply more and more different things as problems arise but the totality of things all together and all at once? But, according to Blanshard, the intellectual impulse cannot be satisfied with a plurality of wholes. So long as there is the slightest possibility of some unattached island the intellectual drive requires that we go on. But must we deny the oceans to recognize the land?

At any rate, the dominant trend in Blanshard's thought appears to be an absolutistic emphasis, but from time to time there is a suggestion that we can put our questions to nature on a more limited scale. The questions may arise from the materials of a specific situation, and the immanent goal of satisfying the impulse responsible for them just possibly may be met within that context and that not simply for sloppy minds. For example, if a mathematician puzzles "over his problem until he arrives at an insight that brings its elements into a certain order" and then stops because "he has found in this final order what satisfies the desire that moved him" (*Nature of Thought,* 1:489), it would appear that on occasion specific questions have a specific answer and the theoretic impulse does not have to move on to the Absolute. But how far is the mathematician's quest, as Blanshard sees it, an authentic instance of reason's being satisfied within a limited context?

In terms of his criticism of the claim of the logical atomists that a full knowledge of the world pulverizes it into atoms (*Reason and Analysis,* 145), I gather that both Blanshard as an objective idealist and I as a contextualist have misgivings over the type of analysis that seeks to break something up into discrete elements or atomic units. Perhaps we agree that analysis, far from being a matter of reducing a whole into indivisible units, is rather an affair of tracing connections or strands of reference from a given texture into control textures. If so, for him the ultimate control texture is the Absolute. For me less extensive control textures are feasible. We agree that human thought and action are purposive and that it is important to note the end or goal being sought. Analysis may proceed by delineating the initiating conditions, the stages or phases of development, and the end aimed at.

One further set of queries may be posed concerning Blanshard's notion that knowledge requires absorption of thought in its object. According to him, when "we say that an idea is *of* an object, we are saying that the idea . . . is a potentiality which this object alone would actualize, a content informed by an impulse to become this object" (*Nature of Thought,* 1:473). And there are systemic reasons for his adopting such a theory of knowledge. But does not this raise doubts about both the theory of knowledge and the metaphysical system? Are the alternatives—say, for example, the view of Dewey and the pragmatists— that bad? Is to understand something to become identical with it? Must I become a rotten egg to tell that one is rotten?

## 3. Change?

We are surrounded by the contingent, the indeterminate, the inarticulate, and the changing; and yet there appears to be no place for them in the real world described by Blanshard. If thought is always implicitly identical with its object, which is ultimately the Absolute, how is it that, say, change is a conspicuous and pervasive feature of the world we live in and yet has no place in the ultimately real? Change, novelty, and contingency are all around us. Are they only appearances?

Change and contingency are troublesome notions on Blanshard's worldview. On the one hand, his dynamic or progressive categories, the ones characterizing the movement from fragments or lesser wholes to more inclusive wholes on the way to the Absolute, seem to require them. The realization of the immanent end is a gradual process, taking time to work itself out. The potential and contingent idea of one stage changes, develops, grows into one with a greater degree of necessity. If a problem is solved, this is done not instantaneously but sometimes slowly, with one's knowledge growing more adequate from one stage to a later one.

On the other hand, his ideal categories, the ones characterizing the Absolute in its completeness, present it as beyond time, changeless, unchanging, completely necessary, and not subject to change. So once we have arrived at the Absolute, we see that it has been present at least implicitly all along. At this point the idea has become one with, is fully realized or absorbed in, the Absolute, and it is realized that the Absolute has been present in it all the while. The fragments, the changing, the incomplete, the contingent, the indeterminate are transcended in a fully determinate, completely necessary, all-embracing totality. And what we thought were indications of change, development, growth, fulfillment, temporally successive stages, and the like are said to be logical terms, ways of expressing a logical rather than a temporal relationship. Such a non-temporal teleology may indeed be, as he claims (*Nature of Thought,* 1:520), a perfectly clear notion, but is it therefore acceptable? Can all real change be disposed of in this way?

If we say that the Absolute is not subject to change, how does this square with the doctrine of internal relations and the internal relation between myself or my idea and the Absolute? Initially, my idea attempts to pass beyond its present content to what it would be but is not yet. The search, the striving, for identification with that end seems to be predicated on the assumption that in some sense the idea is not now one with that end. If later my idea becomes one with that end, the Absolute, it may then be seen that the Absolute was present all along, necessarily implicated in the idea, and the seeking was really unnecessary. But whether the search was necessary or not, at one stage I thought I was seeking and at another I saw that I already had what I sought. There is at least a difference in level of comprehension in me between the two stages, a change in the extent of my understanding. Does this make no difference to the Absolute? To say that it does not appears to deny the internality of the relation between myself or my idea and the Absolute. To say that it does is to admit change in the Absolute.

At any rate, it would be good to have something more from Blanshard on his view of the ontological status of change. He sometimes gives the impression that he thinks being rational is like being pregnant: one either is or is not; there is no such thing as the not fully real or rational? And does reason require that there be either a fully necessary world or an anarchic, chaotic one with no connections between things? Is there nothing in between? Is there no place for some mixture of contingency and necessity? Why should there be no possibility of any necessary connections or requirements except in a fully determined, completely necessary world? Is there no place for real change in an intelligible order?

## 4. Pots, Pans, and Persons

The search for the Aristotelian substantial bearer or carrier of qualities, on Blanshard's view, is bound to be a frustrating one (*Nature of Thought*, 1:122). For there is but one true particular, and that is the Absolute (1:639). According to Blanshard, "all that we commonly call particulars, pots and pans, mountains and rivers, are . . . seen to be universals" (1:639). Indeed, neither individuals nor instances or particulars can avoid being dissolved into universals (1:626–27). For both the argument that particulars are directly apprehended in sense and that they are required by difference of position in space and time prove to be confusions rather than cogent arguments (1:631). Hence his position is that "there are no particulars," presumably except for the Absolute. "For what gives apparent particularity to any character or complex is itself always universal" (1:631). What happens, then, on this view, to pots, pans, and persons? They would appear to be clusters of universals, characters in relation (*Philosophical Interrogations*, 255).

This account raises some questions as to the status of individuals and poses once more ancient questions concerning the one and the many. Which is primary in our world, unity or multiplicity? What constitutes an individual, and how many such individuals are there in our world? It seems clear that for Blanshard all minds are members of one intelligible order (*Nature of Thought*, 2:520), and that for him and other absolutists all things and all minds are components of a single mind (1:377), that of the Absolute; and if for Blanshard, Bradley, Royce, and company the true subject of every judgment is not this or that finite person or thing but rather the Absolute (1:647), the one is certainly preserved, but what about the many? Are they simply swallowed up in the Absolute? How junior is their membership in the one? Does one do justice to the individuality of the many finite persons and things in holding that there is only one particular, only one subject, the Absolute? Does it do justice to, say, Blanshard, Bosanquet, Bradley, Royce, Hegel, and Plato to treat them as only modes of the one ultimate reality?

For Josiah Royce the Absolute may be interpreted as the great community of intercommunicating, mutually interpreting persons or minds; an interpretation which he hoped would maintain the reality of both the one and the many. But what is the case for Brand Blanshard? Would Royce's version, in whole or in part, be acceptable to him? For Blanshard how are the many related to the Absolute, or what is the Absolute's relation to them? Is the relation that of reality to appearances, reality to potentialities, real to ideal, fully real to partially real, reality to realities, whole to parts, subject to predicates, less actual to fully actual, construct to constructs, substance to modes, determiner to determined, or what?

## 5. Can the Absolute Be Bad?

Not even a sketchy account of Blanshard's worldview would be complete without some consideration of the place of value in it and the relation between the most real and the most valuable, the more especially since traditionally the objective idealists have had something distinctive to say in this regard. In spite of the fact that he has written extensively and illuminatingly on problems of moral conduct, moreover, I have found relatively little in Blanshard's writings directly concerned with the relation between the intelligible order of the world and the shoring up of values in it. In addition, his brief discussion of this topic in the final pages of *Reason and Analysis* suggests that he may be taking a different turn than his idealistic predecessors; it would be interesting to see whether this is definitely the case and if so, how much of a break he is making with them. So I am eager to hear something further from him on this topic.

Traditionally, the objective idealists have held that the notion of an organic whole of internally related parts, supremely illustrated by the Absolute, is central for an account of the good and the beautiful as well as of the true and the real. The Absolute is the peak of perfection, the culmination at once of value and of the intelligible and the real. It provides the standard of what truly is as well as of what is valuable. Accordingly, Bradley, for example, as Blanshard notes, held that "The best life, like the truest thought, is that which approaches most nearly the Absolute."[7]

The Absolute exemplifies the ideal of the fully integrated whole, embracing the totality of facts and events in a logically necessary system, each fact and event internally related to or implied by every other. Whatever the materials, whether judgments, acts, feelings, or something else, the ideal of integration or organization of diverse contents into a unified whole remains the same. The higher the degree of integration and the larger the amount of relevant material integrated, the more nearly we approach the Absolute: the more real, the more true, the more intelligible, the more valuable. In Bosanquet's words, the basic method of philosophy is everywhere the same, namely, "to expand *all* the relevant facts, taken together, into ideas which approve themselves to thought as exhaustive and self-consistent."[8]

If "intelligence finds an answering intelligibility" in our world,[9] is there no answering chord for our value aspirations and hopes, or, in Jamesian phraseology, could only a tender-minded yearning for a moral holiday lead us to ask? If necessity "holds in degree everywhere," being "the characteristic, not of special forms, but of a whole or system into which everything apparently enters" (*Nature of Thought,* 2:335), is value somehow exempt or inoperative in this framework? If in accepting the rationalist's postulate we are committed to a world in which "every fact and event is connected with its context, and ultimately with every other fact and event, in a way that is logically necessary" and "every fact and event is ultimately connected with all others by internal relations" ("Internal Relations," 228), can this system be limited to logical connectedness? Does not the presence of values in it make a difference?

If all the contradictions, fragments, incoherencies, and contingencies are transcended in the Absolute and all the parts or lesser wholes are combined into an intelligible structure, a coherent totality, without omitting what is distinctive in each (*Nature of Thought,* 2:442), will this be without regard to value content? When the Absolute as the perfect and all-embracing totality supersedes lesser systems, absorbing and extending their gains (2:438), does this apply only to the intellectual gains? William James somewhere says that since the Absolute contains all errors and mistakes and silly things as well as the true and the real, it must contain more rubbish than desirable content; but if nevertheless all this is transcended in the perfection of the Absolute, giving us truth and reality in their completeness, is there no comparable transcending and maximization of values?

Blanshard sees the theoretic drive as having far greater sweep than, say, the moral or aesthetic interest. And in a rational world reason, far from being simply a slave of the passions, enters into everything and exerts a shaping influence. So it is that for him our goods "lie in the fulfilment not of bare impulses, but of desires into whose nature thought has entered once for all, with its own demands for consistency, integration, and expansion."[10] He defines the good in the sense of the ethical end as "*the most comprehensive possible fulfilment and satisfaction of impulse-desire,*" and by comprehensive fulfillment he means "one that takes account not only of this or that desire, but of our desires generally, and not only of this or that man's desires but of all men's."[11] If these desires are rational, is there no place in the nature of things for them? Indeed, is there not a logically necessary place for them, one which assures the conservation and optimalization of values in the universe? If the world is, as Bosanquet, for example, maintained, "a single individual whose parts are connected with each other by a necessity so intimate and so organic that the nature of the part" depends "on its place in the Absolute" (*Reason and Analysis,* 145), does not this insure an optimal place for values? Or could such a world be bad?

Blanshard concedes that many persons have found in the belief that the world is a necessary system, and thus in a sense rational, "a source of ethical and religious reassurance"; but he questions whether this reassurance is warranted. He argues, first, that "between the rational as the logically necessary and the rational as the morally right, there is an abyss of difference," and secondly, that "to pass from 'everything is rational,' in the sense of necessity, to 'everything is rational,' in the sense of right, is to stultify one's moral perception" (*Reason and Analysis,* 491). I am not disposed to deny that there are significant differences between the senses mentioned, but whether in terms of the implications of his general view the differences are so abysmal I am less certain. Blanshard's characteristic tendency to face up to facts squarely is, of course, admirable, but one wonders why one who can in effect deny the reality of change should have this much difficulty with the problem of evil. Is reason somehow more fully manifest in logic and the causal structure of nature than in art or morals?

At any rate, philosophers differ in their characterizations of the Absolute. Some, as Blanshard notes in his *Encyclopaedia Britannica* article on "The Absolute," agree with Royce in holding that it is morally good whereas others side with Spinoza, great naturalist and rationalist, in affirming that it is above all distinctions of value. How would Blanshard describe it? As neither good nor bad? Would he hold with Bosanquet that the highest and most appropriate value characterization of the Absolute is perfection? Is the world a perfect whole logically but not morally?

*Notes*

*Bibliography of Works by Lewis E. Hahn*

*Index*

# Notes

## Introduction: Broadening Our Philosophic Vision

1. Professor Sandra Rosenthal is one pragmatist who is not deterred by such terms. She has written several excellent works with such titles as *Speculative Pragmatism* (La Salle, Ill.: Open Court, 1990) and *Time, Continuity, and Indeterminacy: A Pragmatic Engagement with Contemporary Perspectives* (Albany: State University of New York Press, 2000). With the classical American pragmatists, Charles Peirce, William James, John Dewey, C. I. Lewis, and G. H. Mead, she centers on lived time and shows how through a pragmatic reconstruction of temporality we can better understand and interrelate the key issues of time and thereby greatly enhance our worldview and philosophy of life.

I should add that, with Patrick L. Bourgeois, she has produced yet another outstanding book that sheds fresh light on pragmatism; namely, *Mead and Merleau-Ponty: Toward a Common Vision* (Albany: State University of New York Press, 1991).

2. Dewey himself, for example, writes that in a few pages in the last chapter of *Experience and Nature* (Chicago: Open Court, 1925), he "attempted to state a view upon which the words *metaphysics* and *metaphysical* would make sense on experiential grounds, instead of upon the ground of ultimate Being behind experience serving as its underpinning." He adds: "I now realize that it was exceedingly naive of me to suppose that it was possible to rescue the word from its deeply engrained traditional use." *John Dewey: The Later Works, 1925–1953,* ed. Jo Ann Boydston (Carbondale: Southern Illinois University Press, 1989), 16:387–88.

In further references to the Critical Edition of the *Collected Works of John Dewey, 1882–1953,* published by Southern Illinois University Press, under the general editorship of Jo Ann Boydston, I shall use the standard abbreviations for the five volumes of *The Early Works,* 1882–98, the fifteen volumes of *The Middle Works,* 1899–1924, and the seventeen volumes of *The Later Works,* 1925–19: *EW* for *The Early Works, MW* for *The Middle Works,* and *LW* for *The Later Works.* In citations, the initials *EW, MW,* and *LW* will be followed by the volume and page numbers.

Incidentally, there is a thirty-eighth volume that provides an index for the thirty-seven volumes of text. It was edited by Anne S. Sharpe, with the assistance of Associate Editor Harriet Furst Simon and Assistant Editor Barbara Levine.

3. Since writing the other chapters in this volume, I have read Raymond D. Boisvert's very suggestive and immensely helpful essay, "Dewey's Metaphysics: Ground-Map of the Prototypically Real," in *Reading Dewey: Interpretations for a Postmodern Generation,* ed. Larry A. Hickman (Bloomington: Indiana University Press, 1998), 149–65. His map metaphor seems to me quite apt.

4. Ray Lepley, ed., *Value: A Cooperative Inquiry* (New York: Columbia University Press, 1949).

5. This statement is from the John Dewey Papers, Special Collections, Morris Library, Southern Illinois University Carbondale.

6. Henry Nelson Wieman, *The Source of Human Good* (Chicago: University of Chicago Press, 1946; reprinted in Carbondale: Southern Illinois University Press, 1964), 297.

7. Henry Nelson Wieman, *Religious Inquiry: Some Explorations* (Boston: Beacon, 1968), 189.

8. Henry Nelson Wieman, *Man's Ultimate Commitment* (Carbondale: Southern Illinois University Press, 1958; reprinted in Carbondale: Southern Illinois University Press, 1963), 79.

9. See my introduction to the first volume of *Dewey's Early Works,* "From Intuitionalism to Absolutism," in *EW* 1:xxiii–xxxvii, for a succinct account of his early views; and for somewhat more, see my "Dewey's Philosophy and Philosophic Method" in *Guide to the Works of John Dewey,* ed. Jo Ann Boydston (Carbondale: Southern Illinois University Press, 1970), 15–25.

# 1. Contextualism and Cosmic Evolution-Revolution

1. Cf. John Dewey, "The Development of American Pragmatism," in *Philosophy and Civilization* (New York: Minton, Balch, 1931), 13–14; cf. *LW* 2:3–5.

2. *Collected Papers of Charles Sanders Peirce,* ed. Charles Hartshorne and Paul Weiss (Cambridge: Harvard University Press, 1934), 5.414.

3. John Dewey, *Experience and Nature* (Chicago: Open Court, 1925), 71; cf. *LW* 1:63.

4. Dewey, *Experience and Nature,* 28.

5. Lewis E. Hahn, *A Contextualistic Theory of Perception,* in *University of California Publications in Philosophy,* ed. George P. Adams et al. (Berkeley: University of California Press, 1942), 22:8–9.

6. The name may well have been suggested by Dewey's George Holmes Howison Lecture for 1930, "Context and Thought," Berkeley, Jan. 14, 1931; *LW* 6:3–21.

7. For a fuller account, see Hahn, *A Contextualistic Theory of Perception,* 6–19.

8. See, for example, Stephen C. Pepper, "The Conceptual Framework of Tolman's Purposive Behaviorism," *Psychological Review* 41 (1934): 108–33, especially 111, or his chapter on contextualism in *World Hypotheses: A Study in Evidence* (Berkeley: University of California Press, 1942).

9. Philip P. Wiener, *Evolution and the Founders of Pragmatism* (New York: Harper and Row, Harper Torchbooks, 1965; originally published by Harvard University Press, 1949), 6.

10. John Dewey, "The Influence of Darwinism on Philosophy," in *The Influence of Darwin on Philosophy and Other Essays in Contemporary Thought* (New York: Henry Holt, 1910), 1–19; originally published as "Darwin's Influence on Philosophy," *Popular Science Monthly* 75 (1909): 90–98; *MW* 4:3–14.

11. Cf. George Kimball Plochmann, "Darwin or Spencer?" *Science* 130 (Nov. 27, 1959): 1452–56.

12. See, for example, William James, *A Pluralistic Universe* (London: Longmans Green, 1909), 79.

13. Cf. John Dewey, "Context and Thought," *LW* 6:3–21. In this essay, he maintains that "the most pervasive fallacy of philosophic thinking goes back to neglect of context" (5).

14. James, Dewey, and various other pragmatists have written at length on analysis, but for excellent succinct accounts of analysis for the contextualist, see Pepper's "The Conceptual Framework of Tolman's Purposive Behaviorism," 112–13, and *World Hypotheses*, 248–52.

15. Dewey, "The Influence of Darwinism on Philosophy," *MW* 4:10.

16. George Herbert Mead, *Movements of Thought in the Nineteenth Century*, ed. Merritt H. Moore (Chicago: University of Chicago Press, 1936), 344–59, especially 351.

17. Cf. my "Psychological Data and Philosophical Theory of Perception," *Journal of Philosophy* 39 (May 1942): 296–301; reprinted in this volume as chapter 6.

18. Edward C. Tolman, *Purposive Behavior in Animals and Men* (New York: Century, 1932), 12.

19. Hahn, *A Contextualistic Theory of Perception*, 28–29.

20. I wrote this essay some twenty-seven or twenty-eight years ago, and since then I have read Professor Thomas M. Alexander's excellent book *John Dewey's Theory of Art, Experience, and Nature: The Horizons of Feeling* (Albany: State University of New York Press, 1993). His account in this book of the principle of continuity in Dewey's writings is the most suggestive and illuminating one I have seen. It sheds fresh light not merely on Dewey's view of experience and his aesthetics but on his philosophy as a whole. See, for example, 94–103.

21. See Dewey, *Experience and Nature*, 261–62; *LW* 1:200.

22. John Dewey et al., "The Need for a Recovery of Philosophy," in *Creative Intelligence: Essays in the Pragmatic Attitude* (New York: Henry Holt, 1917), 3–69; *MW* 10:3–48; see p. 6 for the list of five points.

23. Stephen C. Pepper, *Aesthetic Quality: A Contextualistic Theory of Beauty* (New York: Charles Scribner's Sons, 1937), 29.

24. John Dewey, "Qualitative Thought," *Philosophy and Civilization*, 93–116 (101); first published in *Symposium* 1 (Jan. 1930): 5–32; *LW* 5:243–62 (249).

25. Iredell Jenkins, *Art and the Human Enterprise* (Cambridge: Harvard University Press, 1958).

26. Larry A. Hickman, in his *John Dewey's Pragmatic Technology* (Bloomington: Indiana University Press, 1990), also finds these fruitful but broadens them to cover Dewey's technological landscape, and in terms of Dewey's critique of technology, he offers an illuminating survey of the great pragmatist's thought. In his introduction, however, he took off from a metaphor of John J. McDermott's, which he says proved invaluable for his later work. McDermott, of course, over the years has shed fresh light for many of us on numerous points in Dewey's philosophy.

At least three things struck me in connection with Hickman's introductory remarks: (1) the suggestion that metaphors may help us understand a philosophy; (2) how McDermott's figure of Dewey's philosophy as an elaborate spider's web of junctions and lineaments helps explain why the uninitiated may find the interconnections and ramifications of his philosophy difficult; and (3) Hickman's noting that appreciation for Dewey is as much an act of technological production as is the construction of what is to be appreciated.

27. Pepper, *World Hypotheses*, 225–60.

28. Cf. Thomas S. Kuhn, *The Structure of Scientific Revolutions,* in *International Encyclopedia of Unified Science,* vol. 2.2, ed. Otto Neurath et al. (Chicago: University of Chicago Press, 1962).

## 2. Metaphysical Interpretation

1. Stephen C. Pepper, *World Hypotheses: A Study in Evidence* (Berkeley: University of California Press, 1942).

2. Dorothy M. Emmet, *The Nature of Metaphysical Thinking* (London: Macmillan, 1945; New York: St. Martin's, 1957).

3. For example, Alfred North Whitehead, *Modes of Thought* (New York: Macmillan, 1938), chapter 1.

4. See, for example, A. E. Murphy, "Whitehead and the Method of Speculative Philosophy," in *The Philosophy of Alfred North Whitehead,* 2d ed., ed. P. A. Schilpp (LaSalle, Ill.: Open Court, 1951), 353–80.

5. Otto Neurath, "Universal Jargon and Terminology," *Proceedings of the Aristotelian Society,* n.s., 41 (1940–41): 127–48.

6. Neurath, "Universal Jargon and Terminology," 129.

7. Neurath, "Universal Jargon and Terminology," 131.

8. John Wisdom, "Metaphysics and Verification, I," *Mind,* n.s., 47 (Oct. 1938): 452–98.

9. Wisdom, "Metaphysics and Verification, I," 494.

10. Wisdom, "Metaphysics and Verification, I," 497.

11. John Dewey, "Qualitative Thought," *Philosophy and Civilization* (New York: Minton, Balch, 1931), 96; *LW* 5:245.

12. See, for example, Gustav Bergmann, "Logical Positivism," in *A History of Philosophical Systems,* ed. Vergilius Ferm (New York: Philosophical Library, 1950), 471–82.

13. Walter T. Stace, "Can Speculative Philosophy Be Defended?" *Philosophical Review* 52 (1943): 123.

14. Stace, "Can Speculative Philosophy Be Defended?" 123.

15. J. Loewenberg, "Artifacts of Reason," in *Reason,* University of California Publications in Philosophy (Berkeley: University of California Press, 1939), 21:67.

## 3. Metaphysical Inquiry

1. D. F. Pears, ed., *The Nature of Metaphysics* (New York: St. Martin's, 1957), 1.

2. For an extended account of the merits of metaphysics, see W. Somerset Maugham, *The Summing Up* (New York: Doubleday, 1946), 238–39.

3. For example, Alfred North Whitehead, *Modes of Thought* (New York: Macmillan, 1938), chapter 1.

4. Lewis E. Hahn, *A Contextualistic Theory of Perception,* in *University of California Publications in Philosophy,* ed. George P. Adams et al. (Berkeley: University of California Press, 1942), 22:8–9.

5. Cf. J. Urmson, *Philosophical Analysis: Its Development Between the Two World Wars* (Oxford University Press, 1956), 165–78.

6. Morris Lazerowitz, *The Structure of Metaphysics* (New York: Humanities Press, 1955), 23–24.

7. Lazerowitz, *The Structure of Metaphysics*, 11–12.

8. Dorothy M. Emmet, "The Use of Analogy in Metaphysics," *Proceedings of the Aristotelian Society*, n.s., 41 (1940–41): 30–31.

9. Stephen C. Pepper, *World Hypotheses: A Study in Evidence* (Berkeley: University of California Press, 1942), 91.

10. Morris R. Cohen, *A Preface to Logic* (New York: Henry Holt, 1944), 83.

11. Emmet, "The Use of Analogy in Metaphysics," 41.

## 4. Philosophy as Comprehensive Vision

1. John Dewey, "The Logic of Judgments of Practice," *MW* 8:14–82, especially 59; first published in 1915; revised and reprinted in *Essays in Experimental Logic* (Chicago: University of Chicago Press, 1916), 335–442.

2. Since presenting this address, I have read Professor Diane Gillespie, *The Mind's We: Contextualism in Cognitive Psychology* (Carbondale: Southern Illinois University Press, 1992); and it provides ample evidence that psychologists and philosophers may reinforce each other. For a number of reasons, it is the best, the most important, and the most exciting book on knowing and the known I have read in years. Written in a delightfully clear, straightforward, and engaging style, with a minimum of technical jargon, it fills a significant gap in the literature. It underscores the importance of psychology for worldviews in philosophy and shows the relevance of an understanding of these worldviews for psychological and philosophical accounts of perception, memory, and concepts. In particular, it shows what a fine job a cognitive contextualist can do on these topics.

3. Friedrich Waismann, "How I see Philosophy," in *Contemporary British Philosophy*, ed. H. D. Lewis (New York: Macmillan, 1925), 464–65.

## 5. Metaphysical Categories: Of Shoes and Ships and Sealing Wax, and Cabbages and Kings

1. Albert Hofstadter, "The Question of Categories," *Journal of Philosophy* 48 (Mar. 1951): 173.

2. Stephen C. Pepper, *World Hypotheses: A Study in Evidence* (Berkeley: University of California Press, 1942).

3. Dorothy M. Emmet, *The Nature of Metaphysical Thinking* (London: Macmillan, 1945; New York: St. Martin's, 1957).

4. See Lewis E. Hahn, *A Contextualistic Theory of Perception*, in *University of California Publications in Philosophy*, ed. George P. Adams et al. (Berkeley: University of California Press, 1942), 22:6–19; cf. "Contextualism and Cosmic Evolution-Revolution" in chapter 1 of the section on contextualism of this volume.

5. See, for example, Stephen C. Pepper, "The Conceptual Framework of Tolman's Purposive Behaviorism," *Psychological Review* 41 (1934): 108–33, especially 111, or his chapter on contextualism in *World Hypotheses*.

6. See Lewis E. Hahn, "Metaphysical Interpretation," *Philosophical Review* 61.2 (Apr. 1952): 176–87; reprinted in this volume as chapter 2.

7. Eugene Freeman, *The Categories of Charles Peirce* (Chicago: Open Court, 1934), 4.

8. Alfred North Whitehead, *Process and Reality* (New York: Macmillan, 1929), 28.

9. Whitehead, *Process and Reality,* 36.

10. Whitehead, *Process and Reality,* 33.

11. See, for example, Archie Bahm, "Organicism's Nine Types of Philosophy," *Proceedings of the Eleventh International Congress of Philosophy,* Brussels (Aug. 1953) 3:52–56.

12. See, for example, R. G. Collingwood, *An Essay on Metaphysics* (Oxford: Clarendon Press, 1940), 65–68 (76).

## 6. Psychological Data and Philosophical Theory of Perception

1. John A. McGeoch, "The Formal Criteria of a Systematic Psychology," *Psychological Review* 40 (1933): 1–12 (1).

2. John Dewey, *Essays in Experimental Logic* (Chicago: University of Chicago Press, 1916), 402–13.

3. Dewey, *Essays in Experimental Logic,* 402.

4. George Herbert Mead, *Movements of Thought in the Nineteenth Century* (Chicago: University of Chicago Press, 1936), 351.

## 7. Neutral, Indubitable Sense-Data as the Starting Point for Theories of Perception

1. H. H. Price, *Perception* (London: Methuen, 1932), 19, 37. All page references in this paper are to this work unless specifically stated otherwise.

2. G. Dawes Hicks, "Sensible Appearances and Material Things," *Proceedings of the Sixth International Congress of Philosophy* (1926): 224–36 (225).

3. See, for example, Price, *Perception,* 103.

4. George Santayana, *Scepticism and Animal Faith* (New York: Scribner, 1923), 45: "That which is certain and given is something of which existence can not be predicated." Or again, in the same work, Santayana announces that he will deny "existence to any datum, whatever it may be; and as the datum, by hypothesis, is the whole of what solicits my attention at any moment, I shall deny the existence of everything, and abolish that category of thought altogether" (35).

5. David Wight Prall, "The Inaccessibility of Truth," *University of California Publications in Philosophy* 11 (1929): 201–32: "Existence is predicable only of what is in change" (221). And Mr. Price denies that sense-data change.

6. Hicks, "Sensible Appearances and Material Things," 231: "Considered, then, in abstraction from the physical object, sensible appearances [Dawes Hicks's name for the given] are not, I should urge, existents; they are not entities that have characteristics, they *are* characteristics."

7. See, for example, Price, *Perception,* 116 n. 2.

8. Prall, "The Inaccessibility of Truth," 219.

9. Virgil C. Aldrich, "Are there Vague Sense-Data?" *Mind,* n.s., 43.172 (1934): 477–82.

10. Aldrich, "Are there Vague Sense-Data?" 478.

11. Aldrich, "Are there Vague Sense-Data?" 481.

12. Perhaps, in this connection, we should remind Mr. Price of a statement he makes: "Of course certain characteristics may be given which some philosopher thinks *ought not* to be given [e.g., shall we say?, indeterminate frontal shapes and certain indeterminate

distances].... So much the worse for him, that is all. He must have held a false theory of what is 'giveable.' If something is given, it is given, and we must just make the best of it. In a matter of this kind we can not and will not accept the dictation of theorists" (10). What is giveable, however, it should be added, has a strange way of varying with different theories; and until the ardent seeker for the given takes explicit cognizance of his own theoretical grounds and those of others, he will be at the mercy of thinkers who realize how much of a difference the dictates of different theorists make in what is giveable.

13. I borrow this term from Professor Loewenberg, "Pre-Analytical and Post-Analytical Data," *Journal of Philosophy* 24 (1927): 5–14.

14. Cf. John Dewey's *Experience and Nature* (Chicago: Open Court, 1925), 144: "Sensory data, whether they are designated psychic or physical or, it might be added, neither, are thus not starting points; they are the products of analysis . . . moreover every step of analysis depends upon continual reference to these empirical objects"; cf. *LW* 1:116.

15. Edward Strong, "Signs of Mind," *University of California Publications in Philosophy* 19 (1936): 115–42 (129).

16. As a matter fact, Mr. Price's actual starting point is better than his professed one, though he loses sight of the former in his insistence upon the latter until he gets into difficulty. Actually he starts not with data *simpliciter* but with such experiences as those of looking at a tomato, touching it, smelling it, and so on (3). And these experiences include a great deal more than indubitable sense-data. In any one of these situations, he has a perceptually accepted object, and from it he analyzes out sense-data for the purpose of answering such questions as "What is there in this experience which can serve as the basis for reliable inference?"

17. Prall, "The Inaccessibility of Truth," 224.

18. For example, Dewey, *Experience and Nature,* 327 ff.; cf. *LW* 1:246–47.

19. Clarence Irving Lewis, *Mind and the World-Order* (New York: Scribner's, 1929): 120–21.

20. Bertrand Russell, *The Analysis of Mind* (London: Allen and Unwin; New York: Macmillan, 1921), 145: "The distinction between images and sensations [Russell's name for sense-data in this work] is . . . by no means always obvious to inspection."

21. Russell, *The Analysis of Mind,* 148–49. Mr. Russell maintains that sensations cannot be distinguished from images on the ground that the former lead us to believe in their "physical reality" and the latter do not, for our feeling of unreality for the image results from our having already realized on other grounds that we are dealing with an image.

22. In connection with Mr. Price's claim that "the given is still given, however much we know about it" (18), which attempts to preserve indubitability by suggesting that his account may be doubtful but not the data, I should like to quote a passage from Pepper's "Middle-Sized Facts," *University of California Publications in Philosophy* 14 (1932): 3–28 (10–11), in which he is discussing the claim that facts are stubborn and indubitable, however fallible our knowledge may be. After indicating the possibility that the purity of facts may be illusory, he takes up the answer of the defenders of such facts:

> To this the exponent of the descriptive method will object that I am con-
> fusing the fact with the knowing of it. The knowing of a fact is admittedly
> fallible. . . . A fact is one thing. The knowing of it is another and an added
> thing that has nothing to do with the fact. The identification or the fusion
> of a fact with the knowing of it is a fallacy.

I reply that the theory that all facts are dependent on the knowing of them is indeed a theory. To assume that a fact is dependent on the knowing of it is unwarrantable. To assert that thesis as an indubitable fact is as absurd as the assertion of any other indubitable. But I note that the theory that no facts are dependent on the knowing of them is equally a theory. The one theory is as dubious as the other. Either or both of them may be good theories. But there is no legitimate way of establishing either of them on the basis of indubitable facts.

Moreover, the ascription of the apparent transitoriness or variability of a fact entirely to the knowing of it is not the sole possible interpretation. . . . There is no self-evident reason why a fact in its very nature, even apart from the knowing of it, might not be variable or amorphous.

23. Hicks, "Sensible Appearances and Material Things," 224–36, especially 224–25. Professor Hicks objects to the term *sense-data* on two scores: (1) It is suggested that what is thus designated is "given," whereas the specific entities denoted by the term never are, as such, "given"; and (2) it is implied that the entities in question are existents, whereas this is an assumption that should be avoided at the outset at least.

24. Dewey regards this as one of the major confusions of traditional theories of epistemology. See "A Naturalistic Theory of Sense Perception," in *Philosophy and Civilization* 188–201 (189–92); cf. *LW* 2:44–45, 45–47, 50–51; see also *Experience and Nature,* 340, in which Dewey maintains that "in every case, the basis of classification is extrinsic, an affair dependent upon a study, often hard to make, of generating conditions and of subsequent careers"; *LW* 1:255–56. It is not a matter of immediate inspection of the intrinsic characters of sense-data.

25. Cf., for example, Price, *Perception,* 146–47: "So far as we have yet shown, it [the material thing we take to exist] may never in any instance exist, and perceptual consciousness may be nothing but an inevitable and continuing error."

26. Though he holds that sense-data are phases of no substance, Price admits that there is a non-spatial sense in which they may be said to be "in" the mind and says that "to dismiss this as a mere metaphor for 'apprehended by the mind' is not sufficient," pointing out that "many philosophers have held that sense-data are 'in' the mind in a sense in which other people and external objects are not," though all these are apprehended (124). He suggests that the word *in* marks a difference between acquaintance and other forms of consciousness, saying that "what we apprehend in other ways has to be sought out, and as it were fussed after," whereas "what we are acquainted with is just present of itself" (124). Hence the upshot of his discussion is that "the statement we are examining needs only a change of emphasis: the truth being not so much that sense-data are *in* the mind, as that they *are* in the mind, and do not have, so to speak, to be brought before it by a process as the conclusion of an argument, for instance, does" (125).

Incidentally, the denial that sense-data are phases of physical substances is at least part of what traditional dualists have meant in saying that these data were in the mind.

27. See Stephen C. Pepper, "A Criticism of a Positivistic Theory of Mind," *University of California Publications in Philosophy* 19 (1936): 211–32 (213 ff.). Pepper suggests the following as the mechanistic categories: (1) a spatio-temporal field of locations, (2) a set of efficient or primary characters of nature, (3) laws of motion determining sequences of primary characters in the field, (4) secondary characters, (5) laws holding among secondary characters, and (6) a principle describing the relation of secondary to primary characters.

28. "For the purposes of the discussion we shall obviously have to assume the existence of various material objects [though, of course, on his view there may be no such material things], particularly of living creatures, although we have not yet been able to give a satisfactory account of the way in which we are conscious of them. But as we hope to offer one later, and as in any case we certainly do have this consciousness, whether philosophers succeed in understanding it or not, perhaps this lapse from strict methodological propriety may be pardoned" (105).

## 8. A Contextualistic View of Experience and Ecological Responsibility

1. I have discussed the contextualistic categories at length in *A Contextualistic Theory of Perception,* in *University of California Publications in Philosophy,* ed. George P. Adams et al. (Berkeley: University of California Press, 1942), 22:6–19, and in "Contextualism and Cosmic Evolution-Revolution," *The Philosophy Forum* 11 (Mar. 1972): 3–8, 15–35; see also the opening chapter in *Evolution-Revolution: Patterns of Development in Nature, Society, Man and Knowledge,* ed. Rubin Gotesky and Ervin Laszlo (New York: Gordon and Breach Science Publishers, 1971), 3–39.

2. See, for example, Stephen C. Pepper's "The Conceptual Framework of Tolman's Purposive Behaviorism," *Psychological Review* 41 (1934): 108–33, especially 111, or his chapter on contextualism in *World Hypotheses: A Study in Evidence* (Berkeley: University of California Press, 1942).

3. "Contextualism and Cosmic Evolution-Revolution," 7–8; reprinted in this volume as chapter 1.

4. John Dewey, "Context and Thought," *LW* 6:5.

5. Lewis E. Hahn, "Contextualism and Cosmic Evolution-Revolution," 25.

6. John Dewey, *Logic: The Theory of Inquiry, LW* 12:152.

7. John Dewey, "The Need for a Recovery of Philosophy," *MW* 10:5–6.

8. Irwin Edman, *Arts and the Man: A Short Introduction to Esthetics* (New York: W. W. Norton, 1939); John Dewey, *Art as Experience, LW* 10; Stephen C. Pepper, *Aesthetic Quality: A Contextualistic Theory of Beauty* (New York: Charles Scribner's Sons, 1938); and Hahn, *A Contextualistic Theory of Perception,* chapter 5.

9. Al Gore, *Earth in the Balance* (Boston: Houghton Mifflin, 1992).

10. Gore, *Earth in the Balance,* 75.

11. Gore, *Earth in the Balance,* 1.

12. Gore, *Earth in the Balance,* 259.

13. Gore, *Earth in the Balance,* 305–7.

14. Gore, *Earth in the Balance,* 291.

## 9. Creating: Solving Problems and Experiencing Afresh

1. George E. Axtelle, "John Dewey's Conception of the Religious," *Religious Humanism* 1 (1967):66–67.

2. George E. Axtelle and Joe R. Burnett, "Dewey on Education and Schooling," in *Guide to the Works of John Dewey,* ed. Jo Ann Boydston (Carbondale: Southern Illinois University Press, 1970), 263.

3. John Dewey, "Context and Thought," in *University of California Publications in*

*Philosophy* (Berkeley: University of California Press, 1931), 12:203–24; reprinted in *LW* 6:3–21, especially 11 and 5.

4. I have discussed the contextualistic categories at length in *A Contextualistic Theory of Perception,* in *University of California Publications in Philosophy,* ed. George P. Adams et al. (Berkeley: University of California Press, 1942), 22:6–19, and in "Contextualism and Cosmic Evolution-Revolution," *Philosophy Forum* 11 (Mar. 1972): 3–39; see also the opening chapter in *Evolution-Revolution: Patterns of Development in Nature, Society, Man and Knowledge,* ed. Rubin Gotesky and Ervin Laszlo (New York: Gordon and Breach Science Publishers, 1971), 3–39; reprinted in this volume as chapter 1.

5. John Dewey, *Experience and Nature* (Chicago: Open Court, 1925), 71.

6. Cf. Hahn, *A Contextualistic Theory of Perception,* 28–29, or "Contextualism and Cosmic Evolution-Revolution," 32–33.

7. Cf. John Dewey, "The Development of American Pragmatism," in *Studies in the History of Ideas,* ed. Department of Philosophy, Columbia University (New York: Columbia University Press, 1925), 2:353–77; *LW* 2:3–21, especially 12–13.

8. Hahn, "Contextualism and Cosmic Evolution-Revolution," 22.

9. John Dewey, "My Pedagogic Creed," *EW* 5:86.

10. Irwin Edman, *Arts and the Man: A Short Introduction to Esthetics* (New York: W. W. Norton, 1939); John Dewey, *Art as Experience, LW* 10; Stephen C. Pepper, *Aesthetic Quality: A Contextualistic Theory of Beauty* (New York: Charles Scribner's Sons, 1938); and Hahn, *A Contextualistic Theory of Perception,* chapter 5.

11. See Thomas M. Alexander, *John Dewey's Theory of Art, Experience, and Nature: The Horizons of Feeling* (Albany: State University of New York Press, 1987), 94–103.

12. See, for example, "Aesthetics and Education," *Chinese University of Hong Kong Education Journal* 12.2 (Dec. 1984): 71–76.

13. David Lee Miller, *Philosophy of Creativity* (New York: Peter Lang, 1989), 119.

14. Larry A. Hickman, *John Dewey's Pragmatic Technology* (Bloomington: Indiana University Press, 1990, 1992), 61.

15. Dewey, *Experience and Nature,* chapter 5; *LW* 1:132–61.

16. John Dewey, "Creative Democracy–The Task Before Us," in *The Philosophy of the Common Man: Essays in Honor of John Dewey to Celebrate His Eightieth Birthday,* ed. Sidney Ratner (New York: G. P. Putnam's Sons, 1940), 227; cf. *LW* 14:224–30, especially, 229.

## 11. John Dewey and Our Time

1. John Dewey, *Experience and Nature* (Chicago: Open Court, 1925), 71; 2d ed. (New York: W. W. Norton, 1929); *LW* 1:1–326.

2. Dewey, *Experience and Nature,* 28.

3. John Dewey, "The Need for a Recovery of Philosophy," in *Creative Intelligence: Essays in the Pragmatic Attitude* (New York: Henry Holt, 1917), 3–69; *MW* 10:3–48.

4. Dewey, "The Need for a Recovery of Philosophy," *MW* 10:46.

5. John Dewey, "Philosophy and Civilization," *LW* 3:4.

6. John Dewey, "Creative Democracy—The Task Before Us," *LW* 14:229.

## 12. Dewey's View of Experience and Culture

1. These drafts are in the John Dewey Papers, Special Collections, Morris Library, Southern Illinois University Carbondale.

2. John Dewey, *Experience and Nature* (LaSalle, Ill.: Open Court, 1929), 8.

3. Dewey, *Experience and Nature,* 2a.

4. See, for example, *A Contextualistic Theory of Perception,* in *University of California Publications in Philosophy,* ed. George P. Adams et al. (Berkeley: University of California Press, 1942), 22:6–19; "Dewey's Philosophy and Philosophic Method" in *Guide to the Works of John Dewey,* ed. Jo Ann Boydston (Carbondale: Southern Illinois University Press, 1970), 15–60, especially 40–51; and "Contextualism and Cosmic Evolution-Revolution," in *Evolution-Revolution,* ed. Rubin Gotesky and Ervin Laszlo (New York: Gordon and Breach Science Publishers, 1971), 3–39.

5. Dewey, *Experience and Nature,* 2a.

6. John Dewey, "The Need for a Recovery in Philosophy," in *Creative Intelligence: Essays in the Pragmatic Attitude* (New York: Henry Holt, 1917), 3–69; *MW* 10:3–48.

7. John Dewey, "A Short Catechism Concerning Truth," in *The Influence of Darwin on Philosophy and Other Essays in Contemporary Thought* (New York: Henry Holt, 1910), 156; *MW* 6:5.

8. John Dewey, *Reconstruction in Philosophy* (Boston: Beacon Press, 1957), 91; cf. *MW* 12:131–32.

9. John Dewey, "The Need for a Recovery of Philosophy," in *Art as Experience* (New York: Capricorn Books, 1934), 246; cf. *LW* 10:251.

10. Dewey, *Art as Experience,* 247; cf. *LW* 10:252.

11. This assertion and the remaining quotations in this paper are from John Dewey Papers, Special Collections, Morris Library, Southern Illinois University Carbondale.

# 13. Wieman's Empiricism

1. Henry Nelson Wieman, *The Source of Human Good* (Chicago: University of Chicago Press, 1946; reprint, Carbondale: Southern Illinois University Press, 1964), 297.

2. Henry Nelson Wieman, *Religious Inquiry: Some Explorations* (Boston: Beacon, 1968), 189.

3. See, for example, Robert W. Bretall, ed., *The Empirical Theology of Henry Nelson Wieman* (Carbondale: Southern Illinois University Press, 1969), 262–63.

4. Wieman, *Religious Inquiry,* 188. Additional material on this topic is provided in Huston Smith's "Empiricism Revisited" and Wieman's reply to it in *Empirical Theology* (New York: Macmillan, 1963) 244–64.

5. Cf. Bretall, ed., *Empirical Theology,* 111.

6. Stephen C. Pepper, *World Hypotheses: A Study in Evidence* (Berkeley: University of California Press, 1942).

7. Henry Nelson Wieman, *Man's Ultimate Commitment* (Carbondale, Ill.: Southern Illinois University Press, 1958), 82–83.

8. Wieman, *Man's Ultimate Commitment,* 91. See also Wieman, *Source of Human Good,* 298–99.

9. Henry Nelson Wieman, "Can God Be Perceived?" *Journal of Religion* 23 (Jan. 1943): 27 n. 3.

10. William James, preface to *The Meaning of Truth* (London: Longmans, Green, 1911), xii.

11. Henry Nelson Wieman, "Experience, Mind, and the Concept," *Journal of Philosophy* 21 (Oct. 1924): 561–72; reprinted in *Seeking a Faith for a New Age: Essays on the*

*Interdependence of Religion, Science and Philosophy,* ed. Cedric L. Hepler (Methuchen, N.J.: Scarecrow, 1975), 40.

12. Wieman, "Experience, Mind, and the Concept"; reprinted in *Seeking a Faith for a New Age.*

13. Wieman, "Knowledge, Religious and Otherwise," *Journal of Religion* 38 (Jan. 1958): 12–28; reprinted in *Seeking a Faith for a New Age,* 273.

14. Wieman, "Knowledge, Religious and Otherwise," 279.

15. Wieman, "Knowledge, Religious and Otherwise," 275.

16. Henry N. Wieman Papers, Special Collection 17, Morris Library, Southern Illinois University Carbondale.

## 14. Stephen C. Pepper's World Hypotheses

1. Stephen C. Pepper, *World Hypotheses: A Study in Evidence* (Berkeley: University of California Press, 1942).

2. Stephen C. Pepper, *The Basis of Criticism in the Arts* (Cambridge: Harvard University Press, 1945).

3. Stephen C. Pepper, *Aesthetic Quality: A Contextualistic Theory of Beauty* (New York: Charles Scribner's Sons, 1938).

4. This is part of the very extensive body of Pepper manuscripts and correspondence in Special Collection 106, Morris Library, Southern Illinois University Carbondale.

5. Special Collection 106, Morris Library.

6. A. J. Reck, "Pepper and Recent Metaphilosophy," *Journal of Mind and Behavior* 3 (Summer 1982): 208.

7. Stephen C. Pepper, "Metaphor in Philosophy," *Journal of Mind and Behavior* 3 (Summer 1982): 200; reprinted from *Dictionary of History of Ideas,* vol. 3 (New York: Charles Scribner's Sons, 1973).

8. Stephen C. Pepper, *Concept and Quality: A World Hypothesis* (La Salle, Ill.: Open Court, 1967).

9. Donald S. Lee, "Adequacy in World Hypotheses: Reconstructing Pepper's Criteria," *Metaphilosophy* 14.2 (Apr. 1983): 151–61.

10. Richard Rorty, "Pragmatism, Relativism, and Irrationalism," *Proceedings and Addresses of the American Philosophical Association* 53.6 (Aug. 1980): 719–38.

11. Richard Rorty, *Philosophy and the Mirror of Nature* (Princeton: Princeton University Press, 1979).

12. Special Collection 106, Morris Library.

13. Stephen C. Pepper, *A Digest of Purposive Values* (Berkeley: University of California Press, 1947).

14. Stephen C. Pepper, *The Sources of Value* (Berkeley: University of California Press, 1958).

15. Stephen C. Pepper, *Principles of Art Appreciation* (New York: Harcourt, Brace, 1949).

## 15. Brand Blanshard's Worldview

1. Stephen C. Pepper, *World Hypotheses: A Study in Evidence* (Berkeley: University of California Press, 1942), 283.

2. Brand Blanshard, *Reason and Analysis* (La Salle, Ill.: Open Court, 1962; London: Allen and Unwin, 1962; La Salle, Ill.: Open Court paperback, 1973), 383.

3. Brand Blanshard, *The Nature of Thought,* 2 vols. (New York: Macmillan, 1940), 1:473.

4. *Encyclopaedia Britannica* (1967 ed.), 1:50.

5. Sydney Chester Rome and Beatrice Rome, eds., *Philosophical Interrogations: Interrogations of Martin Buber, John Wild, Jean Wahl, Brand Blanshard, Paul Weiss, Charles Hartshorne, and Paul Tillich* (New York: Holt, Rinehart and Winston, 1964), 212.

6. Brand Blanshard, "Internal Relations and Their Importance to Philosophy," *Review of Metaphysics* 21.2 (Dec. 1967): 227.

7. Brand Blanshard, "Francis Herbert Bradley," *Journal of Philosophy* 22.1 (Jan. 1, 1925): 15.

8. Bernard Bosanquet, *Three Lectures on Aesthetic* (London: Macmillan, 1915), 3.

9. Brand Blanshard, "Current Strictures on Reason," *Philosophical Review* 54.4 (July 1945): 361.

10. Brand Blanshard, *Reason and Goodness* (London: Allen and Unwin, 1961), 347.

11. Blanshard, *Reason and Goodness,* 311.

# Bibliography of Works by Lewis E. Hahn

## Books

*A Contextualistic Theory of Perception*. University of California Publications in Philosophy. Vol. 22. Ed. George P. Adams et al. Berkeley: University of California Press, 1942.

(with Cecil H. Miller) *The Elements of Logic*. Columbia, Mo.: Lucas Brothers, 1946.

(with Ray Lepley, John Dewey, and others) *Value: A Cooperative Inquiry*. New York: Columbia University Press, 1949.

*Enhancing Cultural Interflow Between East and West*. Collected Essays in Comparative Philosophy and Culture (in Chinese and English). Ed. and Trans. George C. H. Sun. Thomé H. Fang Institute, 1998.

## Articles and Essays

"Neutral, Indubitable Sense-Data as the Starting Point for Theories of Perception." *Journal of Philosophy* 36 (1939).

"Philosophy and Scientific Method." *Proc. of the Missouri Academy of Science* (1940).

"Psychological Data and Philosophical Theory of Perception," *Journal of Philosophy* 39 (1942), 296–300.

"Remedial Logic," *Journal of Higher Education* 17 (Nov. 1947): 423–28.

"Developing Critical Thinking in the Secondary Schools." *Educational Administration and Supervision* 34 (Nov. 1948): 421–24.

"Elementary Logic as Remedial and Functional." *The Teaching of Philosophy*. Proceedings and Addresses of the Conference on the Teaching of Philosophy, Western Reserve University, Oct. 14–15, 1949. Ed. Frederick P. Harris, 74–76, Cleveland, Ohio, 1950.

"Metaphysical Interpretation." *Philosophical Review* 61 (Apr. 1952), 176–87.

"Of Shoes and Ships and Sealing Wax, and Cabbages and Kings." *Journal of Philosophy* 55.2 (Jan. 16, 1958): 45–57. Presidential Address for Southwestern Philosophical Society.

"What is the Starting Point of Metaphysics?" *Philosophy and Phenomenological Research* 18 (Mar. 1958): 293–311.

"The Pursuit of Graduate Degrees by Members of the University Faculty." *Proc. of the Midwest Conference on Graduate Study and Research*, 1960.

"Philosophy as Comprehensive Vision." *Philosophy and Phenomenological Research* 22 (Sept. 1961): 16–25. Presidential Address for Southern Society for Philosophy and Psychology.

"Graduate and Professional Education During the Next Ten Years." *Proc. of the Missouri Conference on Higher Education*, 1962.

"Criteria for the Establishment of New Ph.D. Programs." *Proc. of the Council of Graduate Schools in the United States,* 1963.

"Philosophical Inquiry and the Sociology of Knowledge." *Proc. of the Second Extraordinary Interamerican Convention of Philosophers,* San Jose, Costa Rica, 1963.

"Truth, Choice, and Despair." *Pacific Philosophy Forum* (Feb. 1963), 85–90.

"Metaphysical Inquiry." *Memorias del XIII Congreso International de Filosofia* (Mexico, D. F., 7–14 Septiembre de 1963). Ciudad Universidad, Mexico 20, D. F., Universidad Nacional Autonoma de Mexico, 1964.

Foreword to *Whitehead on Education,* by Harold B. Dunkel. Columbus: Ohio State University Press, 1965, vii–xii.

"Creativity in Hartshorne's World View." In *Charles Hartshorne and Henry Nelson Wiema,* ed. William S. Minor. Philosophy of Creativity Monograph Series, Vol. 1. Carbondale: Foundation for Creative Philosophy, 1969.

"From Intuitionalism to Absolutism." Introduction to *The Early Works of John Dewey, 1882–1898.* Vol. 1. Ed. Jo Ann Boydston, xii–xxxvii. Carbondale and Edwardsville: Southern Illinois University Press, 1969.

"John Dewey on Teaching Philosophy in High School." *Educational Theory* 17.3 (July 1967): 219–21. Reprinted in *Journal of Critical Analysis* 1 (Oct. 1969): 115–18.

"Dewey's Philosophy and Philosophic Method." In *Guide to the Works of John Dewey.* Ed. Jo Ann Boydston, 15–60. Carbondale and Edwardsville: Southern Illinois University Press, 1970. Arcturus Books Edition, 1972.

"Contextualism and Cosmic Evolution-Revolution." In *Evolution-Revolution: Patterns of Development in Nature, Society, Man and Knowledge.* Ed. Rubin Gotesky and Ervin Laszlo, 3–39. New York: Gordon and Breach Science Publishers, 1971; also in *Philosophy Forum* 11 (Mar. 1972): 3–39.

"Contextualism and Cosmic Evolution-Revolution." *Philosophy Forum* 11 (Mar. 1972): 3–39; also the opening chapter in *Evolution-Revolution: Patterns of Development in Nature, Society, Man and Knowledge.* Ed. Rubin Gotesky and Ervin Laszlo.

"Advice to the New Philosophy Teacher." In *Philosophy and the Civilizing Arts: Essays Presented to Herbert W. Schneider.* Ed. Craig Walton and John P. Anton, 365–69. Athens: Ohio University Press, 1974.

"Does Philosophy Have a Future?" *Proceedings of the Fifteenth World Congress of Philosophy,* 1973, Varna, Bulgaria, Vol. 4, 417–20; Sofia, Bulgaria: Sofia Production Centre, 1974. Reprinted in *Darshana International.* Vol. 14 (Apr. 1974).

"A Flair for Philosophy." *Midwestern Journal of Philosophy* (Spring 1974): 1–12. Presidential Address of the Illinois Philosophy Association.

"Reflective Inquiry and Language." In *Abstracts of Papers to be Presented in Sectional Meetings.* Ed. K. K. Mittal, Golden Jubilee Session, Indian Philosophical Congress, World Philosophy Conference, Dec. 28, 1975–Jan. 3, 1976. "Points of View: IV." Delhi: 110007: Department of Philosophy, University of Delhi, 1975.

"Reflective Inquiry and Language" (chapter 26 of part 2). In *Knowledge, Culture and Value.* Ed. R. C. Pandeya and S. R. Bhatt. Papers Presented in Plenary Sessions, Panel Discussions, and Sectional Meetings of World Philosophy Conference (Golden Jubilee Session of the Indian Philosophical Congress), Dec. 28, 1975–Jan. 3, 1976. Delhi, Varanasi, and Patna: Motilal Banarsidass, 1976.

"Dewey's View of Experience and Culture." In *Philosophy in the Life of a Nation: Abstracts of Contributed Papers [and] Biographies of Participants.* New York: Bicentennial Symposium of Philosophy, 1976.

"Dewey's View of Experience and Culture." In *Philosophy in the Life of a Nation: Papers Contributed to the Bicentennial Symposium of Philosophy,* Oct. 7–10, 1976. New York: Bicentennial Symposium of Philosophy, 1976.

"Piping Pragmatically." Introduction to *The Middle Works of John Dewey,* Vol. 4. Southern Illinois University Press, 1977.

"John Dewey and Our Time." *Baylor Educator* (Spring 1978): 1–7, 14.

"Brand Blanshard's Worldview." In *The Philosophy of Brand Blanshard.* Ed. Paul Arthur Schilpp, 878–91. The Library of Living Philosophers. LaSalle, Ill.: Open Court, 1980.

"A Contextualistic Interpretation of the Self." In *El Hombre y Su Conducta: Ensayos Filosóficos en Honor de Risieri Frondizi (Man and His Conduct: Philosophical Essays in Honor of Risieri Frondizi).* Ed. Jorge J. E. Gracia, 169–79. Rio Piedras, Puerto Rico: University of Puerto Rico Press, 1980.

"Dewey's View of Experience and Culture." In *Two Centuries of Philosophy in America.* Ed. Peter Caws, 167–73. American Philosophical Quarterly Library of Philosophy, Basil Blackwell, 1980. Reprinted from *Philosophy in the Life of a Nation.*

Introduction to *The Middle Works of John Dewey, 1899–1924.* Vol. 10. Ed. Jo Ann Boydston, ix–xxxix. Southern Illinois University Press, 1980.

"John Dewey's World View." *Religious Humanism* 14.1 (Winter 1980): 32–37.

"The Stephen C. Pepper Papers, 1903–1972." *Root Metaphor: The Live Thought of Stephen C. Pepper. Paunch,* nos. 53–54 (1980): 73–80.

"A Contextualistic Philosophy of Life." In *Symposium of the International Congress of Philosophy, Fu Jen Catholic University,* Dec. 28, 1979–Jan. 1, 1980. Hsin Chuang, Taipei Hsien, Taiwan: Fu Jen Catholic Universit, 1981, 168–82.

(with Jo Ann Boydston) "The Center for Dewey Studies." *Religious Humanism* 15.2 (Spring 1981): 50–57.

"A Contextualistic View of the Self." In *La Filosofía en America, Trabajos presentados en el IX Congreso Interamericano de Filosofía.* Vol. 2. [June 1977 in Caracas, Venezuela]. Caracas: Sociedad Venezolana de Filosofía, julio de 1979 [distributed in 1981].

"Reflective Inquiry and Language." *Indian Philosophical Quarterly* 9.3 (Apr. 1982), 245–49. Reprint of chapter 26 of part 2 in *Knowledge, Culture and Value,* Ed. R. C. Pandeya and S. R. Bhatt. Papers Presented in World Philosophy Conference (Golden Jubilee Session of the Indian Philosophical Congress), Dec. 28, 1975–Jan. 3, 1976 (Delhi, Varanasi, and Patna: Motilal Banarsidass, 1976).

"Wieman's Empiricism." *Creative Interchange.* Ed. John A. Broyer and William S. Minor, 97–106. Carbondale and Edwardsville: Southern Illinois University Press, 1982.

"Aesthetics and Education." *Chinese University of Hong Kong Education Journal* 12.2 (Dec. 1984): 71–76.

"Contextualism and Chinese Philosophy." *Comparative Studies of Eastern and Western Philosophy.* 2 vols. International Symposium on Comparative Studies of Eastern and Western Philosophy, Sponsored by the Graduate Institute of Philosophy, Chinese Culture University, Aug. 16–18, 1989, Taipei, Taiwan, R.O.C. [publication date and publisher not specified; received Feb. 1993], Vol. 1, 31–60.

"John Dewey's World Hypothesis." *Chinese University of Hong Kong Education Journal* 13.1 (June 1985): 82–87.

"Philosophy, Education, and the Art of Leadership." *Philosophy of Thomé H. Fang*. Ed. Executive Committee of the International Symposium on Thomé H. Fang's Philosophy, 173–81. Taipei: Youth Cultural Enterprises, 1989.

"Thomé H. Fang and the Spirit of Chinese Philosophy." *Philosophy of Thomé H. Fang*. Ed. Executive Committee of the International Symposium on Thomé H. Fang's Philosophy, 9–20. Taipei: Youth Cultural Enterprises, 1989 (Chinese translation in Chinese portion of book, 5–15).

"Of a Shared Desk and Advancement of Philosophy." Proceeding and Addresses of the American Philosophical Association 65.3 (Nov. 1991): 48–52.

"Contextualists and Chinese Philosophers." *Comparative Studies of Eastern and Western Philosophy*. Continued Edition. Graduate Institute of Philosophy, Chinese Culture University, The Second International Symposium on Comparative Studies of Eastern and Western Philosophy, June 10–12, 1993, Taipei, Taiwan, R.O.C. [publication date and publisher not specified; received Apr. 8, 1994], 21–33.

"Interview of Lewis E. Hahn by John M. Abbarno." *Journal of Value Inquiry* 29.2 (June 1995): 255–68.

"A Contextualistic View of Experience and Ecological Responsibility." In *Religious Experience and Ecological Responsibility*. Vol. 3, American Liberal Religious Thought. Ed. Donald A. Crosby and Charley D. Hardwick, 173–87. New York: Peter Lang, 1996.

Foreword to *An Analysis of Dr. Martin Luther King, Jr.'s Letter from Birmingham Jail: "Why We Can't Wait,"* by Dr. Melvin Tuggle. Memphis: Tuggle Books, 1996, vii–ix.

Foreword to *The Evolution of John Dewey's Conception of Philosophy and His Notion of Truth,* by Dr. Melvin Tuggle. Lanham, Md.: University Press of America, 1997, v–vii.

"Interview of Lewis E. Hahn by Marilyn Davis." *Perspectives: Research and Creative Activities at Southern Illinois University Carbondale,* Spring 1998, 10–15.

"The Living Philosopher: An Interview with Lewis Edwin Hahn on the Occasion of His Ninetieth Birthday by Michael W. Allen and Janet Elizabeth Handy." *Kinesis, Graduate Journal in Philosophy, Southern Illinois University Carbondale* 25.2 (Fall 1998): 5–35.

"Ambassador of Dialogue. In *A Parliament of Minds*. Ed. Michael Tobias, J. Patrick Fitzgerald, and David Rothenberg. Albany: State University of New York Press, 2000, 274–79.

## Edited Volumes

*The Proceedings and Addresses of the American Philosophical Association*. Vols. 22–39, 1960–66. Yellow Springs, Ohio: Antioch Press.

*The Early Works of John Dewey, 1882–1898*. Vols. 1–5. Carbondale: Southern Illinois University Press, 1967–72; paperbound edition, Aug. 1975.

(with P.A. Schilpp) *The Philosophy of Gabriel Marcel*. The Library of Living Philosophers, Vol. 17. La Salle, Ill.: Open Court, 1984.

(with P.A. Schilpp) *The Philosophy of W.V. Quine*. The Library of Living Philosophers, Vol. 18. La Salle, Ill.: Open Court, 1986.

(with P. A. Schilpp) *The Philosophy of Georg Henrik von Wright*. The Library of Living Philosophers, Vol. 19. La Salle, Ill.: Open Court, 1989.

(with Harold M. Kaplan and Ralph E. McCoy) *Charles D. Tenney's The Discovery of Discovery*. Lanham, Md.: University Press of America, 1991.

*The Philosophy of Charles Hartshorne.* The Library of Living Philosophers, Vol. 20. La Salle, Ill: Open Court, 1991.

*The Philosophy of A. J. Ayer.* The Library of Living Philosophers, Vol. 21. La Salle, Ill: Open Court, 1992.

*The Philosophy of Paul Ricoeur.* The Library of Living Philosophers, Vol. 22. La Salle, Ill: Open Court, 1994.

*The Philosophy of Paul Weiss.* The Library of Living Philosophers, Vol. 23. La Salle, Ill: Open Court, 1995.

*The Philosophy of Hans-Georg Gadamer.* The Library of Living Philosophers, Vol. 24. Chicago: Open Court, 1997.

*The Philosophy of Roderick M. Chisholm.* The Library of Living Philosophers, Vol. 25. Chicago: Open Court, 1997.

*The Philosophy of P. F. Strawson.* The Library of Living Philosophers, Vol. 26. Chicago: Open Court, 1998.

## Book Reviews (selected list)

"Talking Properly about Perceiving." A Review of Chisholm's *Perceiving. Contemporary Psychology,* Jan. 1959.

"On Psychological Atomism." A Review of Peter Alexander's *Sensationalism and Scientific Explanation. Contemporary Psychology* 9 (1964): 74–76.

"Cats' Grins Without Cats?" Review of Maurice Merleau-Ponty's *The Structure of Behavior. Contemporary Psychology* 10 (1965): 422–23.

"Irrational Man, Rational Society?" Review of A. O. Lovejoy's *Reflections on Human Nature. Contemporary Psychology* 10 (1965): 83–84.

Review of Paul Weiss's *Philosophy in Process. Philosophy and Phenomenological Research* 28.3 (Mar. 1968): 458–59.

Review Discussion of Stuart Hampshire's *Freedom of the Individual. Philosophy Forum* 7.2 (Dec. 1968): 68–71.

Review of Victor Kestenbaum's *The Phenomenological Sense of John Dewey: Habit and Meaning. Review of Metaphysics* 31.4 (June 1978): 677–78.

Review of Nelson Goodman's *Ways of Worldmaking. Review of Metaphysics* 33.4 (June 1980): 785–86.

Review article on Hermann Lübbe, ed., *Wozu Philosophie? Stellungnahmen eines Arbeitskreises. Contemporary German Philosophy* 4 (1984): 320–26.

Review of David Ray Griffin, John B. Cobb, Jr., Marcus P. Ford, Pete A.Y. Gunter, and Peter Ochs's *Founders of Constructive Postmodern Philosophy: Peirce, James, Bergson, Whitehead, and Hartshorne. Southwest Philosophy Review, The Journal of the Southwestern Philosophical Society* 9.2 (Aug. 1993): 145–47.

## Papers and Presentations

"Stephen C. Pepper's World Hypotheses." Annual Meeting of the Society for the Philosophy of Creativity, American Philosophical Association, Eastern Division, Boston, Mass., Dec. 28, 1983.

"Paul Arthur Schilpp and the Library of Living Philosophers." Schilpp Recognition and Open Court Centennial Symposium, Peru, Ill., May 15–17, 1987.

"Philosophy, Education, and the Art of Leadership." International Symposium on Thomé H. Fang's Philosophy, Taipei, Taiwan, Aug. 16–18, 1987.

"Thomé H. Fang and the Spirit of Chinese Philosophy." International Symposium on Thomé H. Fang's Philosophy, Taipei, Taiwan, Aug. 16–18, 1987.

"The Fiftieth Anniversary of the Publication of the First Volume of the Library of Living Philosophers." American Philosophical Association, Chicago, Apr. 28, 1989.

"Perceiving and Creating." Paper presented for Foundation for Philosophy of Creativity, American Philosophical Association, Chicago, Apr. 28, 1989.

"Contextualism and Chinese Philosophy." International Symposium on Comparative Studies of Eastern and Western Philosophy," Taipei, Taiwan, Aug. 16, 1989.

"Creating: Solving Problems and Experiencing Afresh." American Philosophical Association, New Orleans, Apr. 26, 1990.

"Of a Shared Desk and Advancement of Philosophy." American Philosophical Association, Chicago, Apr. 25, 1991.

"Enhancing Cultural Interflow between East and West." Keynote Address for the International Symposium on East-West Cultural Interflow, Macao, Mar. 4, 1993.

"Contextualists and Chinese Philosophers." Keynote address for the Second Chinese Culture University International Symposium on Comparative Studies of Eastern and Western Philosophy, Taipei, Taiwan, June 10, 1993.

"A Contextualistic View of Experience and Ecological Responsibility." Highlands Institute for American Religious Thought Second International Conference on Philosophical Theology, University of St. Andrews, Scotland, Aug. 5, 1993.

"Creativity, Dialogue, and Philosophy." Society for Philosophy of Creativity Colloquium, Nineteenth World Congress of Philosophy, Moscow, Aug. 22, 1993.

"The Library of Living Philosophers and World Dialogue." Round Table on Philosophical Reconstruction in a Changing World: Achievements and Prospects. Nineteenth World Congress of Philosophy, Moscow, Aug. 27, 1993.

"A Contextualistic View of Creativity." Forum on Philosophy of Creativity and Ideation, Tokai University, Honolulu, Aug. 1994.

"Promoting World Dialogue in Philosophy." Citizen Ambassador Program to Russia and Hungary, Sept. 15–28, 1995.

"Contextualism and Anti-Substantialism." Second Symposium on Field-Being and the Non-Substantialistic Turn, Fairfield University, Fairfield, Conn., Aug. 1998.

"Contextualism and Field-Being." Third Symposium on Field-Being and the Non-Substantialistic Turn, Fairfield University, Fairfield, Conn., Aug. 1999.

## Talks and Addresses

"Coping with Change: A Philosophy of Life." Unitarian Fellowship of Waco, Tex., Feb. 24, 1980.

"Why a Liberal Church in 1987?" Unitarian Fellowship of Carbondale, Mar. 1, 1987.

"A Visit to Japan and Taiwan, Summer 1987." Philosophy Colloquium, Southern Illinois University Carbondale, Sept. 10, 1987.

"Report on XVIII World Congress of Philosophy, Brighton UK, Aug. 1988." Student Society for Creative Communication and Philosophy Colloquium, Southern Illinois University Carbondale, Sept. 15, 1988.

"Restructuring, Hopes, and Philosophy in the Soviet Union." Philosophy Colloquium,

Southern Illinois University Carbondale, Nov. 3, 1988.

"Confucius's World View and Some American Outlooks." Unitarian Fellowship of Carbondale, Jan. 7, 1990.

"The Library of Living Philosophers." Address for Phi Sigma Tau Philosophy Honors Students, Sept. 25, 1992.

"Chicago's 1893 World Parliament of Religions." Unitarian Fellowship of Carbondale, Feb. 19, 1993.

"The Library of Living Philosophers and World Dialogue in Philosophy." Philosophy Colloquium, Chinese University of Hong Kong, Mar. 1, 1993.

"John Dewey, Hu Shih, and Thomé H. Fang." Address Cosponsored by Taiwan Regional Development Institute and China TV, Taipei, Taiwan, Mar. 7, 1993.

"Extending Our Legacy of Values." Address for Illinois Beta Association of Phi Beta Kappa and Southern Illinois University Carbondale Liberal Arts and Sciences Honor Society, Apr. 4, 1993.

# Index

Absolute, xvii, xviii, 14, 19, 145, 147–48; categories and, 150–53; explanation and, 149–50; subject and, 154–55; values and, 155–57
absolute novelty, 29–30
aesthetics, 46–48, 99–103, 108, 135
Aldrich, Virgil C., 76–77
Alexander, Thomas M., 100
analogy, x, 43, 46–48, 61
analysis, 12–13, 16–19, 26–27, 84, 152; detective metaphor and, 96, 115–16; forms of, 95–96; metaphysical interpretation and, 31, 38; and scientific method, 42, 97–98; sense-data and, 77–78
Anglo-American analytical philosophy, 140
antimetaphysicians, 31, 33, 38–39
a priori reasoning, 38, 131
Aristotle, 59, 131, 151
atomism, 142, 152
Axtelle, George E., 92–93, 113

Bahm, Archie J., 67
behaviorism, xiii, 20–21, 86
behavioristic psychology, 20–21, 86
Being, 22, 41, 59
Bentley, Arthur F., xii
Bergson, Henri-Louis, 26–27
Blanshard, Brand, xiv, xvii–xviii, 145–57; works: *Nature of Thought,* 146–56; *Philosophical Interrogations,* 150, 154; *Reason and Analysis,* 147, 148, 152, 155, 156
Bosanquet, Bernard, 155
Boydston, Jo Ann, 114
Bryan, William Jennings, 8

categories, xi, 18, 43–44, 47, 58–68, 128; and Absolute, 150–53; characteristics and, 59–63; contextual, 6–7, 61–63, 83, 84, 94; empirical relevance of, 63–65; root metaphor theory and, 61, 66–67, 138; and sets or systems, 65–67; universality and, 64–65; worldview and, 60–66
certainty, 14–15, 32–34, 135, 142–43, 166n. 4
change, xiv, xvi, 13–14, 93–94, 106–7; Blanshard on, 152–54; and continuities/discontinuities, 29–30, 100, 107, 138; Dewey on, 99, 114–15; evolution as, 12, 28–29; experience and, 14, 108; and potentialities, 23–24
Chesterton, Gilbert Keith, 106
clarity/obscurity, 55–56
Cohen, Morris R., 47
coherence, 138
Collingwood, R. G., 67
commitment, 132
common sense, 38, 64, 70–71, 135–36
consciousness, 74, 77, 79, 80
consistency, 42–43, 48, 138
consummations, 6–7, 62, 83, 85, 94
contextualism, ix, 3–7, 121–22, 137, 142, 144; analysis and, 12–13, 16–19, 26–27, 84; categories and, 6–7, 61–63, 83, 84, 94; change and, 13–14, 93–94; evolution and, 13–30; experience and, 82–91; Wieman on, 128, 129
*Contextualistic Theory of Perception, A* (Hahn), xi, 27, 42, 62
contingency, 152–54

continuities/discontinuities, 29–30, 100, 107, 138
correspondence theory, 140
corroboration, 135–37, 138, 143, 144
creativity, xiv–xvii, 32, 47, 87; aesthetics and, 99–103; and creative interchange, 143–44; critical thinking and, 96–99, 104; growth and, 92–93, 96; metaphysics and, 128–30; order and, 130–31
critical thinking, xiv, xv, 16, 24–28, 36, 90, 116–17; creativity and, 96–99, 104; experience and, 25–26, 85; steps in, 24–25, 42, 53, 98–99, 117–18

danda, 135, 136, 140
Darrow, Clarence, 8
Darwin, Charles, 7, 113
deduction, 25, 67
democracy, 104–5
Descartes, René, 24, 79–80, 96, 97
Dewey, John, xiv, 72, 100, 107, 113–26, 132; on change, 99, 114–15; on context, 84, 93–94; on critical thinking, 116–17; on Darwin, 11–12, 19; on education, 104–5, 119–20; on events, 5–6; on experience, 87–88, 118–19, 121–26, 161n. 2; letter to Hahn of, xi–xii, 73; naturalism of, 121–22; pragmatism of, 4–5, 114–15; on problem solving, 27–28, 42, 53, 97; on psychology, 51; on sense-data, 167n. 14, 168n. 24; worldview of, 114–15; works: *Art as Experience,* 119, 121, 123; *A Common Faith,* 19, 87; "Context and Thought," 93; *Experience and Education,* xv, 22–23, 121–24; *How We Think,* 24, 85, 96, 116; *Logic: The Theory of Inquiry,* 24, 85, 87, 96, 116; "The Need for a Recovery of Philosophy," 26, 88, 118, 122, 125; *Philosophy and Civilization,* 35–36; "Qualitative Thought," 27; *The Quest for Certainty,* 14; *Reconstruction in Philosophy,* 123; "Some Questions about Value," xii
Dewey Center (Southern Illinois University Carbondale), 114
diffusion perception, 100–101

dogmatism, 135, 136, 141–42
doubt, 24, 96–97; sense-data and, 74–77, 79–80
drives, 97
dualism, 22, 54, 85, 86, 95, 122

*Earth in the Balance* (Gore), xiii, 89
eclecticism, 139
Edman, Irwin, 89, 100
education, 104–5, 119–20
emergent-qualitative novelty, 29
emergent-textural novelty, 29–30
Emmet, Dorothy M., 46, 48, 61
empirical relevance, 63–65
*Empirical Theology of Henry Nelson Wieman, The* (ed. Bretall), xv–xvi
empiricism, 88, 119, 121–22; Wieman's, 127–33
enhanced quality, 100–102, 108
environment, xiii–xiv, 62, 83, 85, 87; goals for, 90–91; naturalism and, 21–22, 94–95; and pollution, 89–91, 93
epistemology, 70–71, 73, 140–41, 168n. 27
events, 4–7, 29, 84–85, 94, 114–15, 124–25
evidence, 55, 135–36
evolution, 3, 7–13, 27; as change, 12, 28–29; contextualism and, 13–30; and naturalism *vs.* supernaturalism, 9–11, 87, 94; and natural selection, 8–9; theology and, 7–10
existence, levels of, 22–23
experience, 13, 64, 77, 82–91, 118–19, 130; biological matrix of, 19–24, 28, 86; change and, 14, 108; critical thinking and, 25–26, 85; Dewey on, 87–88, 118–19, 121–26, 161n. 2; events and, 124–25
experiencing afresh, xiv, xv, 92–105
experimental approach, 16, 27, 97–98
explanation, 148–52
external world, 53–54, 79–80, 86

facts, 52, 135, 166n. 4; epistemological view of, 70–71, 73; metaphysical inquiry and, 42–44; metaphysical interpretation and, 32–38

Fiske, John, 19
formism, 137, 142
Freeman, Eugene, 64
frustrations (blocking), 6–7, 62, 83, 85, 94
fusion, 6–7, 62, 83

genetic hypothesis, 19–20
Gestalt psychology, 141–42
Gillespie, Diane, 165n. 2
God, 8, 10–11, 19, 87, 107, 131
goods, 109, 119
Gore, Al, xiii, 89, 90–91
Greeks, 50
grounding, 140

habit patterns, 99–103
having, 132
Hegel, Georg Wilhelm Friedrich, 41, 151
Hickman, Larry A., 103, 114, 163n. 26
Hicks, Dawes, 75, 78, 166n. 6, 168n. 23
Hofstadter, Albert, 58
"How to Make Our Ideas Clear" (Peirce), 4, 96
human growth, xv, 92–93, 119–20
humanism, xvi, 6
hypotheses, 25, 42–43, 46–47, 141; scientific, 36–37; world, 134–36

idealism, xvii, xviii, 78, 145, 155
immanence, 148, 152, 153
implications, 145, 147, 153
importance, 32, 38–39, 41
"In a Station of the Metro" (Pound), 102
inclusiveness, 36–37, 53, 124, 145
indubitability, xi, xvi, 4–5, 15, 70–71, 96, 135; consciousness and, 74, 77, 79; Pepper on, 142–43; sense-data and, 74–81, 167–68n. 22
inference, 72, 88, 123
information, 42–44, 48
initiations, 6–7, 62, 83, 85
instrumentalism, 4, 5, 114–15
instruments, 6–7, 62, 83, 85
integrative process, 146–48, 150
intelligence, 11, 20, 155
internal relations, 153, 155–56

interpretation. *See* metaphysical interpretation
"Intimations of Immortality" (Wordsworth), 101–2
*Introduction to Metaphysics* (Bergson), 26–27
introspective philosophy, 85
intrusive novelty, 29
intuition, 26–27

James, William, 4, 14, 87, 106, 151, 156; on Dewey, 114; on events, 29, 94–95; pragmatism of, 4, 82, 132
Jenkins, Iredell, 27
John Dewey Foundation, 114

Kant, Immanuel, 4, 40, 59
Kantianism, 144
knowledge, 20, 26–27, 53, 77, 135; Blanshard on, 148–52; experience and, 132–33; metaphysical inquiry and, 41, 43, 48
Koffka, Kurt, 142

language, 33, 35, 54
Lazerowitz, Morris, 45
Lee, Donald S., 138
Lepley, Ray, xii
Lewis, C. I., 131
Loewenberg, Joe, 38
logic, 50
Lotze, Rudolf Hermann, 51, 71
Lovejoy, A. O., 4, 7

Markham, Edwin, 102
material things, 23, 79–80
Maugham, Somerset, 40
McGeoch, John A., 69
Mead, George Herbert, 20, 73, 86, 141–42
means (instruments), 6–7, 62, 83, 85
mechanism, 137, 142
mechanistic naturalism, 17, 54, 64, 71, 79
metaphors, 46–47, 163n. 26
metaphysical inquiry, x, 40–41; as an art, 46–48; knowledge and, 41, 43, 48; as a science, 41–45
metaphysical interpretation, ix, x, 31–39, 47; importance and, 32, 38–39; scien-

metaphysical interpretation (*continued*) tific hypothesis and, 36–37; worldview and, 32–35

metaphysics, ix, 40–41; creativity and, 128–30; and diversity of opinion, 45, 56; empiricism and, 127–31; and questions asked, 44–45; scope of, 44, 52, 53, 138; subject matter of, 44, 52, 59–60

*Metaphysics and the New Logic* (Wick), 37–38

"Metaphysics and Verification, I" (Wisdom), 35

methodology, 41, 42, 48, 52

Miller, David Lee, 103

Minor, William S., xv

Morris, George Sylvester, xvii

naturalism, 9–11, 13, 19–20, 87, 107–8, 129–30; Dewey's, 121–22; environment and, 21–22, 94–95; mechanistic, 17, 54, 64, 71, 79

*Nature of Thought, The* (Blanshard), xvii

Neurath, Otto, 33

"Neutral, Indubitable Sense-Data as the Starting Point for Theories of Perception" (Hahn), xi

neutrality, 37–39, 69–70, 74, 78, 139

novelties, 14, 28–30

object, 22, 77, 78, 152

order, 32–33, 42, 130–31

organicism, xvii, 67, 137, 141, 142, 145, 147

*Origin of Species, The* (Darwin), 7, 12, 113

Peirce, Charles Sanders, 4, 15, 24, 96, 135

Pepper, Stephen C., xiv, xvi–xvii, 6, 17, 27, 29, 61, 89, 100, 134–44; contributions to worldviews of, 128–29, 141–43; creative interchange and, 140–41, 143–44; on epistemology, 140–41, 168n. 27; and metaphilosophy, 134–41; on metaphysical hypotheses, 46–47; works: *Aesthetic Quality,* 134, 142; *Basis of Criticism in the Arts,* 134; *Concept and Quality,* 137, 139, 142; *Digest of Purposive Values,* 142; "History of Stephen C. Pepper, A Philosopher," 134, 141–42; "Middle-Sized Facts," 167–68n. 22; "The Philosophy of Criticism," 135; *Principles of Art Appreciation,* 142; *The Sources of Value,* 142; "Wieman's Contextual Metaphysics," 129, 131; *World Hypotheses: A Study in Evidence,* xvi, 128–29, 134–42

perception, xi, 26–27, 42, 53–55, 69–73; sense-data and, 74–81; types, 100–101

permanence, 107, 115

*Philosophy and the Mirror of Nature* (Rorty), 140

physico-chemical level, 22–23

pluralism, 14–15, 143, 151

poetry, 46–48, 101–3

positivism, 37, 53, 136

Pound, Ezra, 102

practical drive perception, 100–101

pragmatism, xi, xv, 3–6, 77, 82–84, 114–15; criticism of, 70, 71–73

*Pragmatism* (James), 82

"Pragmatism, Relativism, and Irrationalism" (Rorty), 140

Prall, David Wight, 76

precision, 138

Price, H. H., xi–xii, 74–81, 166–69nn. 12, 16, 22, 25, 26, 28

probabilism, 15

problem solving, xiv, 24–28, 88–89, 96–99; Dewey on, 27–28, 42, 53, 97; perception and, 54–55; and pseudo-problems, 53, 54; stages in, 98–99, 117–18

*Process and Reality* (Whitehead), 67

process philosophy, 82–83

psychological data, 69–73

psychology, x, xi, 49–53, 55, 124–25, 165n. 2; behavioristic, 20–21, 86; Gestalt, 141–42

purposive behavior, 21, 30, 86, 94, 137

*Purposive Behavior in Animals and Men* (Tolman), 21, 86

qualities, xiv, 6–7, 18, 27, 29, 62, 83, 89; and aesthetics, 46–48, 99–103, 108; enhanced, 100–102, 108; metaphysical interpretation and, 35–36

reality, 32, 130, 132, 150–51

reason, 11, 50, 153–54, 156–57
Reck, A. J., 135
references, 6–7, 22, 26, 62, 83, 84, 94
reflective thinking. *See* critical thinking
relativism, 16–17
root metaphor theory, xvi–xvii, 32, 46–48, 83, 136–41, 143–44; categories and, 61, 66–67, 138
Rorty, Richard, 140–41
Rosenthal, Sandra, 161n. 1
Royce, Josiah, 154
Russell, Bertrand, 77, 167nn. 20, 21

Santayana, George, 166n. 4
Schiller, F. C. S., 6
science: metaphysical inquiry as, 41–45; philosophy as origin of, 50–53, 57
scientific hypothesis, 36–37
scientific laws, 15–16
scientific method, 42, 97–98
scope of metaphysics, 44, 52, 53, 138
Seattle, Chief, 89–90
selectivism, 137, 139, 142
sense-data, 27, 74–81, 123, 167–68n. 22; as indeterminate, 76–77; as postanalytical, 77–78
sets (systems), 65–67
Southern Illinois University Carbondale, 113–14
Spinoza, Baruch, 67
Stace, Walter T., 38
strands, 6–7, 17–18, 22, 29, 62, 83
Strong, Edward, 77
subject, 22, 154–55
subject matter, 44, 52, 59–60
supernaturalism, 9–11, 19, 30, 87, 94, 107, 129

taste, 109–10
terminations, 83, 94
textures, 6–7, 17–18, 22, 62, 83, 152; context of, 93–95; novelties and, 29–30

theology, 7–10, 127
thought, movement of, 146–47
time, 4–6, 76, 93–94, 122–23, 153
Tolman, E. C., 21, 86, 142
transcendence, 148, 156
transformation, 127–28
truth, 26, 43, 47, 132, 140

understanding, 65, 148–52
universality, 64–65, 154
"Universal Jargon and Terminology" (Neurath), 33

*Value: A Cooperative Inquiry* (Lepley), xii
values, xii–xiii, 19, 27, 48, 118, 143–44; Blanshard on, 155–57; misconceptions about, 108–10
verification, 25

Waismann, Friedrich, 55–56
Whitehead, Alfred North, 66–67, 131
Wick, Warner, 37–38
Wieman, Henry Nelson, xiv, xv–xvi, 19, 87, 107, 127–33; works: "Can God Be Perceived?", 131; "The Empirical Method in Religion," 133; *Empirical Theology,* 129, 131–33; *Man's Ultimate Commitment,* 130–31, 133; *Religious Inquiry,* 128, 130; *The Source of Human Good,* xvi, 129–32
Wiener, Philip, 7
Wisdom, John, 35
Wordsworth, William, 101–2
world hypotheses, 134–36
*World Hypotheses: A Study in Evidence* (Pepper), 128–29
worldviews, x, 86–87, 134–35; adequacy of, xvii, 32–34, 42–43, 45, 57, 128–29, 137–40; categories and, 60–66; metaphysical interpretation and, 32–35; Pepper's contributions to, 141–43; perception and, 54–55

**Lewis E. Hahn** has taught most of the standard undergraduate courses in philosophy along with many advanced courses, but his particular teaching and research interests have been worldviews, philosophical ideas in literature, aesthetics, value theory, epistemology, American philosophy, and contemporary philosophy. As editor of the Library of Living Philosophers since 1981, he is especially interested in world dialogue.